CHRISTIAN SOCIALISM
1848—1854

CHRISTIAN SOCIALISM
1848—1854

CHARLES E. RAVEN

FRANK CASS & CO. LTD.
1968

Published by
FRANK CASS AND COMPANY LIMITED
67 Great Russell Street, London WC1
by arrangement with Macmillan and Co. Ltd.

First edition   1920
New impression   1968

SBN 7146 2129 3

Printed in Great Britain by
Thomas Nelson (Printers) Ltd., London and Edinburgh

TO MY PARENTS
WITH LOVE AND GRATITUDE

PREFACE

THIS book is founded upon the Donnellan lectures delivered by me at Trinity College, Dublin, in May 1919, and my grateful thanks are due to the authorities there for the opportunity thus afforded to me and for their many acts of kindness. In particular I am indebted to the late illustrious Provost, the Rev. Sir John Pentland Mahaffy, whose warm welcome and large-hearted generosity to his young and unknown visitor gave me my first experience of Irish hospitality. It was in consultation with him that my subject was originally chosen ; he expressed the hope that the lectures might be expanded before publication ; and his letters, the last of them written a day or two before his illness, have inspired me to carry on the work in spite of the pressure of many other duties. The completion of it has seemed in some sort the fulfilment of a promise to one who will always be remembered with reverence and affection. In addition my thanks are due to Major Bowes, to the Rev. John Carter, to Professor Foxwell, to Mr. C. R. Fay, and to Sir Norman and Lady Moore for the loan of letters and books and for many valuable suggestions, to Mr. A. W. Pollard and Mr. E. Duchesne for their courtesy in regard to the libraries of the British Museum and the Working Men's

College, and especially to Dr. R. H. Murray and Mr. G. T. Bennett, who have read the book in proof and whose criticisms upon it have been of the greatest assistance. My debt to the many writers from whom I have quoted is apparent from the footnotes, and is particularly large in respect of the first chapter. Finally, I wish to express my deep gratitude to my colleagues at Emmanuel College whose kindness in setting me free from the pressure of College business has enabled me to undertake the research necessary for the completion of this work.

CONTENTS

CHAPTER I

CHAPTER II

CHAPTER VI

CHAPTER VII

CHAPTER VIII

CHAPTER IX

CHAPTER X

CHAPTER XI

CHAPTER I.

INTRODUCTORY: LAISSEZ-FAIRE AND ITS CHAMPIONS.

' In their strictest sense Christianity and Socialism are irreconcilable.' [1] ' It is a profound truth that Socialism is the natural enemy of religion.' [2]   Those are the deliberate opinions expressed in a recent Bampton Lecture and in the official pronouncement of the British Socialist Party; and though many, Christians and Socialists alike, would fiercely repudiate them, they represent a strong and until lately a general attitude.

Indeed there are still, as there were in the days of Maurice, many to whom Christian Socialism seems the statement of a contradiction in terms.   To the Christian the very word Socialist will conjure up memories of Mr. Blatchford or Mr. Belfort Bax, and visions of tub-thumping revolutionaries pouring blasphemy upon the cause of the Crucified or of long-haired sensualists planning the dethronement of chastity and domestic life.   To the Socialist the Church still seems a body of privileged hypocrites valiant only in defence of their emoluments, the bond-slaves of vested interests, offering to starving souls the consolations of an antiquated mythology and to starving bodies the crumbs of a rich man's charity.

[1] Rev. F. W. Bussell, *Christian Theology and Social Progress*, p. 324. This statement is taken as self-evident.

[2] *Socialism and Religion*, p. 6.

Even those who have passed beyond the stage of blind
hostility are conscious of a vast gulf between the two
creeds.   Christians may well feel that Christ's teaching
supplies at once the whole programme of the reformers
and the only incentive adequate to establish it ; and that
Socialists, in their many lapses into self-seeking, spoliation
and violence, have only proved the futility of following
the Christian ethic without the support of the Christian
faith.   Socialists are not wholly unjust when they declare
that the alliance between Church and Capital is a new
union of Pharisees and Sadducees, and that its result is
not the worshipping of the Christ but the nailing of Him
afresh upon the Cross.   Christians still sneer at the
Labour Movement as a search for loaves and fishes.
Socialists still retort that daily bread is at least a more
scriptural aim than heavenly harps and crowns of gold.
And yet both alike are pledged champions of that Kingdom of God upon earth which the Poor Man of Nazareth
proclaimed, and of those principles of love and liberty and
life for which He was condemned.

The quarrel is an irony, the pathos of which both parties
are at last beginning to realise.   The misunderstandings
and exaggerations from which it springs, and the suspicions
and violence which embitter it, will be indicated in the
study of our subject.   Suffice it to say for the present
that they were the inevitable consequence of the rapid
change of environment to which the Church and all other
ancient institutions were exposed during the nineteenth
century.   Organised religion had grown conventional :
its vitality and elasticity were at a low level : it was ill-
prepared to adapt itself without danger and acute dis-
comfort to the needs of a new time.   Just those elements in
the Gospel which were most closely akin to the aspirations
of democracy and had been so strong a feature of apostolic

Christianity had fallen into neglect. And, as has happened a hundred times, when any aspect of truth is forgotten its rediscovery must be effected at the cost of struggle and of schism. Heresy is the inevitable reaction against a one-sided preaching ; for the reformers are received with bitter suspicion and obstinate refusal and driven into the over-emphasis of the revolutionary features of their doctrine ; the whole matter is confused with strife and the real points at issue are lost to sight ; only after the lapse of years and the deaths of the protagonists does the flimsy character of the dispute appear ; then and not till then can readjustments be made and the gulf be bridged. So in the present case, if Christianity be a universal religion, it must be that the Socialists, however crude their opinions or unjust their antagonism, have discovered some real need of the human heart which that religion ought to recognise and satisfy. As we study the first and pre-mature attempt at combining the two and discover the ground of its failure, we shall have gone some way towards clearing our minds of prejudice, discerning where we have fallen short, and learning on what terms and to what extent the two great movements can co-operate for the regeneration of society.

Before we can consider the work and lessons of those earliest professed Christian Socialists we must briefly summarise the circumstances under which their protest was made and the attitude of Churchmen and politicians towards the problems of contemporary industrialism. Such a summary has been admirably compiled by Mr. and Mrs. Hammond in their two invaluable books,[1] and is briefly presented in the historical chapter of the Archbishops' Fifth Committee's Report : but for

---

[1] *The Village Labourer 1760–1832* and *The Town Labourer 1760–1832*.

our purpose it is necessary to cover the ground once
more ; for the Hammonds are not specially interested
in the views of Church parties (which are important for
our purpose) and an individual can speak of them more
freely than a Committee.

Progress, whether in the physical or the spiritual sphere,
is not the smoothly continuous movement that some
theories of evolution would suggest.   Seeds of change lie
dormant for years, perhaps for centuries, until at last
their winter sleep ends and a new life bursts suddenly
upon the world.   Whether it be in the production of new
species or the growth of the individual soul or the process
of human history, we can observe a series of revolutionary events, due to causes previously unrecognised and
even now often obscure—events which mark the opening
of new chapters in development.   Such a period of rapid
transition took place in the last quarter of the eighteenth
century ; and it is from the French Revolution that we
to-day have to start any enquiry into present conditions.
For the new era then born and baptised in blood is still
that under which we live ; and even if its reign be nearly
over, at least it marks the scene of the events with which
we are concerned.   To understand the genesis of Christian
Socialism we must go back to it.

' The liberty of each citizen ends where the liberty
of another citizen begins ' : so Victor Hugo [1] has
summed up the grand axiom of the Convention.   The
old theories of the rights of monarchs and of the relation
of the State to its members were guillotined with
Louis XVI., but it was not only political life that was
shaken to its foundations.   The Revolution was itself
only a symptom, a sudden and horrifying symptom, of

[1] *Ninety-three*, ii. 3, 9.

a change in the whole constitution of European civilisation. As it was at the Renaissance when every human activity, every human relationship, was remade, so now the movement from which sprang the Terror made itself felt in every sphere of thought and life. In the fifteenth century the rediscovery of Greek and the invention of printing, in the eighteenth the development of the inductive method and the use of steam-power revolutionised man's intellectual outlook and profoundly modified his way of life. But the break-up of feudalism was neither so rapid nor so revolutionary as the appearance of democracy. Industrialism was a change wholly unparalleled, and the speed of its coming found the old civilisation unprepared, and threw it into something like chaos. When our blood boils at the hellish iniquity of the factories and the sweating dens, at the smug blindness of the responsible leaders in Church and State, at the complacent indifference of the educated and the wealthy, we need constantly to remind ourselves of the kaleidoscopic changes and catastrophic energy of the time. No wonder men born in the quiet of the eighteenth century were unable to grapple effectively with the tumult of new problems that accompanied the Napoleonic wars ! No wonder that they took refuge in a despairing belief that Nature had best be left to find her own remedies, in a plaintive clinging to whatever relics of authority seemed to promise security, in an eager acceptance of the nostrums provided by statesmen or economists or divines hardly less bewildered than themselves !

And in religion most of all do men hold fast to tradition in times of general uncertainty. When the world around them is shattered to its foundations, even the normally indifferent seek a resting-place in the long-established doctrines and usages of the Churches. And priest or prophet is tempted to take as his text the message that 'the things that are seen are temporal but the things that are unseen are eternal,' and to emphasise the contrast by maintaining a rigid and immovable conservatism. Others may flinch and faint before the things that are coming upon the earth : old landmarks may be swept away amid the confusion and disaster that usher in a new age : he at least will lift up his head, for his redemption from neglect is near and the ancient truths committed to him are being justified : when men are yearning for stability and assurance, it is not the time for him to hesitate or to reinterpret : they must find the faith uncontaminated by novelty, a steadfast protest against the tyranny of progress. In a period of revolution religious institutions, however full of genuine vitality, will always be expected to provide a stronghold for the lovers of the past, and their most zealous champions will find it hard to accept and respond to the motion of the time. So long as men look upon religion as something essentially static and comforting and grandmotherly, ' our balm in sorrow and our stay in strife,' a shelter from the storm and adventure of secular affairs, the Churches will naturally be tempted to follow the principle of supply and demand. Christian soldiers who were surely meant to be God's 'storm-troops' in the forward movement of mankind will find themselves employed rather in the task of ministering to the wounded and providing recreation for the war-worn. Too often they have deliberately enrolled themselves among the forces of reaction, as conscientious objectors to the age-long struggle for the betterment of the race.

And this was particularly the case at the opening of the industrial epoch. The Church of England had for nearly a century been singularly lacking in spirituality or inspiration. Her position under the Hanoverian kings was that of a respectable though little respected department of the State. Her traditions decried enthusiasm as dangerous or even vicious, relegated piety to fixed days and places and persons, inculcated a slavish adherence to the Crown and nobility and a loyal support to privilege and the *status quo*. Her bishops were deliberately chosen either for reasons of birth and political service or because they were known to be sound and sleepy. Her clergy were the well-groomed, well-meaning sons of the well-to-do, men in whose eyes all was well in this best of worlds—or if not there was always the hereafter.

While the countryside was being depopulated and the new manufacturing towns were springing up, indeed during the whole eighteenth century, no great Churchman and, save Methodism, no great religious movement, breaks the level—the very low level—of English Christianity : and the treatment of the Methodists was enough to condemn the Church. The Wesleys and their supporters, and even Whitefield, were men in whose souls burned the authentic fire of the Spirit and whose constant prayer was that they might set the realm aflame ; and not only so but they were ordained, and for a long time loyal, clergy. They were met with sneers and suspicion, apathy and neglect, as disturbers of the peace, as enemies of moderation, as fanatics who were making faith a matter of emotion and inward conviction, and were sacrificing reason and dignity in their insane desire to win the souls and uplift the lives of those whom God had ordained to be poor. They, like St. Paul, were forced to realise that not many rich nor wise nor mighty were called, that political prelates and comfortable incumbents would not accept a creed which threatened to interfere with their legitimate indulgence, and seemed to involve more than the performance of the legal minimum of duties. A little sympathy, a little statesmanship, during the half century of Wesley's crusade would have averted the schism and enabled the Church to retain and absorb the masses whom the Methodist preachers gathered.[1] But no sign was given, no steps were taken ; the preachers were thwarted and discountenanced, and their followers forced first into irregularities and finally, though not till 1795, into separation. And the Church expressed her gratitude with a sigh of relief and returned to her slumbers.

Very typical of her state are the two great writers on religious matters at that time. Gibbon treats Christianity with a cold and confident insolence which must amaze any believer until he studies Paley and recognises that if this represented the faith then contempt was all it deserved. Gibbon's attack upon religion is drastic enough ; but his indictment is far less damning than his rival's defence. Paley's worldliness and sycophancy, Pharisaism and dulness, his praise of the British Constitution with its placemen and pensioners and rotten boroughs and filthy corruption, his counterblast to the French Revolution, the notorious *Reasons for Contentment addressed to the Labouring Part of the British Public*, his sermon on the ' Distinction of Orders in the Church,' in which episcopacy is supported solely because it attracts into holy orders the younger sons of the nobility[2]—these things make a Christian burn with shame and indignation. And the tragedy is that they were written not by some specially scandalous hypocrite or heretic but by the chosen defender of the faith, the man who was selected by the panic-stricken aristocracy to proclaim on their behalf the doctrines of

[1] Southey, for whose importance in social history cf. pp. 48-50, declared boldly that the Church ought to have treated Wesley and the Methodists as the Papacy treated St. Francis and the Franciscans.

[2] For this sermon and Cowper's stricture upon it cf. G. W. Meadley, *Memoirs of Paley*, Appendix, pp. 85-93.

' that truly excellent religion which exhorts to contentment and submission to the higher powers.' [1] Such a
text, though it may have been appropriate enough
during the ' quinquennium Neronis,' becomes simply
grotesque when applied to George III. and his successor :
yet at no other time in all the long and evil history of its
misuse has it been so overworked by Churchmen. On
this one commandment, according to Paley and his kind,
hung all the law and the prophets, and in this faith they
were ready to prostitute religion at the bidding of the
politicians and in the interest of security and pre-
ferment. [2]

Nevertheless even then the Church was beginning to
awake. Several of Wesley's supporters never left her,
and the revival of personal religion due to his work was
wider than the Methodist societies. Men like John
Newton or Henry Venn or Isaac Milner, or somewhat
later their most remarkable leader Charles Simeon, formed
a distinct group whose numbers grew rapidly, not only
from their long hold upon the University of Cambridge
but also from the accession to their ranks of numbers of
quiet and earnest clergy to whom the example of the
Methodists had brought a new vision of the living power
of the Gospel. At a time when morals were generally
loose, conversation crude and coarse and pursuits often
brutal and degrading, these men by reviving a strongly
puritanical habit and insisting that religion was a matter
not of the lips or reason but of the heart and life, did a
great work in redeeming the failure of the Church. They
were at least whole-hearted and sincere : their personal

[1] Quoted by Hammond, *Town Labourer*, p. 234, from Young, *Inquiry
into the state of mind amongst the Lower Classes.*

[2] For all his sycophancy Paley was by no means worse than his contemporaries : he was called ' Pigeon ' Paley for an honourable reason
(cf. *Life of Dr. Paley*, p. 341).

devotion to Jesus Christ and their zeal for the saving of souls were beyond question ; they were lamps shining in a naughty world. And if their doctrines were few and rigid and their theology in consequence ill-balanced and stereotyped, at least they renewed the spiritual life of the Church, afforded noble examples of earnest simplicity and practical philanthropy, and ' helped to form a con-science, if not a heart, in the callous bosom of English politics.' [1]

Yet even so the Evangelicals like the Latitudinarians, though for much nobler reasons, were weak in treating the diseases of the body politic. From the societies that they founded—the Society for the Reformation of Manners, the Religious Tract Society, the Church Missionary Society, the Bible Society—we can see where their interests lay. Primarily they were missionaries, whether in the slums of England or in the deserts of Africa, and their mission aimed solely at individual conversions. The heroic but sententious sisters Hannah and Martha More, the prototypes of generations of district visitors, are representative enough. They cared little for the physical environment of their converts, and nothing for the causes that produced it. Their work happened to be in the Men-dips ; but their attitude would have been the same if it had been in Melanesia. God had made some men poor, just as He had made some men black : Scripture guaranteed that poverty and blackness were alike immutable : the Christian was no more concerned with the white man's hovel or wages than with the Ethiopian's skin : his duty was to bring to white and black alike the blessed news of salvation from sin and of a glorious immortality for

---

[1] Morley, *Life of Gladstone*, i. p. 163, where is contained a short, but striking, comparison of the Evangelicals with the Tractarians in this respect.

those that believe.[1] Over individual souls he would
yearn with an intensity of passion ; brands here and there
might be plucked from the burning : but of corporate
sin or corporate betterment, of the capacity in men to
alter their own environment and so promote growth in
goodness, of the hopelessness of working on purely individualistic lines, he had in common with the general
thought of his time no understanding whatever.

Nor was the content of Evangelical preaching likely to
satisfy those whose consciences had been stirred by the
evidences of social evil. Not only were they individualistic,
but they were actively anti-revolutionary. Their doctrine
of salvation came almost entirely from St. Paul, and from
him they derived also the quietism and other-worldliness
which gave such offence to would-be reformers. No
doubt the great Apostle supplements his injunctions to
peace and submission, to contentment and patience and
meekness, by much that is more in keeping with his own
restless activity and high courage. No doubt he had
reason to know the futility of any attempt at revolutionary
action by his following of slaves and petty tradesmen
against the throned might of Caesar. But the Evangelicals
took every word of his literally and added to them
a contempt for this life which is altogether alien from his
thought. Earth became ' a vale of tears,' its pursuits
' vanity and vexation of spirit,' its pleasures ' snares
and traps,' its circumstances a divine gift to be accepted
with as good a grace as possible. The praises of Zion,
the pilgrimage to the promised land, the passage of
Jordan, the joys of its farther shore, the wistful hopes,
the exhortations to patience, the stress upon the meekness

---

[1] It ought to be noted that in the foreign mission field also the individualistic method has long been abandoned by the more enlightened
societies, in favour of educational and social efforts.

and gentleness of the Redeemer—these depressing features of our hymn-books are eminently developed in the poetical effusions of Evangelicalism. At its best such a doctrine might be called unpractical and pietistic ; at its worst it became a mere device for repressing honest aspiration and obstructing every attempt at progress. No doubt it helped to save England from the bloodshed and horror which convulsed France, and to this extent served a useful purpose : but it did so at the cost of divorcing religion from life and fostering the alliance between reformers and secularists.

And their concentration upon the future world blinded them to the horrors around them. Very characteristic is their great hero William Wilberforce,[1] whose private life was a shining example of consistent and earnest goodness, who had a real belief in freedom and spent years in the struggle for the abolition of slavery, and who never realised that, while he was bringing liberty to negroes in the plantations, the white slaves of industry in mine and factory were being made the victims of a tyranny a thousandfold more cruel. Persons who think reverently of the hero of the anti-slavery movement should remember such facts as those revealed by Richard Oastler in his letters on *Slavery in Yorkshire* ;[2] and should remember too that Wilberforce had consistently opposed every single attempt to benefit the condition of the workers by legislation and was reckoned by Cobbett to be the worst enemy of the people then living : as a writer in *Politics for the People* remarked, ' the negro slaves had black faces and lived a great way off, and therefore people felt for

[1] Cf. Hammond, *The Town Labourer*, pp. 231-246.

[2] Published in the *Leeds Mercury* and *Leeds Intelligencer* in 1830 and as a pamphlet in 1835. They may be regarded as the starting-point of the Ten Hours Movement. Cf. Hutchins and Harrison, *History of Factory Legislation*, pp. 43-46 (2nd edition).

them.'[1] In the next generation when the Evangelicals had become the dominant party in the Church, there was among them all scarcely one save Lord Shaftesbury who did not acquiesce in Wilberforce's dictum that the existing social order combined 'the greatest measure of temporal comforts and spiritual privileges,' and did not echo his message of resignation and humility to the poor 'since their situation, with all its evils, is better than they have deserved at the hands of God.'[2] It was from men of this school that the Christian Socialists received their fiercest persecution, and by their organ, the *Record*, that Maurice was hounded from his post at King's College because he dared to maintain that eternal life was a state in which men could live here on earth, and to act up to his belief.

On its intellectual side the Evangelical movement was not only hampered in the acceptance of new ideas but driven into opposition to them. It was from the Bible that it drew then as now its strength, and the Bible like every other authority was being rudely criticised by the revolutionary spirits of the age. The new learning, and especially the new scientific studies, refused to take anything on trust. Honest enquirers could not long be put off and could never be satisfied by current apologetics or by an array of aptly-quoted texts. The story of the controversies over the inspiration of Scripture lies outside our scope, but the matter bears closely on social problems. The democratic and liberalising tendencies in politics were naturally combined with liberal views upon literary

---

[1] *Politics*, p. 55. The case of the journeymen bakers is being compared with black slavery. For a similar case cf. Hammond, *Town Labourer*, p. 160.

[2] *Practical view of the prevailing religious system of Professed Christians in the higher and middle classes of this country contrasted with real Christianity*, ch. vi. p. 302 (edition of 1834).

and historical subjects, and particularly so in religion, because the dominant theory laid stress upon just those elements of Old Testament teaching, the conception of the monarchy as a thing of divine decree and the insistence upon submission to law, which the reformers were driven to dispute. It is hard to say which of Tom Paine's two books, *The Rights of Man*, his defence of the French Revolution, or *The Age of Reason*, his attack on orthodox Christianity, aroused the greater consternation; but it is clear that their motive was the same, the liberation of mankind from the rule of unreason, from hereditary aristocracy backed up by sycophantic priestcraft. Kingsley is not exaggerating when he speaks of the Bible as having been turned into ' a mere special constable's handbook —an opium-dose for keeping beasts of burden patient while they were being overloaded.' [1] The Scriptures and the social *status quo* were supposed to stand or fall together : Bible and Throne were the two great pillars on which the nation rested : criticism of either was an attack upon both : social reformers were branded as atheists and often driven into atheism ; while, even less justly, biblical critics were suspected of sinister designs against the realm. That the record of the reformations of Israel, the social preaching of Amos or Isaiah, the Gospel of the Kingdom, and the history of the little band who turned the world upside down could ever have been used to bolster up the doctrine of *laissez-faire* and the righteousness of unrestricted competition, is a paradox which no cynic would dare to invent, had it not in fact happened in the story of Evangelical Christianity in the first half of the last century.

None the less it is from their devotion to the Bible

---

[1] Parson Lot's *Second Letter* in *Politics for the People*, p. 58.

that the Evangelicals made their chief contribution to the
social redemption of the country : they made it invol-
untarily, but that does not diminish its effectiveness.
Believing with fervour that the privilege of free study of
God's word was the proudest heritage of Englishmen,
they set themselves to make this possible. To read
Scripture it was necessary first to read the alphabet ;
and masses of the people were still illiterate. So there
arose the Sunday School, an institution founded from
purely religious motives but contributing powerfully to
the cause of democracy by giving to the workers that
corporate consciousness and possibility of concerted
action which only education can bestow. The motive
may have been to teach them contentment and the
consolations of religion by opening to them the knowledge
of a better world : the result was to enlighten them to
the evils of this world and to bestow upon them in some
degree the means of reforming it. Evangelicals must
always be honoured as the pioneers of national education ;
unknowingly in their Sunday Schools they were promoting the very revolution which they desired to resist,
and doing so in the most useful fashion.

And if Evangelicals, for all their philanthropy, were
likely to look askance at social reformers, the Oxford
Movement was definitely hostile to them. The work
of the great Tractarians has loomed large in the recent
history of Anglicanism—so large that at least one
popular manual of Church History [1] treats it as the
only event worthy of mention between 1830 and 1895.
The persons of the three great leaders, Keble, Newman,
and Pusey have been crowned with haloes, eulogised
and idealised until it is hardly possible to see them

---

[1] Wakeman, *Introduction to the History of the Church of England.*

in perspective. Certainly they were men who have
in their several ways some claim to that rare quality
which we call saintliness—Keble for the humility and
gentleness of his character and the simplicity of
his devotion, Newman for the sincerity, sensitiveness
and subtlety of his nature and the long agony of his
spiritual conflicts, Pusey for his assiduity, his energy, and
his self-discipline. And their Movement has unquestionably borne rich fruit. At a time when the conception
of the Church as a great brotherhood with a life and
constitution of its own had been almost lost, when the
great heritage of the past, the corporate and continuous
witness of Catholic experience, was slighted and set
aside, when order and discipline in life, and dignity
and beauty in worship were sadly lacking, and when
the sacramental principle, upon which God has constructed the universe, and Christ modelled His preaching
and founded His Church, was scarcely recognised, these
men had the courage and the ability to claim that such
things were integral parts of the Christian religion. They
delivered us from the complacent Erastianism, the arid
intellectualism, and the solemn ugliness of Hanoverian
Churchmanship, and from the narrow individualism, the
one-sided theology, the sentimentality and the Bible-
worship of the Evangelicals. It is indisputable that
we owe to them the recovery of much that is vital and
still more that is valuable in Christianity, that they have
both enlarged and deepened the spiritual life of the Church,
and that they have enlisted in the service of religion much
that can rightly be dedicated to it. But that is by no
means the whole story.

It is probably unfair to follow J. A. Froude [1] unre-

---

[1] ' The Oxford Counter-reformation ' in *Short Studies*, Series IV.

servedly and to depict Tractarianism as solely or even mainly a reaction against the liberal movement. No doubt there is truth in his claim that its object was to strengthen the corporate life of the Church in order to make her an adequate bulwark against the assaults of the reformers. No doubt its champions recognised that ' Protestantism was the chrysalis of Liberalism,' [1] and with this in view determined that ' the Church was to be unprotestantised.' No doubt from one aspect Tractarianism was simply ' Toryism in ecclesiastical costume.' [2] We shall show in a moment that this is not a complete account of their motives. But it must first be admitted that it is not wholly unjust. The genesis of the Movement proves it. Oxford University has always been noted for its Tory politics and its intense respect for tradition. The ' home of lost causes ' had passed unscathed through the upheavals of the first quarter of the century. Of all the great prophets and singers of liberty very few were Oxford men : and of these Southey declared that he ' learned two things only at Oxford—to row and to swim ; ' [3] Arnold barely escaped the influence of the place by leaving it ; Landor and Shelley were sent down. Not until the repeal of the Test Acts and the passing of the Reform Bill did the University realise that the world was changing around it. And while it was in a state of restive alarm came the attack upon the Irish bishoprics and Keble's sermon of protest. Had it not been for the terror of liberalism his words might have passed unnoticed ; as it was the atmosphere was tense and on the whole sympathetic. In the early *Tracts* it

---

[1] L.c. p. 167.   [2] L.c. p. 175.

[3] *Life and Correspondence of R. Southey*, i. p. 176. Cf. Coleridge's remark that Southey at Oxford was ' a nightingale among owls ' (l.c. p. 213) ; cf. Dowden, *Southey*, pp. 29, 30.

is clear enough that the Tories are being summoned to
rally, that a challenge is being flung at ' the shallow and
detestable liberalism of the day ' [1]—liberalism in politics
which had infringed the vested interests of the Church,
liberalism in social matters which was a direct attack
upon ' gentlemen of county influence,' [2] liberalism in
thought which was undermining the remnants of authority
that Evangelical individualism had spared and was leading
to a sceptical and materialistic rationalism. Men were
ready enough to take refuge from the new learning, from
the ' hodge podge of philosophers ' as Keble called the
British Association, in a mediaevalism which ascribed
a quite unhistorical consistency to Catholic authority and
set it up as the only alternative to downright unbelief.
The Tractarians, in bidding Churchmen to hold fast the
faith once delivered and authoritatively interpreted, were
responding to the panic of the times.

But it is not on this account that we need regard their
influence with disapproval. In the current liberalism
there was much that Christians were thoroughly justified
in resisting with all their power. In his individualist
interpretation of freedom and gospel of enlightened
selfishness the liberal was in fact the enemy of social
morality ; he was still more obviously unchristian and
anti-christian. We may regret that in undertaking the
defence of the Catholic faith the Tractarians were not
able to concentrate their opposition upon the evil elements
in the spirit of the new age, that they took up an attitude
of thoroughgoing hostility, and sought to obstruct rather
than guide, to reject good and bad alike. Yet even if

---

[1] *Tracts for the Times*, iii. p. 1.

[2] Newman to Pusey, letter of 19th March,1833. Cf. Newman, *Apologia*,
p. 30 (ed. of 1873), ' The vital question was, How were we to keep the
Church from being liberalised ' ; Church, *Oxford Movement*, pp. 89-92 ;
Sarolea, *Cardinal Newman*, pp. 18-21.

their action was in part dictated by fear of change and blind resistance to current tendencies, there was abundant warrant for it, and we must repudiate the attempt to write it down as obstinate and reactionary obscurantism.

Nor is it more than very partially true to say that their dominant motive was dislike of liberalism. They were essentially positive not negative. Genuine devotion to the ideal of Catholic Churchmanship was the inspiration of the whole Movement. The sceptic's craving for finality, the scholar's passion for minute investigation, the legalist's desire for precise definition, the antiquarian's reverence for the curious customs of the past, the artist's love of beauty and dignity in word and worship, architecture and music, the devotee's delight in the treasury of religious experience and the records of saints and doctors,—all these interests were focussed by them upon the history of the Church. They were looking for a golden age, and with a somewhat pathetic credulity assumed that it was to be traced in the records of undivided Christendom and particularly of the Fourth and Fifth centuries. While Evangelicals were applying St. Paul's more quietistic sayings to the circumstances of the industrial era, Pusey was labouring to reconstruct in nineteenth-century England the religion of St. Ambrose or St. Cyril of Alexandria—a much less desirable proceeding. He and his friends found in their favourite Fathers much that was interesting and much that was Christian, though in the centuries which they specially admired religion was at a very low ebb : but from their increasing concentration upon the past they involved themselves and the Church in consequences gravely harmful. In the first place they lost all faith in progress, in the living and present guidance of the Holy Spirit, and so confirmed themselves in their hostility to liberalism :

and secondly, which is more important, they diverted
the attention of the Church from the crying needs of the
time into meticulous and often unedifying arguments
upon matters of archaeology.

'Their error,' said Maurice [1] in 1837, 'I think consists
in opposing to τὸ πνεῦμα τοῦ αἰῶνος τούτου the spirit
of a former age, instead of the ever-living and acting
Spirit of God,' To set up 'the child-like spirit of the
Fathers against the intellectual spirit of these times—
the spirit of submission to Church authority against the
spirit of voluntary association,' seemed to him to be a
denial of the present organic life of Christianity, and so
of that very principle of continuity on which the
Tractarians rightly laid stress. They were allowing the
vintage of the Catholic religion, which might have been
for the refreshment of the nations, to remain sealed up
and useless, while its discoverers engaged in learned dis-
quisitions and heated controversies over the shape and
ornamentation of the bottles in which it was contained.
Their story is a sad example of how men can lose all
sense of proportion, and from real devotion can descend
into such a whirl of petty strifes, of subterfuge and
policy and intrigue, that insignificant details are magnified
into vital issues, means are exaggerated into ends, and
the cause itself is obscured and forgotten. When the cry
of the oppressed was ringing in men's ears and when
Christians might have listened to the prophets of social
righteousness or to the victims of social evil, fifty years
were wasted in lawsuits over 'regeneration' and ritual,
vestments and incense, and the precise meaning of sixteenth
century rubrics. In Christ's time also there were some
who were so earnest about the washing of chalice and

[1] *Life of Maurice*, i. p. 225 (4th Edition).

paten and the tithing of mint and anise and cummin that
they neglected justice and mercy and faith.

Even the greatest and best of them was singularly
blind to the industrial problems of the time. Newman,
late in life, declared that he ' had never considered social
questions in their relation to faith, and had always looked
upon the poor as objects for compassion and benevolence.'[1]
Pusey regarded their degradation similarly as a pretext
for the foundation of sisterhoods ; Ward as an argument
for the importance of dogmatic theology.[2] The outlook
of the Tractarians was conditioned by the circumstances
of their experience. They were dons, men whose lives
were fragrant with an old-world and cloistered virtue.
The Church Catholic was to them simply Oxford on a
large scale—a grand heritage rich in the stored graces
of the past, preserved immaculate in a world of error
and brutality, a possession into which men might enter
and which they must keep and hand on to their successors
unchanged. The minutiae of academic studies were quite
genuinely the most important things in life ; the narrow
circle of academic interests was their world. Outside
there might be chaos : within, at least, was calm. The
remedy was plain ; let the universe model itself upon
the university ; Oxford should give its spirit to Church
and kingdom. This was their mission, and in following
them the Church was side-tracked for half a century
with consequences for which all the benefits of the
Oxford Movement fail to compensate us.

Thanks to this diverting of her energies the Church

[1] Quoted by Marson, God's Co-operative Society, p. 71 ; Ward's Life
of Cardinal Newman bears out this admission.

[2] If Hurrell Froude's Remains be regarded as typical of the first
phase of the Movement, we shall have to convict it not merely of
indifference but of downright hostility to the humanitarian reforms
for which Fowell Buxton and his friends were agitating. Cf. Remains, i.
pp. 258, 348, 355, 377, 382.

lost her opportunity to understand and lead the aspirations of the people : thanks to it her interests were narrowed down to matters concerning her own constitution and ceremonials, and she ceased to reckon it her duty to care for the well-being of those outside her own borders : thanks to it social reform followed Marx and not Maurice, and the masses lost all confidence in institutional religion. It is not altogether surprising that Pusey was driven to declare that he and Maurice ' did not believe in the same God,' [1] or that Maurice [2] for all his diffidence admitted readily that it was so.

That the principles of the Catholic faith do not in themselves involve any such narrow ecclesiasticism, and are not necessarily dependent upon the belief that inspiration ceased with the holding of the last Oecumenical Council, or that democracy is of the devil, has been proved by the lives and labours of many who look back to the Tractarians with filial reverence. A Movement which gave to the Church priests like Dolling or Stanton, which carried the Gospel in all its beauty and brotherhood to the slums and the outcasts, and which has developed in its later phases a social enthusiasm as pure as Maurice's own, cannot be condemned root and branch. Ultimately its emphasis upon corporate life and the duties of membership in a society made it a potent factor in the development of collectivist ideas.[3] Yet it is apparent that the want of faith and charity, the concentration upon trivialities, and the blindness to large issues which characterised its early supporters did grave disservice to Christianity. The

[1] Liddon, *Life of Pusey*, iv. p. 60.
[2] *Life of Maurice*, ii. pp. 466, 467.
[3] Cf. Dicey, *Law and Opinion in England*, pp. 407-409 (2nd edition).

fact is that the Catholicism of the Tractarians was almost as completely individual a creed as the Protestantism of the Evangelicals. They substituted membership of the Church, observance of discipline, and sacramental communion with Christ for conversion, puritanical strictness, and ecstatic consciousness of Christ's presence ; but of man's corporate relationships and responsibilities, of those social sins which the individual shares in but cannot personally cure, and of the social righteousness which flows from the awakening of the common conscience, they knew almost nothing. They made possible a wider conception of the meaning of religion by bringing back the ideals of catholicity and exposing the shortcomings of individualism : but they failed to apply those ideals where they were most needed and themselves exhibited a sectarian spirit as narrow as any dissenter's. Maurice's [1] cry is just—' Oh that our High Churchmen would but be Catholics ! At present they seem to me three parts Papist and one part Protestant ; but the *tertium quid*, the glorious product of each element, so different from both, I cannot discern even in the best of them.' His own influence upon the younger school of High Churchmen has supplied in some measure the answer to his prayer : but in his lifetime he was rejected by the Tractarians almost as decisively as by the Evangelicals, and for his social work he received no help from either party.

It was with a Church dominated by these two schools that the early social reformers were brought into contact ; and they were not likely to be received with open arms. It is perhaps natural, considering the current presentations of Christianity, that Robert Owen, the pioneer of Socialism

[1] *Life of Maurice*, i. p. 188.

in England, should have started without any expectation
of help from organised religion.[1] With men like Phill-
potts, bishop of Exeter, on the bench, or like Brindley,
the anti-Owenite lecturer, on the platform, the doctrines
of his school would become more and more hostile to
orthodoxy. The Socialists were met from the first with
misrepresentation and abuse. ' Do you care nothing for
the stability of the social order ' said the Tory prelate
in the House of Lords, ' or if not, have you lost all respect
for the ordinances of religion or for the dignity of the
sovereign? This Socialist may be doing philanthropic
works—of that I know nothing. But his community
is illegal, his writings are revolutionary, blasphemous,
obscene. He holds loose views on the sanctity of the
Church and of the marriage tie. A government which
refuses to condemn him is unworthy of the confidence
of the country. It is guilty of treason to God and the
Queen.' Brindley is briefer and more brutal. ' Do you
accept the Bible as the inspired word of God?' he demands,
' If so, there are certain words in the first Epistle of St.
Peter. If not—! ' a line of argument which is not dead yet.

That there should have been from the first this total
lack of fairness or of endeavour to understand, this
total blindness to the real conditions which had stirred
the souls of the reformers, this total refusal either to support their efforts or to suggest alternative schemes is
sufficiently tragic and amazing. It becomes almost
incredible when we remember that the terrible condition
of the poor both in manufacturing and in agricultural
districts was not only widespread but well-known.
General studies like those of Aikin [2] and Gisborne [3] in

[1] Cf. F. Podmore, *Robert Owen*, ii. pp. 470-529.
[2] *Description of Country Round Manchester* : cf. especially pp. 156-206.
[3] *Enquiry into the Duties of Man*, ii. pp. 362-397 (3rd edition).

1795 or pamphlets like those of Kay [1] in 1832, Fielden [2] in 1836 and Horner [3] in 1840 revealed conditions as hideous as those denounced in *Yeast* and *Alton Locke*. For twenty years Cobbett had striven to arouse the authorities with his splendid gifts and splendid honesty. Luddites and Chartists had underlined his warnings. The protests of the workers, the constant debates in Parliament, the Reports of three Committees and a Royal Commission,[4] even the newspapers of the time testify to the devilries which were being perpetrated in Lancashire mills, or Staffordshire ironworks, or Durham coal-fields, and repeated in the dens and hovels of every city and every village. These things were not done in a corner. And if we do not here repeat once more the tale of that black epoch in our national life, it is only because the evidence for it is indisputable and by this time familiar. In all the records of human suffering and human shame there is nothing to surpass it. And yet Churchmen, of sound education, delicate sensibilities, and often genuine devotion, closed their eyes and ears and deliberately refused to act, babbling meanwhile of the New Jerusalem and of the Catholic Religion. We must turn to the state of public opinion if we are to condone or at least understand their attitude.

To us who look back to their time with the lessons of their failure and the proofs of the necessity of collective action before our eyes, such an attitude is hard to understand. We can scarcely believe that *laissez-faire* could ever have commanded the support of the country—or

[1] *Moral and Physical Condition of the Working Classes employed in the Cotton Manufacture in Manchester.*

[2] *The Curse of the Factory System.*

[3] *On the Employment of Children.*

[4] House of Commons Committees, 1816 and 1831 ; Lords' Committee, 1819 ; Commission 1833.

even of individuals unless blinded by self-interest : we
can scarcely realise the horror with which State-interference was regarded by men of all classes, parties and
creeds. But the fact remains that for the time individual
liberty, however gross its abuses, seemed synonymous
with progress, and the extension of governmental powers
with reaction.

The general cause of this is plain enough. Until
Adam Smith's time it is not too much to say that the
State had been supreme in industry : and its influence
had been as deadening as its methods were corrupt. The
founder of political economy, like the Physiocrats of his
time, was concerned primarily to contrast the perfections
of the ' natural ' system with the absurdities and wastage
of the artificial laws of the State. His revolt in favour of
liberty, followed up by the smashing attacks of Bentham
against the corruption and iniquity of public life, gave a
strong bias to the whole reforming movement ; and a
bias which under the circumstances was fully justified.
It must be remembered that the State whose supervision
is in question was the unreformed constitution ; if we
want to appreciate its qualifications a brief study of the
speeches in favour of the Reform Bill will furnish us with
a sufficient indictment. Sensible men could hardly be
expected to believe that any good thing could come out
of such a mass of rottenness. Every action of such a
body must have a sinister purpose. Justices might
fix wages ; they would do so in their own interests, and
the workers would do better to trust to the laws of supply
and demand.[1] The State might create communal settlements for the relief of the Unemployed ; the workers

---

[1] Whitbread's proposals in 1795 to assess wages met with little
support : cf. Cunningham, *Growth of English Industry and Commerce*,
ii. pp. 498-501.

would support no paternal reforms until Parliament had
been remodelled.[1] Inspectors might enforce Factory
Acts ; they were appointed by the wealthy in order to
whitewash the employers.[2] Legislators might control
industry ; their laws would only rivet fresh chains upon
the poor.   Rather would men choose freedom to starve
unheeded than such a tyranny.

This general reaction against State-interference was
emphasised by the experience of the Napoleonic wars.
War must always distract attention from social problems,
impoverish the population, impose restrictions upon trade,
send up prices, and strengthen the centralised powers of
government.   The country suffered hideously during the
long struggle : every class had been embittered by the
constraints imposed in the name of national necessity :
rich and poor were united in believing that the State
was the source of all their evils.   After Waterloo, a few
prophets might declare that the war had ' its golden side '
and ' had forced on the people at large the home truth
that national honesty and individual security, private
morals and public safety, mutually grounded each other,
and could not grow or thrive but in intertwine ' ;[3] but
the vast majority clamoured only for the repeal of restrictions ;   and then, when this larger liberty was
accompanied by a huge increase of industrial prosperity,
hailed it as a clear case of cause and effect, and argued

[1] This scheme of Owen's was rejected by two meetings of workers in
1817 : cf. Beer, *History of British Socialism*, i. p. 171.

[2] The Act of 1833 appointing four inspectors was received by the
mill-hands with ridicule : cf. Hutchins and Harrison, *History of Factory
Legislation*, pp. 55, 56.

[3] S. T. Coleridge in an essay published in the *Courier*, July 1816, and
quoted in his second *Lay Sermon*, p. 39.   The passage is startlingly
appropriate to present conditions : for as proof of the awakening of a
social conscience he points to ' the changed condition of manners and
intellect among the young men at Oxford and Cambridge,' and to ' the
predominant anxiety concerning the education of children ' !

that all would be well if only the individual was allowed
to live unhampered. We must not judge them too
harshly. They were confronted with what appeared an
inevitable alternative, either state-control or individual
freedom : they had had a long and unpleasant experience of the former ;   despairing of it, they turned to the
latter in the eager expectation that the private citizen
if left to himself would accomplish what the State was
impotent to achieve, and confident that in any case they
were choosing the lesser evil.

It is interesting to compare the development of public
opinion in England after the French wars with that in
Germany. There it was the evils of disunion and of
unsupported private enterprise which were familiar.
State-control among that mass of petty duchies and small
kingdoms was unknown—and consequently desirable.
All the constructive minds in the country set themselves
therefore to the creation of a single sovereign State and
the transference to it of unlimited powers of interference.
Instead of a half-century of *laissez-faire* they endured a
half-century of increasing governmental control, culminating in the establishment of the German Empire
and of the system of discipline and efficiency with which
we have become painfully familiar. When we blame
our countrymen for the evils of unrestricted individualism,
we must not forget that they might have fared little
better if they had chosen the other alternative.

And if the general condition of public opinion sanctioned
a policy of non-intervention, we can readily understand,
even if we find it hard to pardon, the failure of the Church.
For after all she only accepted and sanctioned with
her blessing the views of those whose knowledge
of such matters she reckoned superior to her own. The
material well-being of its citizens was primarily the busi-

ness of the State, which alone possessed expert information
and power to put its resolutions into force. When
politicians and philosophers, scientists and economists
united to declare that the condition of the poor was
unalterable, that destitution and child-slavery, and
intolerably long hours of work, and reeking warrens of
slums, and the condemnation of masses of human
beings to an utterly inhuman existence, were the logical
outcome of natural law, and that any attempts at
interference or even alleviation would but intensify
the evil, it is perhaps hardly surprising that the religious
world gave up the effort to grapple with the situation
and directed its energies to other and less unsavoury
spheres. Englishmen have always possessed a faculty
for closing their eyes and refusing to see the evil in their
midst and even denying with an air of outraged virtue
that anything is wrong. We have heard much latterly
of the ' Nelson touch' : but our hero was more truly typical
of his race at Copenhagen than he was at Trafalgar.
In those days it was industrial slavery in the north-
country ; a few years back it was prostitution in the
West-end. When a prophet arises and the ugly truth
is thrust upon our notice, we take refuge behind a formula,
as our fathers did behind a text ; and in secret console
ourselves with the belief that things cannot be as bad as
they appear, that even if they are they will soon improve,
that meddling will only make matters worse, and that
anyhow it is none of our business. Having come to
which very satisfactory conclusion we discharge our
duty to the country by writing a complaint to the press
or the parson, and dismiss the topic from our minds with
the reflection that its existence is a necessary evil.

And in the early nineteenth century such a method
was more excusable than it is to-day. For it was

characteristic of the time that the educated classes had
a childlike confidence in the existence and immutability
of law. Their treatises upon Natural Religion, their
political oratory, their standards of conduct, all reveal
a readiness to govern their lives upon a few generally
accepted and often quite fallacious principles which were
given divine authority and obeyed with awe and a sense
of conscious rectitude. When once the experts were
agreed and the verdict went forth, it might remain
unquestioned for generations : for the scientific spirit
which insists that every law must be verified before it
can be approved and sets each student to test for himself
the conclusions of a Newton or a Faraday was yet unborn.
The tyranny of catchwords and generalisations still lies
heavy upon us ; to-day it has become a superstition, but
a century ago it was a religion.

So it was with the politicians of the time. They were
living in an age when progress vastly outstripped their
ability to keep pace with it. ' The story of the changes
that transformed travel, transport, commerce, manufacture, farming, banking, and all the various arts and
means of social life, reads like a chapter from the *Arabian
Nights.*' [1] They selected, as statesmen in difficulties are
swift to select, sounding phrases and solemn enunciations
of principle. ' Liberty ' was the most overworked and
the least understood of them all. Great men like Burke
and small men like Melbourne rolled it ever upon their
tongues and committed their blackest crimes against civilisation and humanity in its name. For liberty to them
meant simply the right of the individual to follow his own
interests restrained by the minimum of interference.
The laws of course must not be broken ; but then they

[1] Hammond, *The Town Labourer*, p. 1.

were framed so as to leave the largest scope for the self-development of the prosperous. It is curious to note how widely the principle of freedom was employed. Wages [1] must not be fixed—that would be to destroy freedom of contract : workers must not combine [2]—that would violate freedom to engage labour or to seek other employment : industry must not be controlled—freedom of competition was the source of national prosperity : child-labour must go on unchecked—even infants should enjoy freedom to spend sixteen hours a day in the mills : poor-relief must be abolished—it interfered with the freedom of the poor to starve. The corn-trade and most imports, meetings, speech, and the printing-press, and until 1824 combination and emigration,—in these things alone freedom was withheld ; one can have too much even of a good thing. And so the cult of *laissez-faire* continued ; and the riots were suppressed ; and the leaders of labour were flung into goal ; and the rich grew fat ; and the trade-returns increased by leaps and bounds. And hardly a word was said in protest until Carlyle [3] lifted up his strident voice and said drily,' Liberty I am told is divine. Liberty when it becomes liberty to die by starvation is not so divine.' Even then, though here and there men listened, the majority shrugged their shoulders at the cranky Scot, and forgave him his blasphemy of their goddess. Years afterwards the Manchester School still haunted the same altars and repeated the same creeds, appealing the while, in support of their cult of liberty, to the swollen income of the country.

[1] The last law fixing wages disappeared in 1824.

[2] So said one section : another led by Place, the Benthamite and Malthusian, argued that it was more truly liberal to repeal the Combination Laws and leave the worker free. They succeeded in 1824 : cf. Graham Wallas, *Life of Francis Place*, pp. 197-240.

[3] *Past and Present*, p. 212 (edition of 1899).

No wonder that Karl Marx grew bitter and wrote fiercely :
for Marx was a German and no devotee of freedom ;
and he was a keen observer, and knew that the profits
of trade were going not to the country but to the Manchester School.

And the policy of *laissez-faire* was buttressed by appeals
to the laws of the universe as interpreted in the works
of Bentham or Malthus or Ricardo. It is one of the
strange survivals of puritan times that men clung to the
determinist outlook, the most unpleasant feature of
Puritanism, even when they had forsaken the faith
which made it endurable. Fatalism has always been
familiar to the Briton, whether it comes in the guise of
the Calvinism of Protestant Reformers, or of the ' iron
laws ' of the early economists, or of the Stoic ethics
of the Victorian agnostics, or of the biological theories
of Weismannists and Mendelians. And it is in the
language of unalterable fate that the politicians justified
their inaction. ' The laws of commerce are the laws of
Nature and therefore the laws of God ' ; [1] Burke's dictum
reappears in various forms for nearly a century, and is
used to excuse every kind of enormity. Marx justly
quotes it as typical of the age, and cannot resist adding
a characteristically savage comment :—' No wonder that,
true to the laws of God and of Nature, Burke always sold
himself in the best market ! ' [2] ' Laissez-faire, Supply-
and-demand—one begins to be weary of all that. Leave
all to egoism, to ravenous greed of money, of pleasure, of
applause :—it is the Gospel of Despair.' [3] But the politicians were not so much to blame. They were only
repeating what was put into their mouths by wiser and not

[1] *Thoughts on Scarcity*, p. 31.
[2] *Capital* (English edition) ii. p. 786.
[3] Carlyle, *Past and Present*, p. 184.

less disinterested persons. Bad philosophy and bad
economics were the chief cause and the chief excuse of
the failure of Church and State.

Among those ultimately responsible for the sins of
laissez-faire Bentham and the Utilitarian philosophy
must bear the heaviest blame.[1]   In spite of the value of
his critical labours in clearing out 'the Augean stable
of the law,'[2] in exposing abuses and demanding radical
reform, and in forcing men to cross-examine traditional
values and free their minds of cant, Bentham's
work popularised if it did not originate an anti-social
ethic, the consequences of which were disastrous.   While
claiming to adopt the principle of ' the greatest happiness
of the greatest number ' as ' the foundation of morals
and legislation,'[3] he eliminated all the altruism which
might be covered by such a phrase, using it only to justify
his own radical politics and eventually shortening it by
omitting all reference to ' the greatest number.'[4]   The
motive of every action was in his eyes not duty but self-
interest, and ethical conduct was to be based solely upon
a cold and calculating egoism.   ' To prove that the
immoral action is a miscalculation of self-interest is the
purpose of the intelligent moralist ' ;[5]   and we are
justified in concluding that ' though adopting the " greatest

[1] Cf. Dicey, *Law and Opinion in England*, p. 147, ' though *laissez-faire*
is not an essential part of Utilitarianism, it was practically the most
vital part of Bentham's legislative dectrine.'

[2] J. S. Mill, *Early Essays*, p. 360.

[3] Bowring, *Works of Jeremy Bentham*, x. p. 142.

[4] Cf. Atkinson, *Jeremy Bentham*, p. 214, quoting Perronet Thompson,
Works, i. p. 136.

[5] Bentham, *Deontology*, i. p. 12 ; Leslie Stephen, *English Utilitarians*,
i. pp. 313, 314, admits the substantial genuineness of this book which
the Mills, in their jealousy of Bowring, had repudiated : cf. J. S. Mill,
Dissertations, i. pp. 364, 365.

happiness " formula, Bentham's logical position is distinctly that of eighteenth century Individualism.' [1]

Such doctrines, despite his ridiculous vanity and
corrosive temper, limited experience and crabbed style,
were eagerly seized upon by the politicians of the time,
and from their influence upon James and John
Stuart Mill became the dominant belief of the
liberal movement. Over and over again the Utilitarian
principle is invoked as a sanction for *laissez-faire*. It is
assumed that enlightened selfishness is the highest that
can be expected from human nature ; that its free development will produce not only the greatest happiness
of the selfish individual, but in some mysterious fashion
the greatest happiness of the community. In this spirit
it is seriously argued that mill-owners, while securing their
own interests by the employment of children, will also
be benefiting not only the country but somehow the
poor little victims of their greed : that farmers may be
relied upon to provide the greatest possible well-being
for their labourers, not from motives of brotherhood, but
simply because they will thus themselves be the greater
gainers : that the best thing to do for the slave is to
leave him defenceless in the hand of his owner, the man
who understands his needs best. Burke had expressed it
in a sinister sentence, ' The benign and wise Disposer of all
things obliges men whether they will or not in pursuing
their own selfish interests, to connect the general good
with their own individual successes : ' [2]—a creed well
calculated to soothe the susceptibilities of the magnates
of industry. ' At last it came to be carelessly accepted
as the teaching both of philosophy and of experience

---

[1] Albee, *History of English Utilitarianism*, p. 181 : cf. L. Stephen,
l.c. pp. 307-318, where this conclusion is virtually endorsed.

[2] Quoted in *Archbishops' Fifth Committee's Report*, § 56, p. 44.

that every man must fight for himself ; and " devil take the hindmost " became the accepted social creed of what was still believed to be a Christian nation. Utilitarianism became the Protestantism of Sociology, and " how to make for self and family the best of both worlds" was assumed to be the duty, as it certainly was the aim, of every practical Englishman.' [1]

And along with the Utilitarians come Malthus and the application of the doctrine of the struggle for existence to the problem of poverty. Though he is recognised by Darwin [2] as in some sense his forerunner, Malthus simply notes the facts of struggle and does not develop the idea of their relation to progress nor the theory of the survival of the fittest : if he had, his influence might have been even more untoward. In his *Essay on the Principle of Population*, the thesis is submitted that mankind will always multiply beyond the limit of subsistence, since the increase of numbers far outstrips the utmost product-ivity of earth, and that the surplus which cannot secure for itself a share in the available food is kept down by the eliminating power of disease, vice, and starvation. The book was first issued in 1798, and its harshness was much softened in the second edition of 1803 when ' moral restraint ' was introduced as a check alongside of the other three ; though even then it was recognised that this would only apply to the educated classes. Until mankind learn self-restraint there must always be a proportion of the people living on the verge of destitution, nor is it possible to remedy their distress except for a

[1] *Fabian Essays*, No. ii. p. 45.   For the resemblance in regard to their individualism between Benthamites and Evangelicals see an article by J. H. Burton on the relations of Bentham and Wilberforce in *Westminster Review*, xxxvii. pp. 289, 290.

[2] Cf. *Origin of Species*, ch. iii. p. 79 (Popular edition 1902).   Cf. L. Stephen, l.c. ii. pp. 162-164.

brief period even if the rate of wages or the quantity of food be increased ; for every improvement encourages a further fecundity and in a few years the dividend will again be insufficient to support life.

The *Essay* had a remarkable success. Six editions appeared by 1826 ; replies were addressed to it by the dozen ; converts to its views came in by hundreds. And among the experts it was the earlier form of the theory that attracted most attention. Torrens [1] and others definitely condemned the concession made in the second edition to the potentialities of man's moral nature ; and for themselves repudiated this part of the work. Malthus was himself a scholar and a parson, a sympathiser with the poor, a man full of benevolence. Occasionally he allowed his heart to get the better of his head, as when quite inconsistently he threw over Ricardo's doctrine of rigid *laissez-faire* by allowing state-interference within certain limits.[2] But he was convinced that the laws of nature had fixed a definite margin to the possibility of food-production, and that poverty depended solely upon the ratio of population to products—the first of which axioms is still tenable, though, thanks to the increase of knowledge, the margin is not yet in sight, while the second would only be true if wealth were equally distributed. He foresaw ' that a doctrine which attributes the greatest part of the sufferings of the lower classes of society exclusively to themselves, may appear unfavourable to the cause of liberty, as affording a tempting opportunity to govern- ments of oppressing their subjects at pleasure and laying

---

[1] Cf. *Essay on External Corn Trade*, published 1815. Malthus' work was originally undertaken as a criticism of Godwin : as such the first edition was unanswerable, whereas the concession ruined the logic of his case : cf. Bagehot's essay on Malthus, *Economic Studies*, pp. 176-196.

[2] Cf. Bonar, *Malthus and his work*, pp. 343, 344.

the whole blame on the laws of nature and the imprudence of the poor ' : [1] but never seems to have realised that such a sentence does in fact exactly describe the effects of his teaching. Southey's conclusion—'His remedy for the existing evils of society is simply to abolish the poor rates and starve the poor into celibacy ' [2]—is by no means unfair. For the politicians accepted Malthus' work in its extreme form, used it as an excuse for refusing all remedial legislation, and eventually under its influence repealed the Poor Laws while leaving the Corn Laws in force, thereby subjecting the workers to twelve years of unparalleled misery. No wonder Cobbett [3] declared with his healthy violence, ' Parson, I have during my life detested many men, but never any one so much as you.' No wonder Carlyle [4] suggested that it would be more rational to establish a ' Parish Exterminator ' and to prescribe ' painless extinction ' for the infants of the poor.

Over-population became in fact the favourite bogey of the *laissez-faire* school, and for nearly a century was employed to scare away every champion of reform. Very significant of its power is the change of attitude towards the question of poor-relief. In 1796 Pitt, introducing his Poor Bill into the House of Commons, used words which might have been spoken by any modern advocate of the endowment of motherhood. ' Let us,' said he, ' make relief in cases where there are a number of children a matter of right and honour instead of a ground of opprobrium and contempt. This will make a large family a blessing and not a curse. Those who

---

[1] *Essay on the Principle of Population*, bk. iv. ch. 6. p. 417 (7th edition).

[2] *Essays Moral and Political*, i. p. 91, written 1816.

[3] ' Letter to Parson Malthus,' *Political Register*, vol. 34, No. 33.

[4] *Chartism*, pp. 201, 202 (edition of 1899).

have enriched their country with a number of children have a claim upon its assistance for support.'[1] Yet in 1800 he was compelled by the influence of ' those whose opinions he was bound to respect '—Bentham and Malthus—to withdraw his bill. And in 1817 Ricardo, quoting his words, contrasts them with the report of the Committee on the Poor Laws, and declares that ' the pernicious tendency of these Poor-laws is no longer a mystery since it has been fully developed by the able hand of Mr. Malthus, and every friend to the poor must ardently wish for their abolition.'[2] At a time when the wealth of the country was increasing with unprecedented speed, the wealthy were solemnly warned that while poor-relief was given it was ' quite in the natural order of things that the fund for the maintenance of the poor should progressively increase till it has absorbed all the net revenue of the country.'[3]

And the spectre once raised was not easily laid. The Christian Socialists had to encounter it, and admitted that the problem of population was ' the root-question of all social science ';[4] though in view of ' our own social arrangements, the state of our farming, the necessity of employing such vast numbers in distribution instead of production, and the present frightful waste of the raw materials of food ' they declined to be terrorised by it. On the economists its grip remained unshaken. In 1852 J. S. Mill repeats Malthus' doctrine almost verbally :—' Poverty, like most social evils, exists because men follow their brute instincts without due

[1] *Hansard*, xxxiii. p. 710.   Cf. Bonar, *Malthus and his work*, pp. 29-44.

[2] *Principles of Political Economy and Taxation* (edited by M'Culloch), p. 58.

[3] Ricardo, l.c. p. 57.

[4] Cf. Kingsley's articles ' The Church *versus* Malthus ' in *Christian Socialist*, i. pp. 170, 179.

consideration'[1] : and after discussing the various remedies
concludes that the only true one is a rigid restriction of
the birth-rate. Over-population and ' the niggardliness
of nature ' [2] remained the conventional excuse for the
miseries of the poor, so that even in 1879 Henry George
complained that this doctrine is ' deeply-rooted and
thoroughly entwined with the reasonings of the current
political economy.' [3]

To follow up the subject, with the further factor, the
possibility of birth-control,[4] which the neo-malthusians,
Francis Place and the younger Owen, have done so much
to popularise, is outside our scope. Suffice it to say that,
if there is still much loose talk about the ' moral value of
the struggle for existence ' (as if the survivors were
necessarily the best instead of the most competitive,
the most human instead of the most animal), we have at
least escaped from the policy of exacerbating the struggle
by condemning all efforts to reorganise society on co-
operative lines, or, failing that, to alleviate the miseries
of the present position: Malthus is no longer used as a
support for *laissez-faire*.

Finally, as the stalwart allies of the cause of non-
interference, came the economists with their theories of
value and wages. Adam Smith, the founder of political
science, had laid down in his *Wealth of Nations* the principle
that wages were fixed by the law of supply and demand,
and would find their natural level if left free from all

[1] *Principles of Political Economy*, bk. ii. ch. 13, p. 446 (3rd edition).

[2] Cf. J. S. Mill, l.c. p. 232.   For the influence of Malthus on Mill cf.
MacCunn, *Six Radical Thinkers*, pp. 46-48.

[3] *Progress and Poverty*, p. 125.

[4] Malthus himself nowhere suggests any preventive checks save the
postponement of marriage and a life of continence.   Contraceptive
methods seem first to have been publicly advocated by Place in *Illustra-
tions and Proofs of the Principle of Population* (published 1822), pp. 165,
173-5.

artificial control. But it was the work of Ricardo, supplementing that of Malthus, which developed this principle into the ' iron law.' ' The natural price of labour,' he maintained, ' is that price which is necessary to enable the labourers, one with another, to subsist and to perpetuate their race, without either increase or diminution. . . . The market price is the price which is really paid for labour, from the natural operation of the proportion of the supply to the demand. However much the market price may deviate from its natural price, it has, like commodities, a tendency to conform to it.' [1] Wages are thus supposed to be naturally fixed at the subsistence level : even if they rise above it through the increase of capital relative to the quantity of labour available, they will not do so for long, because firstly, as Malthus proved, the population will increase until the demand is supplied, and secondly, as Ricardo constantly hints,[2] a rise in the cost of labour will stimulate the introduction of machinery and thus diminish the need for labourers.

Further, although he lays down the general law that ' in proportion to the increase of capital will be the increase in the demand for labour,' [3] a law which was freely quoted to support the belief that the growth of the national wealth would naturally benefit the workers, he is driven to admit that as capital increases ' the ratio will necessarily be a diminishing ratio,' [4] and quotes with

---

[1] *Principles of Political Economy and Taxation*, p. 50. The last sentence is typical of the author's style ! We are not concerned here with Ricardo's work as a whole, nor do we wish to dispute either his eminence as an abstract thinker (for which cf. Bagehot, *Economic Studies*, pp. 197-208), or his real goodness of heart.

[2] Especially in *Principles of Political Economy and Taxation*, ch. 31—a chapter added to the third edition and lamented by M'Culloch. Cf. *Letters of Ricardo to Malthus*, p. 184 (letter 76).

[3] L.c. p. 51 *et passim*.

[4] L. c. p. 241.

approval Barton's argument [1] that as arts and civilisation
develop capital will always become more and more
' fixed ' and be withdrawn from the labour-market, and
that owing to this fixing ' the position that the number of
labourers employed is in proportion to the wealth of the
State has not the semblance of probability.' Thus the
dividend which constitutes wages does not consist of the
whole available capital but only of the ' circulating
capital.' This admission supplies the famous theory of
the Wages Fund, that the amount of capital payable in
wages is strictly limited and that each labourer can only
receive a dividend proportionate to the number of com-
petitors for employment.[2]

Ricardo views with even greater horror than Malthus
all attempts to alleviate the position. There is for him
only one remedy, to diminish the birth-rate. Adam
Smith had pleaded for the right of workers to combine ;
Whitbread in 1795 had urged the fixing of a minimum
wage ; Ricardo will have none of it. His dictum, ' like
all other contracts, wages should be left to the fair and
free competition of the market, and should never be
controlled by the interference of the legislature,' [3] is stated
as a truism on which no discussion can arise. Throughout
his treatise this Jewish stockbroker, who had made his
own fortune by speculation, seems to assume that the
capitalist will never take more than a strictly limited
percentage of profits and that any surplus will find its
way back to the workers—an assumption which any

---

[1] *On the Condition of the Labouring Classes of Society*, p. 16.

[2] Details of the origin and meaning of the doctrine of the Wages
Fund are very obscure. It was preached for some forty years without
ever being clearly understood. Even Leslie Stephen admits the
inadequacy and inconsistencies of the Ricardian school in this matter :
cf. *English Utilitarians*, iii. pp. 203-224.

[3] *Principles of Political Economy and Taxation*, p. 57.

manufacturing colleague in the House must have accepted with his tongue in his cheek.

From such economics the Christian Socialists could extract but cold comfort. As Kingsley most justly remarked in 1857, ' As yet political economy has produced nothing. It has merely said *Laissez-faire.*' [1] Ludlow, the only one of them who knew much of the subject, was very clever in selecting such support as he could from it ; but it was no easy task. The ' iron law,' like Malthus' doctrine, had a long life. Believing it to be true of the existing social order, Marx used it as at once a proof of the futility of palliatives and piecemeal reform, and an incentive to revolution : indeed he based upon its assumptions his case against Capital.[2] Mill accepted it in his *Principles of Political Economy,* though even then practical experience of the working of the various controlling laws that had been wrung from Parliament was beginning to make its security doubtful. Not till 1869 was it finally abandoned, when W. T. Thornton in his book *On Labour* attacked it vigorously,[3] and Mill replied in the *Fortnightly* [4] acknowledging its failure and accepting Thornton's criticism of current economics in regard to the law of supply and demand and the doctrine of the Wages Fund. ' The doctrine hitherto taught by all or most economists (including myself), which denied it to be possible that trade combinations can raise wages—this doctrine is deprived of its scientific foundation, and must be thrown aside.' Wages are at last allowed to come not under ' natural ' but under ' moral ' law. The political economists had repudiated *laissez-faire* at last.

[1] Letter to J. Bullar on association (*Life of Kingsley*, ii. p. 36, 1st edition).

[2] Cf. Foxwell's introduction to Menger, *The Right to the whole Produce of Labour*, pp. xl-xlii, lxxxi-iv.

[3] Bk. ii. ch. i. pp. 43-87.

[4] Vol. V. New Series (1st May, 1869) pp. 505-518, reprinted in *Dissertations*, iv. pp. 25-85.

Under the combined influence of all these champions of ' the obvious and simple system of natural liberty ' it is scarcely surprising that the condition of the workers seemed well-nigh desperate, and that their champions were driven to the advocacy of violent methods. The legislation of the first twenty years of the century is consistently successful in increasing their misery ; and improvements even when they came were for a long time inoperative. State interference, hateful as it was to the dominant political philosophy, had indeed been conceded in the case of child-labour by the Acts of 1802 [1] and 1819 : but it was not until 1833 that these Acts were made effective by the appointment of four factory inspectors, nor till 1847 that the principle was extended and a ten-hours day fixed for women and young persons. The first real benefit which *laissez-faire* conferred on the poor was the repeal of the Combination Laws in 1824 which gave Trades Societies the right to exist once more and so laid the foundation of progress—though the masters' power to suppress attempts at union was, as we shall see in the history of the Engineers' lock-out in 1852, winked at by the authorities. Following this the Reform Act of 1832, though it gave no assistance to the workers directly, did in fact not only abolish some of the worst abuses, but established a precedent for the extension of the franchise and so gave a definite objective to their efforts for betterment, an objective which the Chartists were not slow to attack. By these two Acts an organised Labour movement had become a possibility : *laissez-faire* was not yet forsaken, but there was now the opportunity for such action as would make its overthrow inevitable. The

---

[1] This Act dealt with apprentices and was not strictly a Factory Act : cf. for this and the whole matter, Hutchins and Harrison, *History of Factory Legislation.*

Chartists were almost certainly mistaken in their selection of the political rather than the social or industrial sphere as their scene of operations. Indirectly they did a vast amount of good in opening the eyes of statesmen and of the public to the urgency of their case. But they failed to realise that there was much preparatory work to be done before they were likely to attain the franchise, and that to move step by step along the circuitous path of industrial reform was a surer road to their goal than the attempt to carry the whole position by direct assault. They chose the wrong method. There was already at work one who had been in that respect wiser than they.

Robert Owen, the founder of English Socialism and of the co-operative movement,[1] was for the greater part of his life the foremost among his contemporaries in rebelling against the dominant doctrine. The story of his career first told by his disciple, Lloyd Jones, whom we shall meet hereafter as a prominent supporter of the Christian Socialists, has been so often and so fully retold that we need not dwell long upon it. But he is of supreme interest, not only as the pioneer in much that the Christian Socialists also attempted, but because he illustrates in himself that cleavage with the churches which has been so general a characteristic of socialism. We can in his case follow clearly the stages by which he was driven into revolt.

Starting as a draper's assistant at the age of ten, he showed such energy and ability that before his twentieth birthday he was manager of a cotton-mill, and ten years later, in 1800, settled at New Lanark. There he set himself to uplift the condition of his work-people, his efforts being at first purely experimental and constructive. He founded schools, opened cheap shops, built decent houses,

[1] Yet he 'never took any practical part in promoting co-operation': cf. Ludlow in *Spectator*, lvii. p. 1339.

and encouraged temperance, cleanliness, and thrift. He
was already unorthodox in his views ; for his faith in
human nature would not allow him to accept the current
beliefs as to man's natural depravity. But hitherto
he was content to plead for the purging rather than the
destruction of the churches, advocating this in his early
book, the *New View of Society*.[1] In his schools he respected
the wishes of the parents in the matter of religious teaching, and in private life allowed his wife to bring up his
children in her own presbyterian faith.[2] In 1817 he drew
up a scheme for the organising of industrial communities,
and his proposals were very favourably received and exercised considerable influence. His work contained a
vigorous attack upon Malthus, and all the critics of the
Essay on the Principle of Population rallied to his support.
The differences between Owenites and Benthamites were
widely canvassed and debated : and Maurice, when he
was in London in 1825, found himself in the thick of the
fray, and with his friend, John Sterling, took up an independent position. For a time it seemed as if Owen's
argument that faulty production and distribution were responsible for social evil rather than an excessive birth-rate
would be accepted, and that co-operative methods, such
as he recommended, would be given a fair trial. Unfortunately he had formulated by this time his crude
determinist belief that character was entirely the product
of environment and education, and that these and these
alone conditioned moral quality.[3] So he concluded
that, if he set up utopian communities for colonies of

[1] Pp. 136, 137.

[2] Cf. R. Dale Owen, *Threading my way*, 53-65, 173, 174, and Podmore,
Robert Owen, i. pp. 154, 179.

[3] He was a man of limited education and great self-assurance.
His philosophy is an unpleasant blend of Calvinism and Benthamism :
cf. Dale Owen, l.c. 166-170.

workers, they would respond automatically to the changed surroundings, and without any further moral motive would develop into reliable members of the community. He founded several self-supporting settlements both in Scotland and in America, in which his scheme was tested : but in every case failure was rapid and complete. The disappointment naturally gave his opponents an opportunity ; he was made the subject of much criticism and some ridicule ; and the possibility of getting public support for his work became remote.

He had already in 1817, while at the zenith of his influence, delivered a somewhat wanton and bombastic attack upon religion. Now, embittered by the apathy of the churches and feeling that more drastic methods were necessary, he proclaimed his rebellion by the publication in 1836 of the *Book of the New Moral World*. In this he not only expounded more fully his own system of social and industrial reform, but stated the philosophic basis upon which it rested : and not content with constructive and positive treatment of the theme, developed it in a strongly anti-religious direction, contrasting the harmony and unity of his proposed social order with the priestcraft and superstition of the churches, and his doctrine of circumstances with the orthodox belief in free will and the fall of man.[1] Furthermore, to press home his charges, he published another even more violent work against the institution of the family and indissoluble marriages, criticising fiercely the prudery and false modesty, the conventions and the mercenary unions, which we should nowadays admit to have been characteristic of the early Victorian era, and going on to declare that all these can only be remedied if temporary liaisons are substituted for life-long unions—a doctrine which,

[1] Cf. p. 94, etc.

however palpably absurd, still finds support.[1] His own purity of life was irreproachable ; his faith in the possibility of a righteous social system was an invaluable protest against the counsels of despair which governed the political thought of the time ; his confidence in human goodness and his insistence upon the importance of environment were in striking contrast to the dominant Evangelical theology with its crude individualism and its emphasis upon hell. But so far as his usefulness was concerned, the declaration of war was a fatal mistake. He outraged the sympathies of those who were at one with him in his hatred of *laissez-faire*, and who shared his desire to alleviate the sufferings of the working-classes. Thereafter he was regarded by the charitable as a crank, by the hostile as a danger to the realm and to religion. And under the storm of opposition he degenerated, becoming more and more impatient, obstinate, and doctrinaire.[2] His later years were largely spent in polemics ; and his activities dissipated much of the influence of his earlier work, caused Socialism (a word which he was the first to use) to be regarded as synonymous with infidelity and loose morals, and brought discredit and unnecessary antagonism upon all projects for social reform. Invaluable as was the constructive labour and inspiring influence which he gave to the service of the oppressed, it must be admitted that the suspicion and animosity which subsequent reformers had to meet was mainly due to him, and that it goes far to counterbalance the worth of his achievement.

Before we close this chapter mention must be made of two of Owen's most famous contemporaries who may not

[1] *E.g.* Gilbert Cannan in his recent volume *The Anatomy of Society*.

[2] Cf. Leslie Stephen's brilliantly descriptive phrase : ' He was one of those intolerable bores who are the salt of the earth.' (*Dict. Nat. Biography*, xlii. p. 451.)

unjustly be regarded as in some sort the forerunners of Christian Socialism. Southey, whose poetry we have all been taught to ridicule but not to read, deserves a far higher place than has yet been given to him among the great men of our race. ' He is to us,' says Dicey, ' the prophetic precursor of modern collectivism.' [1]   In his early manhood he was converted to communistic ideas, and although these faded as the revolutionary impulse spent itself they still appear plainly in his *Letters from England*, published in 1807. And their influence coloured his whole life. Introduced to Owen in 1816, and recognising in the Lanark experiment the fulfilment of the ' Pantiso-cracy ' which had amused his undergraduate days, he championed Owen's cause against the Benthamites with generosity, vigour and eloquence. In his essays in the *Quarterly Review*, in the two volumes of his *Colloquies on the Progress and Prospects of Society*, and in his private correspondence, there is abundant evidence both of his hatred of *laissez-faire* and of his belief in the value of co-operative methods of reform. The resources of his well-stored mind and tireless industry were devoted to the problems of poverty. The doctrines of Malthus and Ricardo he rejected with loathing, as false to all the decent instincts and aspirations of humanity : ' as for the Political Economists,' he writes, ' no words can express the thorough contempt which I feel for them. They discard all moral considerations from their philo-sophy, and in their practice they have no compassion for flesh and blood ' : [2] and if his criticisms are sometimes more vehement than logical, at least he does not shrink

---

[1] *Law and Opinion in England*, p. 225. Macaulay's famous essay on Southey's *Colloquies* brings this out very clearly : cf. *Essays*, i. p. 242 (edition of 1870).   So too Dowden, *Southey*, p. 154.

[2] *Life and Correspondence*, vi. p. 58, quoted in the *Christian Socialist* i. p. 79.

from suggesting alternative methods of reform. In doing so, his hatred of the whole manufacturing system, whose soulless commercialism outraged the artist in him as it did later in William Morris, often drove him into support of a reactionary Toryism ; but his insistence upon the value of education, upon the encouragement of emigration, upon the provision of decent houses and upon the development of intensive agriculture, as well as his faith in methods of co-operation, redeem him from the charge of being merely a lover of old times. Moreover he never lost sight of the moral aspect of the problem which the Utilitarians were compelled by their philosophy to underestimate or even ignore. He realised that ' what is spiritual affects men more than what is material ; that they seek more ardently after ideal good than after palpable and perishable realities,' and that for effective reform 'a degree of generous and virtuous excitement is required, which nothing but religious feeling can call forth.' [1] Owen had failed, as he quaintly but truthfully expresses it, because he lacked ' the organ of theopathy.' [2] His own remedies were founded upon the proposed union of Church and State for the moral conversion of mankind and the institution of a Christian social order.

On the philosophical side of his work he was wont to refer his questioners to the teaching of his friend Coleridge whose two *Lay Sermons* have been called ' the first voice of Christian Socialism,' [3] and whose influence as a thinker, whatever estimate we may form of the value of his published works, was admittedly very widespread.[4] It is easy to criticise as vague, dreamy, mystical, one who knew full well how far his own weakness exposed him

---

[1] *Colloquies*, i. pp. 144, 145.   [2] L.c. p. 134.
[3] Beer, *History of British Socialism*, i. p. 137.
[4] Even by so unsympathetic a critic as Leslie Stephen : cf. *English Utilitarians*, ii. pp. 373-382.

to such taunts. Doubtless in all his writings the thought surpasses the power of expression and is most precisely stated only when least original. But not only had he an unchallenged place during his lifetime among the leaders of speculative and religious opinion in England, but in comparison with the cold and narrow rationalism of the Benthamites he is a living man in a world of squeaking ghosts. Neither he nor Southey may have been successful systematisers or even great constructive thinkers : they were at least champions of humanity against the desiccated and dehumanised caricatures of the economists.[1] And their effect upon contemporaries so widely different as Shaftesbury and J. S. Mill lays us deeply under obligation to them. They prepared the way for Carlyle and for Maurice : and the Christian Socialists, so far as they found any support for their views in the writings of their predecessors, found it here. There is an air of triumph, as of one who has found a welcome ally in a long and lonely war, in their appeals to the authority of Southey, the Churchman, the Tory, the historian, and the moralist, against the clamour and scorn of their contemporaries.[2] And the debt of their leaders to Coleridge was greater still : upon Maurice he was one of three chief formative influences and probably the most important of the three,[3] and Kingsley, if he owed more to Carlyle and was never really at home in metaphysics, yet reckoned Coleridge the founder of that school of revived Platonism of which he and his friend were members.

[1] For Coleridge's interest in social evils cf. quotation in Hutchins and Harrison, *History of Factory Legislation*, p. 29. His strongest attack upon Utilitarianism is contained in his *Constitution of Church and State :* cf. Beer, *History of British Socialism*, i. pp. 271-275.

[2] Cf. *Christian Socialist*, i. 38, 39.

[3] Cf. *e.g. Life of Maurice*, i. pp. 176-178 ; *R. C. Trench Letters*, i. p. 164, and especially the dedication prefixed by Maurice to the second edition of his *Kingdom of Christ*.

It is outside our scope to attempt any adequate account of these two prophets, or to trace their influence upon the Tory philanthropists. The heroic struggle over the Factory Acts is the outcome of their work and its only immediate result. But the old Toryism was already a dying creed; and it is in the collectivist school and through their influence upon Christian Socialism that the value of their protest against *laissez-faire* is most plainly felt. Only to-day, when mankind has at last emerged from its wanderings in the wilderness of Benthamite individualism, can we realise and reverence the greatness of those who first pointed the way to the land of promise, and of their successors who had the courage to believe that the exile would not last for ever and to labour through the lonely years for the day which few of them lived to see.

CHAPTER II

THE FOUNDERS OF CHRISTIAN SOCIALISM

' ONE thing I do know : Never on this earth was the relation of man to man long carried on by Cash-payment alone. If, at any time, a philosophy of Laissez-faire, Competition and Supply-and-Demand start up as the exponent of human relations, expect that it will soon end.' [1] So in the darkest years of English social life had Carlyle confessed his faith. And though his voice might seem even to himself to be that of one crying in the wilderness with none to answer or regard him, though his words were unfulfilled for many a weary year and are still awaiting their complete justification, yet when once the prophet had uttered his challenge, the response, though long delayed, did not fail ; and when it came it was in large part a direct result of his own heroic efforts. Before him such opposition as existed to the dominant philosophy had come mainly from rebels like Paine and Godwin, Cobbett and Owen, men whose honesty and courage were too often neutralised by bitterness and lack of balance : even the Owenites, the early co-operators and the socialistic writers like Gray and Thompson and Bray, though they influenced for a time certain groups of skilled artisans, scarcely touched the general public or the educated classes.[2] After him there arise in many quarters thinkers

[1] *Past and Present*, p. 188.

[2] Their lack of influence is proved both by the extreme rarity of copies of their works; and by their failure to direct the Chartist move-

and workers, drawing from him their original impulse, sharing his confidence in humanity, and succeeding more and more in their task of arousing and educating the public conscience and uniting behind them all the progressive elements in the country.

But if Carlyle was in fact the forerunner of a great school of social reformers, it might well seem at first that his message had been fruitless. For almost a decade the only sign that his predictions would be fulfilled was to be found in the Chartist rising ; and the Charter, so far as its direct political object was concerned, had no effect save to consolidate the hostility of the ruling classes to reform. In attempting to accomplish its ends by parliamentary reconstruction and the extension of the franchise it was not only premature but mistaken. To establish social righteousness by the passing of laws has always been an attractive dream, although history proves conclusively that legislation, unsupported by public opinion and unaccompanied by moral sanctions, is foredoomed to futility. The Charter could only have been passed by violence and revolution. If it had been forced upon the country, so long as educated minds were in the grip of a reactionary economic and social theory, and so long as the mass of the people were destitute of any constructive programme and untried in all corporate action, its acceptance could only have been disastrous. Political change must complete, not precede, a change of heart and outlook. And the chief merit of the Charter was that indirectly it aroused misgivings among

ment into co-operative methods. A very complete account of these pioneers is given by Prof. H. S. Foxwell in his introduction and bibliography to Menger's *The Right to the whole Produce of Labour* ; and this is expanded in Beer's *History of British Socialism.* For our purpose a detailed survey of early English socialism is unimportant, as its influence on the group whom we are considering was very slight.

the thoughtful, revealed that all was not well with existing society, and thus stimulated the conscience and directed the studies of the public towards the evils of the time.

Among the first and most potent of the champions of social righteousness is the little group of Christian Socialists with whom we are specially concerned ; and in some respects it is true to say that they owed their inspiration to Carlyle and their opportunity to the Chartists. Certainly their two most prominent leaders were deeply indebted to the historian of the French Revolution : his work, *Chartism*, attracted the attention and influenced the thought of Maurice ; and upon Kingsley he was confessedly one of the greatest formative forces, inspiring both the method and often also the content of the utterances of ' Parson Lot.' If we were content to follow the current view and ascribe to these two great men the origin and guidance of the movement, we should be able to link them up with Carlyle and represent the primary impulse of Christian Socialism as due to him.

Hitherto this has been, for a variety of reasons, the usual practice of writers on the subject. Some, like Kaufmann,[1] have been so carried away by their admiration for Kingsley that they have tried to give him credit for a constructive ability which was wholly outside his powers : others, and with much greater reason, have assigned to Maurice, that notable seer and prophet, the credit for the inception of a movement in which he was confessedly the master-spirit. But the truth is, as has been stated by Benjamin Jones, but by hardly any other, that neither Maurice nor Kingsley was the founder of Christian Socialism, and that it is not to

---

[1] Cf. his two books, *Christian Socialism* and *Charles Kingsley*, especially the latter, pp. 240-251.

Carlyle that it owes any original inspiration. General Sir
Frederick, then Colonel, Maurice corrected a false impression (which a careful reading of his biography of his
father would never have suggested) when he said on
December 21st, 1889, ' John Malcolm Ludlow was the
founder of the movement ; and he brought in my father,
by the force of his strong will, after the first meeting had
been held.' [1] And Furnivall, one of the earliest recruits,
in a manuscript note on the flyleaf of his copy of the
Tracts on Christian Socialism, now in the library of the
British Museum, has given similar testimony ; he has
written, ' J. M. Ludlow was the true mainspring of our
Christian Socialist movement.   Maurice and the rest
knew nothing about Socialism. Ludlow, educated in
Paris, knew all. He got us round Maurice and really
led us.' [2]   And an unprejudiced reading of the documents
bears out this belief to the full.   The great prophet and
the great novelist had each his share, and a very large
and honourable share, in the work.   But it was Ludlow
who was really responsible both for the original creation
and for the subsequent development of the movement ;
he suggested it, he planned its policy, he more than any
other carried that policy into effect. The achievements of
Christian Socialism, though he neither claimed nor received
the credit for them, owe their accomplishment to him ; and
the more closely one studies the records of the work, the
more does one become impressed by his performance and
his personality.

And if he can justly claim to be accounted the true

[1] Quoted by B. Jones, *Co-operative Production*, i. p. 110.

[2] He expressed the same opinion, but with less justice, about the
foundation of the Working Men's College, in a letter to the *People's
Paper* : cf. below, p. 122, and cf. *F. J. Furnivall*, p. xxx.   Needless to
say, Ludlow protested vehemently against this ' preposterous over-
praise ' (*Working Men's College Magazine*, iii. p. 10).

founder of Christian Socialism, his character and ability make him fully worthy to stand alongside his more famous colleagues. Sir Norman Moore, who knew all three men and wrote the account of Ludlow in the *Dictionary of National Biography*, says of them : ' Of the three Ludlow seemed to me the gravest, Maurice equally serious but less clear, Kingsley the least profound. Ludlow left me with a clear impression of the whole group ; Maurice seemed fit to be his colleague ; they seemed to have mysteries and arcana which Kingsley held less seriously. In the Christian world I would have compared Ludlow and Maurice to holy abbots, Kingsley to an itinerant preaching friar, and Hughes to a lay-brother of some attainments.'[1] Mr. E. O. Greening, the champion of co-operation, who knew him intimately for many years and has left a most interesting account of him in the *Working Men's College Journal*,[2] goes so far as to say, ' He was one of the greatest and best men of our time —I speak advisedly,' and explains at length how his modesty and dislike of publicity alone prevented the general recognition of his supreme qualities of ability, energy, devotion and character.

John Malcolm Forbes Ludlow was born at Nimach, India, on March 8th, 1821, and was the second son of Colonel John Ludlow, C.B. His father died shortly after his birth, and his mother, who had many friends in France, took the children to Paris, where they lived for many years. In due course John Malcolm, whose education had been wholly French, went to the Collège Bourbon, and graduated B. ès L. after a very distinguished career. So remarkable was his performance that Guizot, then

[1] In a private letter to the author. So too Johnson, one of the group, calls Ludlow ' our greatest man ' (*Letters of W. Cory*, p. 57).

[2] In a lecture printed in two instalments in vol. xii.

Minister of Public Instruction, whose son was afterwards at the Collège, used regularly to enquire of the British embassy what use his country was making of the ' wonderfully brilliant ' young Englishman.' [1] At this time he had serious thoughts of becoming naturalised, but in deference to his parent's wishes and after a voyage to Martinique he came to London in 1838, threw himself heartily into the agitation against the Corn Laws, read law with Bellenden Ker, and was called to the bar at Lincoln's Inn in 1843.

From the circumstances of his upbringing come several of the permanent characteristics of his outlook. His interest in India, though it has little to do with our subject, supplied him with the material for several sets of lectures at the Working Men's College, and these were elaborated into two books, a large work on *British India, its Races and its History*, published in 1858, and a supplementary volume, *Thoughts on the Policy of the Crown towards India*, issued in the following year. But it was to his education in Paris, then the acknowledged centre of democratic movements in Europe, that he owed the ideals to which he devoted his life, and much of the quality which helped him to put them into practice. As a child he had witnessed the revolution of 1830, and he has described [2] in some of his earliest articles his experience of the soul-destroying influence of Louis Philippe's personal government. During his student days he came into close contact with those schemes of reform which were springing up in France. Fourier especially attracted him [3] ; but he knew something of all the early socialistic enterprises in which in those days the

[1] Mr. E. O. Greening in *Working Men's College Journal*, vol. xii. p. 242.
[2] *Politics for the People*, pp. 14, 15 ; 22-24 ; 60-62.
[3] So Brentano, *Die christlich-soziale Bewegung in England*, p. 25.

French were the pioneers.   Moreover, in the atmosphere
of Paris he grew to understand the meaning of democracy
in a way impossible for his English-trained contemporaries :
monarchy, which was to Maurice a thing divinely sanctioned, as a guarantee of order and discipline, was to
Ludlow simply ' government based wholly upon the
selfish interests of a family, or rather of one old man ' : [1]
we shall have occasion repeatedly to contrast him with his
colleagues in this respect.   In Paris too he had joined
the ' Société des amis des pauvres,' a Protestant guild
for the relief of distress, and had learned that freedom
from class-feeling which made it easy for him to associate
on equal terms with men of all ranks, and to approach the
workers without patronage or awkwardness.[2]   Finally, his
training at the English bar supplied him with a technical
knowledge which was invaluable to his future work.
He intended to take up conveyancing, and began by
specialising in Company Law, his first published
writing, apart from periodicals, being two books on
The Joint Stock Companies Winding-up Acts, issued in
1849-50.   His mastery of this very intricate subject was
a great factor in his social activities.

He was at this time a small, slightly built man, with
dark hair and eyes and a finely shaped head : ' with quiet,
earnest, strong, gentle namner ' [3] : ' so modest that he
would not allow himself to be praised, or even to be
photographed if he could avoid it.' [4] ' He cared not for
the praise of men, but was fearless and most tenacious
of principles, assured in his convictions,' [5] ready to yield
to others the premier place provided they would take and
keep it, but unswerving himself and looking for the same

---

[1] *Politics*, p. 14.   [2] Brentano, l.c. p. 25.
[3] *Life and Letters of F. J. A. Hort*, i. p. 154.   [4] *Times*, Oct. 19th, 1911.
[5] Sir Charles Lucas in *Working Men's College Journal*, xii. p. 195.

strength of purpose in his fellows. It is indeed this remarkable power of concentration and perseverance that was his most marked quality, and that enabled him to collect and control the very mixed group of men who supported the movement ; for repeatedly he shows himself at once outspoken and frank in advocating what he conceives to be the right course, and at the same time ready to withdraw and throw himself heartily into another line of action if they overruled him. And along with his fixity of purpose, and even more notable, is his restless activity and insatiable capacity for hard work. ' If there was work to be done,' says Mr. Greening, ' he would do it, but if it was a question of merely showing himself in the public eye, he would not do it.' [1]. As we trace the history of Christian Socialism we cannot but be amazed at the energy that he displayed. Not only did he get through a vast amount himself, writing, editing, experimenting, supervising, organising, legislating, but he also galvanised his colleagues into a vitality as rich as his own, collecting and shepherding the group, kindling and directing their enthusiasm, interpreting Maurice to them, discussing with him each problem as it arose, submitting the final decision to him and loyally accepting his verdict, never thrusting himself forward or claiming leadership, but none the less steadily carrying out his purpose and patiently marshalling the resources available for its accomplishment.

His mind was fertile and constructive, and, thanks to his wide interests and tireless energy, well-stored with knowledge. Not only was he expert in the study of law, politics and economics, but he had an extensive acquaintance both with men and books. His own writings cover

---

[1] *Working Men's College Journal*, xii. p. 269.

a variety of subjects, and in the letters of Maurice and Kingsley there is abundant evidence that his opinion was asked and given on topics far removed from the usual regions of culture. He made an extensive and methodical collection of papers and reports bearing on social and economic subjects ; and these were acquired after his death by Professor Foxwell, and are now in the Goldsmiths' Library, University of London. Sir Norman Moore, to whose article in the *Dictionary of National Biography* this account of him is greatly indebted, has recorded that he knew more than a dozen languages ; and there is proof in all his later work of his intimate and first-hand study of continental writers upon sociology and politics.

Possessing remarkable capacity as a speaker, but in his modesty leaving this side of the campaign to others, he did a vast amount of writing both then and later. He was a great correspondent, and his letters, written in a small clear hand, are always full of interest. His short articles, though during the years of his Christian Socialist activity they suffer from hurried composition and are sometimes marred by long and ill-constructed sentences, yet reach a wonderfully high level of excellence, are always thoughtful and clear, and frequently rise to passages of splendid eloquence. In later years his work in the *Economic Review*, from which we shall quote at length, and especially his sketches of the characters of his colleagues in the movement, are brilliant pieces of literature. His books are careful and scholarly, and as we have noticed display his versatility in many fields. Few men can have equalled his performance in the years 1865-66, when he published four full volumes, two on *Popular Epics of the Middle Ages*, one on *Women's Work in the Church*, and the last entitled *President Lincoln*

Self-pourtrayed.   Probably it is in his character-studies and criticisms that his most remarkable work is to be found ; and two of these, contained in letters to the Rev. John Carter, and referring to matters relating to Christian Socialism, are worth quoting, to illustrate his insight and soundness of judgment, and because they both refer to published criticisms of his fellow Christian Socialists.   The first, written on March 23rd, 1900, concerns Ruskin's attitude towards Maurice.   He writes : ' Don't you think the laudation of Ruskin is being carried too far ?   I knew him, worked under him in his drawing-class, with him in the council of the Working Men's College, so far as he attended it (which was seldom), and was on ordinary friendly terms with him.   He certainly did a great deal of good in his life.   But I could not even go so far as to call him a good man ἁπλῶς. In fact I don't think he was what I should call a man, but like Froude, a woman's soul lodged in a man's body, attracted invincibly by the purely masculine as in Carlyle, incapable of comprehending the thoroughly manly as in Maurice. . . .   Of his unreliableness, at all events in later years, the following is an instance.   Tom Hughes came to me one day to ask me if I had read the last number of *Praeterita*.[1]   I said no, that I did not care to read all that Ruskin wrote.   " Because," said he, " he gives an account of the one Bible evening at Maurice's which he attended, which is directly contrary to my own recollection."   He showed me the number, and really I could hardly have conceived it possible for a man to publish such a misrepresentation of the facts.   We wrote him a joint letter, of which I kept a copy and which

[1] Cf. vol. iii. pp. 26-30.   Even from Ruskin's description the modern reader will sympathise wholly with Maurice, whom Ruskin accuses of ' infidelity ' because he called Deborah an Amazon and condemned Jael's treatment of Sisera !

Hughes forwarded.   It was never acknowledged.   Afterwards we heard of his mind being gone, and did not press
the matter further.   And now I find the new edition of *Praeterita* contains the old story without a word of alteration.
. . .   Now I am not fond of the part of devil's advocate,
but I do not like a lie to be published, nor the man who
told it to be exalted into a model Christian.'

The second is dated March 8th, 1904, and has reference
to a gross and unjustifiable misquotation of Maurice in
regard to his attitude towards socialism.   Ludlow writes :
' I have been able to contradict some false statements of
Holyoake's in a series on *Bygones worth Remembering*,[1]
which he is publishing in the *Weekly Times and Echo*,
there being only one other man living who could give the
contradiction, and he having refused to associate himself
with me in doing so (I mean Furnivall).   Holyoake
himself I cannot make up my mind about, after all the
years that I have known him.   There must be good in
him, for his daughter,[2] who really seems to me a good
woman, is devoted to him.   But his inaccuracy of statement is such that if he said he had dined off a mutton
chop the chances would be ten to one that it was more
probably a beefsteak.'

' His political creed was based on faith in the people,'
that is his biographer's brief summary.   Of the Christian
Socialists he was the only leader to avow himself a
thorough democrat ;   and his political ideal was clear
and consistent.   He defines it in one of his leading articles
in the *Christian Socialist*.[3]   ' Democracy,' he writes,
' must mean, not the letting loose all the accumulated
selfishness of the many, but the giant self-control of a

---

[1] Since published in book form, and still containing the misquotation
of Maurice's words.   Cf. vol. i. pp. 85, 95, 97.

[2] Mrs. Praill.   [3] Vol. i. pp. 49, 50.

nation, ruling itself as one man, in wisdom and righteousness, beneath the eye of God ' : and ' the truest Democracy
appears to me to be—Socialism,' a word which he, like
Maurice, uses always in a wide and non-technical sense.
The individual is only ' self-governed ' when he is free
not only from the domination of others, from such slavery
as still exists in the industrial world, but from the control
of his own lusts and passions ; to deliver men from the
first alone is not enough. ' Ignorance, conceit, anger,
covetousness, are tyrants ten-fold worse within than
without.' Hence the value of association as ' the great
school of self-government for the people ' : if they learn
to work loyally and unselfishly together in the shop
and factory, they will have proved themselves fit for
political freedom ; if not, what business have they with
the government of the country ? Moreover, free or
slaves, good or bad, ' no one has a right to say, the government of the country is no business of mine . . . since
he shares in it by abstaining to take, as by taking, an
active part in it.' He may be a pauper or a sweated
worker, but in so far as he learns and practises self-
control he is bringing nearer the time when he will be
able to exercise what he has learnt in a wider sphere.
' Let each man learn to govern himself, not in solitude,
but in fellowship with others, and from fellowship to
fellowship, from circle to circle, the privilege of the few
ever widening to admit the many, the collective self-
government of English Democracy is achieved.'

It is this grasp of the double task before mankind, the
task of political emancipation and industrial freedom,
and the task of individual reform and spiritual liberty,
and his recognition of the fact that these two must be
carried on simultaneously, that mark Ludlow as a real
thinker. There were and are many who accept half the

programme; who argue, as Owen argued, that if a man's circumstances were altered nothing more was necessary to enable him to become the perfect citizen; or maintain, as Greg [1] maintained, that the sole change needful is in the heart and life of the individual, that if this is wrought nothing else matters, and that until it comes things had better be left as they are. Ludlow sees that there are two things to do and that they must be done together. A change in the social order will not of itself make men righteous or free. A change of heart cannot be universally accomplished so long as men are living under circumstances which degrade and defile them. He had discovered in history the failure both of the communist's ready-made Utopia, and of the individualist's piecemeal conversions. In doing so he has not lost faith in the ultimate possibility of democracy. And he believes that in the method of association he has found the way to effect the twofold purpose. The social order and its human members will be reformed together; the structure of the one and the characters of the other will change side by side.

He is content to begin in a small way with the material ready to his hand; but this is not because his vision is confined to a few tiny communities. Like Maurice he believes that humanity exists for fellowship, that if once the possibility of co-operation as a substitute for competition is demonstrated it will be welcomed and accepted, and that the method is capable of expansion until the whole constitution of society is rebuilt upon the lines of a world-wide self-governing brotherhood. As the scheme develops, the necessary moral training will be extended; or conversely, as men rise to the requisite

---

[1] W. R. Greg, a prominent critic of the Christian Socialists, whose articles on them, originally published in the *Edinburgh Review* and *Economist*, were collected and issued in 1853 with the title *Essays in Political and Social Science*: cf. below pp. 168, 169.

moral level, they will cast off the competitive system with its concomitant selfishness and slavery and take upon themselves the duty of self-directed and voluntary association. That was the ' promised land ' which he saw before him and to which he set himself to travel.

No account of him—least of all in connection with Christian Socialism—would be adequate which did not lay stress upon his life-long devotion to religion. ' He was firmly attached to Christianity, and his deep religious feelings were apparent in his speeches, writings, and conduct,' says Sir Norman Moore [1] ; and the whole history of the movement and every page of Ludlow's writings bear witness to the truth of the words. His views had been worked out independently, and until he met Maurice were based upon the teaching of Luther and of Arnold,[2] confirmed by his own wide reading and experience. He acutely disliked Tractarianism ; for he had never come under the personal charm of its leaders, and saw it only against a background of French Catholicism : its acceptance was to him an act of moral cowardice and intellectual suicide. But he was equally free from what he calls ' self-deluded word-orthodoxy and bibliolatry, setting up the Bible as a mere dead idol instead of a living witness to Christ.' [3]   And because he had won his way from doubt to faith and knew in whom he believed, he could appreciate both the difficulty and the importance of definite convictions. Moreover, there was about his religion nothing affected or shamefaced. Perhaps it was his French education which freed him from the

---

[1] *Dict. of National Biography.*   [2] Brentano l.c. p. 25.

[3] Article on ' Froude's Nemesis of Faith ' in *Fraser's Magazine*, xxxix. p. 554. This contains a full disclosure of Ludlow's views at the time (May 1849), as well as a sympathetic but strong and searching criticism of the book. Both Maurice and Hort praise this review highly: cf. *Life of Maurice*, i. p. 539 ; *Life of Hort*, i. p. 105.

conventional hesitation of the Englishman when he mentions what he calls 'sacred things.' At any rate he was able to speak of his faith simply and naturally, to treat it as the most important element in man's existence, without becoming in consequence either sentimental or unpractical. This is especially marked in his relations with his clerical colleagues, which are characterised by a complete and most wholesome candour on both sides, and are entirely free from that conventional piety and skin-deep respect for 'the cloth' that make most men unable to deal sincerely with a parson. His intercourse with Maurice is in this, as in other respects, a model of frank and loyal friendship ; where they differed, they discussed the matter fully and freely, with an outspoken directness which could only come from an absolute confidence in one another's honesty and affection. At the Bible-readings especially this directness of his was put to the fullest use. Many of the members, particularly at first, were reticent and restrained, and when they did speak were unable or afraid to express their true feelings : the convention which taboos the mention of religion by the laity and insists that the innocence of the clergy must on no account be disturbed, was even then laying a deadening hand upon the national life. Ludlow, under such circumstances, was ready to act as spokesman : he was not afraid of upsetting Maurice or hurting his feelings, and he thought it important that he should know what men were really thinking. So with a sympathy and insight which could give no offence, he took the part of the questioner upon himself, defended opinions which he knew that others were anxious to hear discussed, raised doubts which seemed to them unfit for clerical ears, and extracted from their leader guidance for which no one else dared to ask. The assistance which he thus rendered to his friend in revealing to him the minds of average laymen and saving him from the fool's paradise in which by a mistaken kindness he might otherwise have been forced to live, is generously acknowledged in the record of Maurice's life.[1]

Before going on to narrate the events of the central episode in his life, it will be well to say a word about his subsequent history : for this explains to some extent the comparative neglect of his work by students of Christian Socialism. Hitherto, as we have already noticed, the movement has been usually presented from the standpoint of Maurice and Kingsley ; and for this false perspective Ludlow himself by his self-effacing narratives of the enterprise has been largely responsible. He outlived all his contemporaries : when he died there was no one left to do for him what he had done for all the others so generously : and during his lifetime it was not possible for any one to pay him the tribute which he had earned, or, in face of his own insistence that the credit for their work belonged to Maurice or to any of his colleagues rather than to himself, to give the full story of the part that he played. How mistaken public opinion has been is nowhere more clearly demonstrated than in the columns of the *Economic Review*.   In its early numbers had been printed the invaluable papers in which he describes and praises the work of all the other Christian Socialists : it had devoted two articles to Hughes' account of Neale, and one to Ludlow's account of Hughes : and yet when he, the greatest of them all, died, there is nothing but a brief editorial paragraph,[2] in which it is intimated that he played only a subordinate part in the

---

[1] *Life of Maurice*, i. p. 404.   Cf. also *Life of Hort*, i. p. 155.

[2] It is only fair to say that the friend for whom he had written was no longer editor.

movement. It is the penalty of extreme old age that it has none to sing its praises with understanding : and, though Ludlow would be the last to complain, it is fully time that his pre-eminent services to the movement and to the religious life of England should be recognised.

After the close of the years with which we are specially concerned, he carried on his connection with social reforms, living for some time with Hughes in two houses with a shared library, on the slope of the Ridgway at Wimbledon, designed for them by Penrose and erected by the North London Builders' Association.[1] Here he saw, and insisted upon the publication of, the manuscript of *Tom Brown*, kept up his work at the Working Men's College, and was largely responsible for those amendments of the Industrial and Provident Societies Act which so greatly promoted the spread of co-operation. During the sixties he did a vast amount of literary work, his most important book for our purpose being the *Progress of the Working Classes*, published in 1867, and the joint work of himself and Lloyd Jones. In 1869 he married Miss Maria S. Forbes, who lived until shortly before his own death.

From 1870 to 1874 he was occupied with the work of the Royal Commission, appointed to enquire into the legal position, organisation and general condition of the Friendly Societies. As secretary to this Commission the largest share of its labour fell upon him : its final Report, a document of 216 folio pages, was mainly due to his efforts, and contains a glowing tribute to the value of his services. In 1875, to the great satisfaction of the workers throughout the country, he was appointed Chief Registrar

[1] Cf. below pp. 203-206.

of Friendly Societies, succeeding J. Tidd Pratt,[1] and thus being entrusted with the administration of the laws which he had so largely helped to draft. This office he held until 1891, receiving the C.B. in recognition of his work in 1887 and exercising an almost unequalled influence over the whole course of industrial development, with every aspect of which he was brought into close touch through his position. In 1892 he was invited to give to the Royal Commission on Labour his impression of the changes in the condition of the workers during the time in which he had studied it. His words prove that the visions of his youth had been in large measure fulfilled : ' I think the condition of the working-class has changed immensely, but not so much, I am happy to say, as the change in public opinion on the subjects relating to that class. I find now that boys and girls fresh from school are at a point of advancement in relation to this question which in 1848 we could not bring grown-up people to, and were considered heretics and revolutionists for trying to bring them to. I think the change has been something perfectly marvellous.' [2] After his retirement he settled in Kensington, and during the next few years wrote the articles descriptive of the movement and its members, from which we shall so freely quote. He still continued to take a deep, and so long as it was possible an active, interest in social questions and in the efforts of the Church to deal with them. His last appearance in public at the Pan-Anglican Congress in 1908 was characteristic. On Monday morning, June 22nd, being then in his eighty-eighth year, he attended the

---

[1] Tidd Pratt had died in 1870 : from that year till Ludlow's appointment the post had been temporarily filled by the Assistant Solicitor to the Treasury.

[2] Cf. E W. Brabrook, *Provident Societies and Industrial Welfare*, p. 213.

public meeting of Section A in the Albert Hall, where the subject was 'Christianity and Socialism.' There, among a generation to whom the Christian Socialists were only names, he, the last survivor, was persuaded to rise ' to protest ' (so runs the official report [1] of his words) ' against any narrowing of the large word Socialism, which stood for the faith that brought men together in one common force—the faith of Frederick Maurice. In those early days they could never have hoped to see such an audience as that gathered for such a purpose. He believed that the true Christian Socialism was the faith of all present.'

He died of an attack of bronchitis on October 17th 1911, being, as he wrote a few months earlier, ' at ninety still in possession of all my faculties—barring a certain amount of deafness.' This letter, written to the Rev. John Carter on the day after his last birthday, contains words which are a fitting close to our account of him : they testify that to the end he kept those qualities of energy and self-sacrifice and devotion to God and his fellow men which had inspired all his work. He says : ' I don't feel that I am any good in the world. However, God knows best, and as I am not yet an actual burthen to any one I cannot complain. Still, though I have a couple of affectionate nieces with me, one of whom looks after the household, and other loving relatives and friends, I cannot feel, as I have said, that I am of any substantial good in the world, and the best news I could hear would be that God was calling me to another, where I should rejoin those whom I have loved most. But do not suppose that I am unthankful for God's blessings, or rebellious against His will. It must be for some purpose that I have fulfilled

[1] *Report*, vol. ii. p. 103.

the tale of fourscore years and ten.   May He give me grace to discover that purpose, and to follow it up.'

His friendship with John Frederick Denison Maurice, which was to have so powerful an influence upon both their lives and was to make possible the whole Christian Socialist movement, began in an unpropitious fashion.   As soon as he settled in Lincoln's Inn his sympathies with the poor were aroused by the disgraceful condition of the courts and alleys around it, and with the help of a scripture-reader named Self he made several attempts to work among them.   In 1846, soon after Maurice's appointment as chaplain, he obtained an introduction to him to ask his assistance in starting regular social activities in the neighbourhood.   Maurice was at this time utterly broken down by the loss of his wife, and bewildered by his new duties as well as by his usual self-distrust.   He had no reserve of vitality to match the enthusiasm and energy of his visitor.   And after the interview Ludlow's comment was, ' A good man, but very unpractical.'   It was not a very hopeful beginning.

At the time nothing more could be done, and during the next year Maurice was occupied over the task of founding Queen's College,[1] and beyond his preaching work had little leisure to give to Lincoln's Inn.   His sermons drew together a band of disciples, and enabled Ludlow to revise his first impression ; but social work seemed out of the question.   Indeed Ludlow was seriously proposing to leave England and return to France, where he had conceived the project of editing a periodical, *La Fraternité Chrétienne*.   But before the scheme matured the revolution of February 1848 had broken out, and he

[1] It was at this time that Tennyson and Maurice renewed their friendship : the poet wrote the *Princess* mostly in Lincoln's Inn Fields, and published it in 1847—an interesting contemporary to Queen's College !   Cf. *Tennyson, A Memoir,* i. p. 247.

had to hasten to Paris, full of anxiety for the safety of his two sisters who were living there. He has described in an article in the *Atlantic Monthly* [1] how he reached the city by the first train that entered it, and found the whole population rejoicing in its new freedom. From his previous knowledge of the French he was able to recognise that socialism, the socialism of Louis Blanc, beneath all the rhetoric and passion which it aroused, represented and satisfied the deeper instincts and higher ideals of the people. Where his English-bred contemporaries saw only ' the red fool-fury of the Seine,' he could descry a real aspiration and striving after brotherhood, a movement that had acquired an unmistakable hold, not only upon the fancies but upon the consciences of the workers, a movement which must be christianised if it were not to shake Christianity to its foundations. And so in the midst of these tremendous happenings he wrote to Maurice the letter which was the true starting-point of the Christian Socialist movement.

How great an impression the receipt of this letter made may be judged not only by the sermon preached on the following Sunday [2] or by the fact that Maurice had it copied and circulated to his friends : in the dedication to Ludlow of his book, *Learning and Working*, he recalls its message and says that it exercised a ' very powerful effect ' upon all his subsequent thoughts. And not only did it pave the way for their social enterprises, but its immediate result was to complete their intimacy. On Ludlow's return the two had several long talks about the social and religious outlook, and during one of these their acquaintance suddenly developed into friendship.

[1] Vol. lxxvii. pp. 109-118. Cf. Brentano, l.c. p. 27.

[2] Preached on 12th March and printed in *Sermons on the Prayerbook and the Lord's Prayer*, pp. 331-347.

Ludlow has simply told us that all at once ' the veil was parted ' [1] and he realised that he was dealing with the greatest and best man he had ever met. Maurice has told us nothing ; but whereas on March 16th he addresses a letter to Ludlow as ' My dear Sir,' on March 24th it has been altered into ' My dear Friend '—a title invariably bestowed upon him thereafter and reserved for a very small circle of the closest and best loved.

Of their friendship we have already said something, and the history of their work will abundantly illustrate it. Maurice's letters reveal clearly enough what it meant to him ; and Ludlow testified his own loyalty and affection alike in words and deeds. Perhaps no occasion is a more complete epitome of the quality of their intimacy than that of the meeting to congratulate Maurice on his appointment to the professorship at Cambridge. Ludlow was always reticent, and hated glib and easy speaking ; but on this theme he was stirred to his very soul, and his feelings found expression in a speech of moving eloquence and sincerity. In the course of it he said [2]—' Without in the least admitting or thinking that, on the many points on which I have often differed from Mr. Maurice, I must have been wrong or he right, I yet, as a proof of the reverence which from long and intimate experience of his life I have acquired of him, who, as I never knew a father, is the only man for whom I have ever felt a sense of reverence, wish here and now to ask his pardon for any words or acts of mine which have given him pain, and to offer him the apologies of a man not much wont to bend the knee to any human authority.' Ludlow's words touched Maurice more than any other tribute, and brought from him the reply, ' I have no words to tell you, as you must

[1] *Economic Review*, iii. p. 488.
[2] *Life of Maurice*, ii. pp. 551, 552.

very well know, what I felt about your loving and generous speech. It was far more than I could well bear to hear all that was said about me by others ; but yours was quite overpowering. I will only thank you for it.'

It was this absolute loyalty, combined with complete independence in the expression of opinions and criticism, which made the partnership of the two men so effective. Ludlow, with his wide knowledge of social problems and impetuous desire for decisive action, was not naturally an easy man to drive : Hughes [1] describes him faithfully as ' a splendid Christian Socialist soldier, but rather like his ancestor the Major General, whom the Protector found somewhat hard to manage ' : and few but Maurice could influence or turn him when once his mind was made up. To Maurice he was always willing to yield, even when the decision contradicted, as it often did, his own wishes. And Maurice, although he felt how galling his warnings and caution might be to younger men, never let himself be driven by affection into hasty or partial verdicts : he may compare himself to Christopher Sly and protest that to govern is not his business ; but none the less as they have made him king he will play the part, and they must bear with his mistakes and obey him. And the result was admirable. Men who would have rebelled against the leadership of a young and relatively unknown man like Ludlow were ready to be guided by Maurice ; and so long as the ' Prophet,' as they called him, could draw upon his friend's knowledge and energy and yet know that he would remain loyal even if his advice was rejected, the group would keep together and follow.

Nor was Ludlow's willingness to submit and to

---

[2] In a letter to Rev. J. Carter of 19th Oct. 1895.

take a subordinate position a matter of policy; it sprang naturally from his intense veneration and love for the man whom he describes as 'the central figure of the movement, towering spiritually by head and shoulders over all the rest.'[1] And it is no small proof of his insight that he recognised in the diffident and, as he thought at first, unpractical theologian that unique character as seer and saint which so many of his contemporaries disregarded or denied, but which we who can judge the great Victorians in truer perspective are learning more and more to appreciate and to admire.

For if Maurice towered above the Christian Socialists he towers also above all others of his time. Among all the Churchmen of the nineteenth century it seems certain that we shall reckon him as incomparably the greatest, alike in life, in vision and in achievement. It has been well said that no words can more exactly describe his mission than those of St. John, 'A man sent from God . . . the same came for a witness to bear witness of the Light,'[2] and in his time the Light was shining in a dark place. In these days when the idols of our grandfathers are being thrown irreverently from their pedestals, he almost alone holds his place secure and attracts to him wider circles of disciples. And not the least proof of his quality is this, that he stands as a test of his contemporaries; by their attitude to him we can with remarkable accuracy determine their true and abiding worth. Upon few characters in history has there been so wide a diversity of opinion. Against Mr. Frederic Harrison's verdict, 'A more utterly muddle-headed and impotent mind I have never known,'[3]

---

[1] *Economic Review*, iii. p. 487.

[2] So writes Sir E. Strachey in *Life of Maurice*, i. p. 201.

[3] *Autobiographic Memories*, i. p. 151. For Tennyson's verdict, cf. *Memoir*, ii. 168; for Hare's, Masterman, *F. D. Maurice*, p. 1.

we may set Tennyson's, ' The greatest mind of them all ' or Hare's, ' The greatest mind since Plato ' : and between these extremes there is an infinite variety of estimate. Men judged him, and in so doing were themselves judged. Those who in his lifetime were ready enough to admit his charm, his sincerity, his saintliness, but yet bestowed upon him the good-natured patronage that is reserved for the unworldly, who treated him rather as a dreamer than a seer, have been refuted by the test of fruits. Maurice's work, the causes to which he gave his life, Christian Socialism, the higher education of women and of the working classes, and above all the reinterpretation of theology in the terms of the Fourth Gospel—these, in all of which he was a pioneer, live and increase to-day. He was a prophet, and in his own generation received the prophet's reward : it is our task to erect a sepulchre worthy of him. Twenty years ago Dean Stubbs,[1] afterwards Bishop of Truro, wrote of him words that are even more appropriate to-day : ' It was the doctrine of Maurice which for forty years kept the whole forward movement in the social and political life of the English people in union with God and identified with religion, a doctrine which, idealised and transfigured in the two great poets of the century, Tennyson and Browning, dominant in the teaching of the Cambridge schools of Lightfoot and Westcott and Hort, assimilated almost unconsciously by the younger Oxford theologians of the *Lux Mundi* school, has during this last decade turned the current of our English Christianity to the consideration of the great social problems of the age, and is at this moment transfiguring the social ideals of the present.'

[1] C. W. Stubbs, *Charles Kingsley*, p. 16.

The facts of Maurice's life and the quality of his mind and character have been made familiar in his son's masterly biography. Few human beings could survive unimpaired the ordeal of so searching and intimate a self-revelation. The evidence of his friends and of the letters so abundantly quoted combine to prove that the record is neither idealised nor incomplete. Readers can study it and judge for themselves ; he has nothing to fear from their verdict.[1]

But there are one or two points which will arise in the course of our narrative upon which it will be well to say a word here.

The outstanding quality of the man, that which is at once the source of his greatness and the ground for the only justifiable criticism of him, is his humility. ' Blessed are the meek, for they shall inherit the earth,' is a paradox upon which the life of Maurice sheds a flood of light. Ludlow accused him on one occasion [2] of being a digger rather than a builder, and complained that Christians ought not to be content with mere digging. The contrast was hardly just ; for it is because he has dug deep and laid his foundations truly that he can and did build imperishably upon them. He was always content to learn, never mistaking phrases for realities, but probing every question to its depths until he can discover its nature and disclose the principle embodied in it. And so what he found was true and lasting, and his works,

---

[1] It must be noted that the article on Maurice in the *Dictionary of National Biography* is one of the few serious cases in that work in which a mistake was made in the choice of a writer. It seems curious that Leslie Stephen should have thought himself qualified to undertake it, in view of the principles on which he had himself selected biographers (cf. Maitland, *Life of L. S.* p. 149), and of his own expressed antipathy to Maurice (e.g. l.c. p. 240). Apparently he yielded to pressure from Sir Sidney Lee, to whom he had just surrendered the editorship (l.c. p. 403).

[2] *Life of Maurice*, ii. p. 135.

the children of his patient and lonely labour, have entered upon a goodly heritage.

This humility with its resulting fear of overstatement and its ability to see both sides of a case gave pretext for the charge of obscurity so generally flung at him. He had been dissatisfied with the Unitarianism of his father, and had set himself without haste or prejudice to seek for truth. Thanks to this he escaped from the formulae of orthodoxy which so many men begin by accepting at second hand and end by persuading themselves that they believe. His theology was a vital part of himself. He had worked over the evidence at a time when his judgment was already mature : he had tested it in his own religious experience : and he had discovered the realities hidden beneath the creeds and definitions of the past. And because he speaks things and not words, because he is not content to deal in the small change of current symbolism without ringing its metal, he seemed to many of his hearers indecisive or obscure. To the super-ficial and the insincere his deep spirituality was not unnaturally unintelligible ; to those who identified Christianity with the forms of it then prevalent, whether they believed in those forms or rejected them, he was speaking of an unknown God; to those who liked dog-matism, his protest against the surface-meaning of terms was a perpetual offence. A study of his contro-versies shows that he was living in a different world from his opponents : their misunderstandings of his use of 'eternal' or of 'the Word'—a use which nowadays has become almost universal—reveal a stupidity that is scarcely credible until one remembers that they were children of a bygone age. Matthew Arnold, who was too pleased with his own culture and felicities of style to be capable of any deep religious experience, might pronounce that 'he passed his life beating the bush with deep emotion and never starting the hare' : but his own efforts in theology warn us that here at least his right to criticise may safely be denied. Ruskin might remark with grandiloquent egotism,[1] ' I do not think of him as one of the great or even one of the leading men of the England of his time . . . his amiable sentimentalism . . . always honest (at least in intention), and unfailingly earnest and kind . . . harmless and soothing in error, and vividly helpful when unerring . . . has successfully, for a time, promoted the charities of his faith and parried its discussion'; a verdict too preposterously mistaken to need discussion, and more appropriate as a description of its author than of Maurice. Gladstone might confess,[2] ' I got little solid meat from him, as I found him difficult to catch and still more difficult to hold ' : and the confession hardly surprises us : but later in life he made amends generously by his glowing tribute to Maurice's spirituality, and by the confession that his failure to understand had been 'greatly my own fault.' To these men, when he is describing simply and clearly the realities of spiritual life, he may seem to be speaking mysteries : when he admits the value of an opponent's views, they may charge him with compromise : in his self-disparagement and refusal to dogmatise, they may see nothing but uncertainty and mental chaos : that is their fault, not his. To others, and the number is not small, even in his own day he appeared the very reverse of this. Here is a typical opinion : ' I, who am a simple person and without

---

[1] *Fors Clavigera II., Letter* 22, pp. 23, 24. For a picture of Ruskin's attitude to Maurice as seen by one who admired them both, cf. *Life of Octavia Hill*, pp. 118-120.

[2] Morley, *Life of Gladstone*, i. p. 55 and p. 456. A number of other criticisms is quoted and refuted by Hughes in his preface to Maurice's *The Friendship of Books*.

learning, judge as I find, and don't feel at all influenced
by the authorities or the majority. I find no man so
simple, so clear, so resolute, to keep himself and his
readers out of limbo. . . . I like him because he has no
mythical explanations, no clever explaining away... I
know that people say he is obscure. I cannot guess why ' [1]
—the verdict of Daniel Macmillan, a man of shrewd judgment and fine spirit, who is answering the charge that
Maurice was dreamy and obscure : and Macmillan at
least must have known that thousands shared his attitude
by the simple test of publishers' returns.

If we are to estimate his work correctly it is important
to have a right decision on this matter. We have not
raked up these old debates merely in order to pay tribute
to his memory, but because our understanding of Christian
Socialism will be powerfully affected by the view which
we take of its leading spirit. If Maurice was a well-
meaning but muddle-headed dreamer, then his work will
have a purely archaeological interest : if he was, as we
are claiming, a prophet, a man who saw and spoke and
acted truth, and whose message has still its lessons,
then we may hope to gain from our study something more
than a knowledge of the past. Fortunately the question
is one which any reader possessed of an average acquaintance with the modern outlook can answer for himself.
Let him take the letters or sermons of Maurice and compare them with those of any of his contemporaries, of
Pusey or Bishop Wilberforce, of Manning or Spurgeon, of
all save his younger fellow-prophet, Frederick Robertson, and he will feel this difference at once, that they
are speaking of things long dead in the language of an

---

[1] Hughes, *Memoir of Daniel Macmillan*, p. 284. Very remarkable
testimony to Maurice's influence is to be found in two such cases as
Fenton J. A. Hort and Octavia Hill.

unknown tongue, while Maurice is fresh and full of meaning, a live man among the ghosts. Like the great Greeks
he has found the eternal behind the phenomenal, and,
having found it, for all his diffidence he cannot but give
it utterance : and his words are true now as then. Any
one who has studied his character and has a sound
appreciation of human greatness will echo Ludlow's
words when he writes [1] : ' Nothing, I must own, irritated
me more in after days than to hear those whose moral
and intellectual height did not reach to the top of his
boot speak of him with patronising superiority ' : but
nowadays at least we may console ourselves with the
knowledge that Time has avenged him ; his critics,
Froude and Jowett, Mill and Huxley and Leslie Stephen,
as well as those already cited, are returning to the dust ;
Maurice lives and grows.

The humility, which thus supplies the explanation of
the criticisms upon his obscurity, is also itself the ground
of the one serious complaint against him among those
who loved him most. Ludlow is perhaps right when he
calls his self-distrust almost morbid ; certainly it must
have been a grave source of anxiety to his colleagues.
At any moment, as a result of some casual or half-jesting
remark, he might be overwhelmed by a paroxysm of
diffidence which would paralyse his action and drive him
to insistence upon resignation. Intensely conscious of
his own shortcomings, genuinely terrified of the idea
that he was in any sense a leader or a great man, shrink-
ing from all publicity and only driven by sheer conviction
and in face of his whole inclination to take overt action,
he was enabled to bear the constant misrepresentation
and abuse to which he was exposed solely because of his

[1] *Economic Review*, iii. p. 488.

profound faith in the truth of the message entrusted to him. Like all the greatest, he had often to travel in loneliness. 'I had a moderately clear instinct,' he says of his first theological pamphlet,[1] 'that I never could be acceptable to any schools in the Church.' That sentence sums up what was to him the sorrow and must be to us the splendour of his life. He suffered hideously; for if few men have been less supported by self-reliance, few have had to bear more wounds. Acutely sensitive to attack he yet schooled himself to incur the certainty of it when he thought it his duty, or in order to champion an unpopular cause; and learnt to avoid that temptation of the persecuted, the tendency to reckon their martyrdom a proof of their righteousness.

But if to Ludlow this humility was 'a spot upon the sun,' there were not many occasions on which it gave rise to any grave difficulty. No doubt to young and vigorous spirits he often appeared, as he warns them that he will, a hesitating leader and a lukewarm combatant. But in fact his care in weighing arguments and his refusal to be hurried into action were of the greatest value; for several of them, not excluding Ludlow himself, were as impetuous as they were resourceful, and without his restraining hand might easily have involved themselves in futile enterprises. Mere expediency and the fear of men counted as little with Maurice as they did with his followers: but he would not go forward until he was sure of his principles, and, when once these were clear, neither sneers nor hostility could give him pause. The self-distrust which haunted him in matters of personal conduct or when the call to him was not plain, left him when he had satisfied himself of the purity of his motives

[1] *Life of Maurice*, i. p. 181.

and of the will of God. And if Ludlow complains of this, at least he goes on to add,[1] ' What I should call positive sin I must say I never saw in him.'

This emphasis upon his humility may seem exaggerated to those who, like Mr. C. F. G. Masterman, find it hard to reconcile it with his many controversies and scathing denunciations of what he regarded as error. Mr. Masterman's book,[2] charming as it is with its wealth of apt quotations and brilliancy of style, is only marred by this failure to understand Maurice's consuming passion for truth : it is a serious flaw in an interpretation otherwise sympathetic and adequate. While yielding to Maurice his right to be called a prophet, he does not realise that a prophet who speaks smooth things is an incredible anomaly. In proportion to the authenticity of his inspiration will be the vigour of his protest against error : it is his business to expose and pillory evil, to explore its roots in his own soul, learning meekness in the process, to wage war upon it there without truce or compromise, and then to confront it in others with the severity which has first been exercised against it in himself. In these days when God's justice has been obscured by His mercy, when Jesus has become a type of gentleness, when charity is confused with amiability, it is the prophet's function to recall to us the ' wrath of the Lamb,' to remind us that sentimentality is the subtlest enemy of love, to restore to us our knowledge of the eternal hideousness of sin. Maurice in the agony of his own spiritual experience had fastened upon certain fundamental principles which he believed to be universal and divine : by them he judged his own life and the society around him :

[1] *Economic Review*, iii. p. 490.

[2] *F. D. Maurice*, in Mowbray's series on *Leaders of the Church, 1800–1900*.

by them he tested the words and actions of his contemporaries. He may have been wrong ; in one or two minor matters his judgment was palpably biassed by the circumstances of his age. But to criticise him because he was as severe to sin in others as he was to it in himself, because he possessed and used a power of righteous indignation towards dominant and fashionable error, is to deny his claim to the prophet's office, and to be blind to the earnestness and depth of his thought.

The second point which must be mentioned if we are to understand his subsequent action, is the bearing of his religious life and thought upon social matters. How was it that at a time when current Christianity in England was almost entirely individualistic and other-worldly, his whole conception of doctrine and conduct was social ? And what were the special ideals which inspired him in the work which he undertook ?

Of his own personal religion, which was at once the source and the consolation of his humility, Professor Brentano's description is the most concise. He wrote : [1] ' Nothing is more common than to meet people who emphatically describe themselves as Christians, and talk about Christianity. Nothing is more rare than men who, in all their decisions and acts, are naturally guided by the Christian spirit. . . . Maurice was not merely guided in his general views of the world by Christian doctrines ; it was impossible for him to think of any aspect of nature or of social life otherwise than from the Christian point of view, nor could he enter into any relation with men in which that Christianity which had transfused itself into his flesh and blood, did not find expression in the simplicity and gentleness which combined with his earnest-

[1] Brentano, *Chr-soz. Bewegung*, pp. 7, 8, and *Life of Maurice*, ii. pp. 2, 3.

ness to form that loving sympathy which was so free from any trace of arrogance or self-seeking. Such a man was evidently marked out by his whole nature to exercise the influence of an apostle.'

It was this 'complete drenching of his whole being in Christianity'[1] that forced him to apply religion socially. This is not the place in which to attempt any full treatment of his theological position or of the possible influences under which it was formed.[2]   Technically speaking his doctrine is thoroughly Johannine, and approximates closely to the Logos-theology of the Greek Fathers, though Maurice lays more stress upon the spiritual and moral, and proportionately less upon the intellectual, aspect of man's relation to God.   This doctrine had practically disappeared from the Church after the close of the third century ; and in its grasp of the principle of evolution and of a progressive and universal revelation, is in strong contrast to that of the Latin Churchmen which superseded it.   Maurice, like the Greeks, regards all history as the record of the education of mankind in the knowledge of God, and delights to trace from age to age and in every field of study the development of that knowledge.[3]   But, though he calls himself a Platonist and obviously admired their work, he did not borrow his belief from them or from any others except the writers of the New Testament.   Rather he took a

[1] Brentano, l.c.   Cf. also V. A. Huber's account of him in *Reisebriefe aus England im Sommer 1854*, ii. pp. 15-17.

[2] For a brief summary and criticism of his theology cf. Storr, *Development of English Theology in the Nineteenth Century*, pp. 340-353.   He defends Maurice from the charge of vagueness or obscurity, but hardly gives him sufficient credit either as a theologian or as an influence.

[3] Hence he was able to welcome Darwin's work as an application of the same principle of evolution to the physical sphere.   Hence too he was censured, neither fairly nor wisely, by J. S. Mill, who had himself a weak sense of history, cf. *Autobiography*, p. 153.

few great ideas, the Fatherhood and universality of God, the oneness of humanity as seen in Christ, the presence of Christ in all men and His revelation of Himself in every good thought and word and deed, and the consequent unity of human society as one body having many members, one body whose head and life was Christ ; and these ideas he applied faithfully and logically to all the details of life, which thus became in the true sense sacramental, an outward embodiment of spiritual truth. It was the sincerity and simplicity with which he followed out his principles to their conclusions that amazed and sometimes perplexed his contemporaries ; for most of us think in compartments, with a different set of principles dominating each, and when we meet one who insists that principles are either true everywhere or not true at all, and moreover forces us to a similar consistency in thought and action, we either stone him or sit at his feet.

This was Maurice's secret, that he saw life whole and saw it in the light of Christ, and that he expressed what he saw in all the relationships of life, personal and social, fearlessly and without compromise. ' I was sent into the world,' he writes in a rare moment of self-revelation, ' that I might persuade men to recognise Christ as the centre of their fellowship with each other, that so they might be united in their families, their countries, and as men, not in schools and factions ' ; and adds with characteristic modesty, ' through forgetfulness of this truth myself, I have been continually separating myself from relations, letting go friendships, and sinking into an unprofitable solitude.' [1]

It is this sense of the corporate oneness of mankind which not only dictated to him his social activities but con-

---

[1] *Life of Maurice*, i. p. 240.

trolled his policy in conducting them.   Class-distinctions
and party-platforms, so far as they are more than the
differentiation of function necessary for organic life, so far
as they divide instead of uniting, he cannot tolerate.
His own thought is always positive and constructive, and
he is not primarily concerned with criticism of others ; but
on the occasions when he does criticise them his motive is
the prevention of schism and partisanship.   Repeatedly
we shall find in the history of Christian Socialism times
when his followers are clamouring for him to express a
clear decision, when Ludlow insists upon definite and
restrictive action : and if he pauses it is solely from his
terror of creating divisions among his colleagues or of
forming them into a political or ecclesiastical faction.
Ignatius once called himself 'a man constituted to
promote unity' : Maurice, whose methods were much
less autocratic, might have received the same title ;
' the desire for Unity both in the nation and in the Church
has haunted me all my days ' he said once to his son.[1]

In working out this ideal he followed in social matters
the same method which he had already elaborated in
reference to parties in the Church.   Satisfied that where
there was discord there must be some radical error, he
set himself to discover the true principles which should
control the relations of Christians one to another, in order
that, if these were formulated and accepted, men might
learn to separate things essential from things secondary,
and while differing in the latter according to their
individual temperaments and upbringing, might agree
and co-operate upon the basis common to them all.
He recognizes to the full the elements of good in every
honest man and party, and often goes out of his way

---

[1] *Life of Maurice*, ii. p. 632.

to do justice to the unpopular and to emphasise the fragment of truth in their errors ; but he does so in the hope of persuading rivals and enemies to discover and build upon that on which they are at one, and by doing so to learn in fellowship the shortcomings and exaggerations which keep them apart.

So in the industrial sphere, he sees that in fact there is war ; that men who should be comrades and fellow-workers are wasting their powers upon strife. He starts from the human and moral, not the theoretical and economic : he is concerned with men, not with problems, and with men who ought to be brothers and are in fact foes. And realising that here is something contrary to the will of God and to the welfare of man, he sets out to diagnose the seat of disease, and soon determines that the whole competitive principle with its postulates of selfishness and conflict is a denial of the law of love, a repudiation of the divine order as revealed in Christ, and a constant source of suffering for mankind. But diagnosis is only part, and the easier part, of his task. When he has found the malady and demonstrated it, he must seek and find its cure. ' To set trade and commerce right we must find some ground, not for them, but for those who are concerned in them, for men to stand upon. That is my formula.'[1] So he writes to Ludlow during the Engineers' lock-out, when he is insisting that eternal principles must not be compromised by temporary and sentimental actions. And with a wonderful, and for his followers almost an exasperating, patience he enters upon the search, never losing sight of the fact that he is dealing, not with abstractions, but with concrete human lives ; that society is not a soulless machine which has got out

[1] *Life of Maurice*, ii. p. 115.

of gear and can be readjusted by ingenious manipula-
tion of its wheels and pulleys, but a corporation of living
souls, each of whom has to be convinced of the folly
and wickedness of faction, and won to the acknowledgment and exercise of his duty of free and brotherly
service. The Body must be restored to health by being
brought back into harmony with its Head, even Christ,
from whom, when it is ' fitly joined and compacted
by that which every joint supplieth,' and when every part
is working effectually and in due measure, it will recover
the power of growth and will be reconstituted ' in love ' : [1]
that is his ideal, and he will prescribe no easier remedy ;
by their conformity with that shall all the details of
treatment be tested.

A quotation from the same letter [2] will illustrate the
application of his method and the difference between him
and most other social reformers. ' What I have tried
to say in the lectures is that the reorganisers of society
and the conservators of society are at war because they
start from the same vicious premises ; because they
tacitly assume land, goods, money, labour, some subjects
of possession, to be the basis of society, and therefore
wish to begin by changing or maintaining the conditions
of that possession ; whereas, the true radical reform and
radical conservation must go much deeper and say :
" Human relations not only should lie, but do lie beneath
all these, and when you substitute—upon one pretext
or another—property relations for these, you destroy
our English life and English constitution, you introduce
hopeless anarchy." '

Equally clear and very characteristic of its author's
outlook is Maurice's definition in the eighth of the *Tracts*

[1] *Ephesians*, iv. 15, 16.   [2] *Life of Maurice*, ii. p. 114.

on Christian Socialism,[1] where he writes : ' These socialist movements seem to us to say, " You must have done with your low grovelling notion, that Christ is the Head of a set of religious men, the Head of a sect of Christians, and you must believe that He is actually the Son of God and the Son of Man." . . . And seeing this is so, and seeing that we are sent into the world to proclaim God's kingdom and to teach men how they may become members of this kingdom, we will with all our hearts and souls help you to work out this principle which you have perceived. We will help you to do it, not in some other land, in some distant Utopia, but here on your own soil ; not by bringing you into some new circumstances, but by encouraging you to struggle in and with those circumstances in which you are placed. We would have you just what you are—tailors, shoemakers, bakers, printers ; only we would have you in these positions be men feeling and sympathising with each other. And we will tell you how you may be this, and what will hinder you from being this. We will help you in fighting against the greatest enemy you have, your own self-will and selfishness. . . . This is what we mean by Christian Socialism.' Few passages more plainly express his social gospel, or more nobly define that ' new spirit in industry ' of which he, like ourselves, acutely felt the need.

The final point to which attention must be briefly directed is his political theory. This was the ground of his chief disagreement with Ludlow, and although he admits that it is a matter on which he cannot speak

---

[1] *A clergyman's answer to the question ' On what grounds can you associate with men generally ? '* pp. 13, 14. This Tract is little known and is not mentioned in Mr. Gray's very accurate bibliography ; there is no copy in the British Museum, nor in the Ludlow tracts in the Goldsmiths' Library. The only copy I have seen is that in the library of the Working Men's College, where there is a complete set of the *Tracts.* For the circumstances of its composition cf. pp. 268, 269.

with authority, it is important to notice his attitude. Ludlow declared that his friend never understood the meaning of democracy or rose above 'the Aristophanic idea of the *demos* ' [1]; and Maurice himself in the most elaborate of his letters [2] on this topic admits that he does not believe democracy to be possible except upon a basis of slavery. Athens had been a slave-state. Modern experiments, in France and America, had only led to chaos and military despotism, or to corruption and negro-servitude. With these examples before him his view is that there must always be some visible embodiment of the principle of authority, and that this is obtained better by monarchy and aristocracy, wherein certain persons are elevated above the normal level, than by democracy and slavery, wherein the same differentiation is reached by depressing one class below the others. Any attempt at a general equalising of status will only produce the same distinction ' illegitimately as a Plutocracy or a Chromatocracy.' ' I must have Monarchy, Aristocracy, and Socialism, or rather Humanity, recognised as necessary elements or conditions of an organic Christian society.' It is as a witness to the permanent value of submission and order, as a type of the lordship of Christ over the individual or of the spirit over the flesh, that he feels the need for these diversities of function in the commonwealth ; and in sending his confession of faith to Ludlow he does it with many apologies and in fear that he will be thought ' only an obstructive.' At the same time he declares that although ' by birth, education, everything, a democrat,' he has arrived

---

[1] *Economic Review*, iii. p. 490.

[2] To Ludlow after his rejection of Goderich's tract, cf. *Life of Maurice*, ii. pp. 128-132, and below p. 165.

at his convictions ' by sheer force of evidence, reflection on history, belief in God's revelation.'

Yet this result, strange as it may at first sight seem when compared with his faith in the equality of every human being in Christ or with the title which he chose for the movement, is in reality inconsistent with neither of them. To him brotherhood and co-operation are the essential things ; men are fellow-workers and members one of another, being united in the one body of humanity. Beside this, and as its necessary sequence, there will be distinction of function, though not of worth, between the members ; else the body will not be co-ordinated or articulated, will not in fact be a body at all. There must be one source of authority, there must be persons appointed to see that authority is duly obeyed ; and in both cases it is better to have these positions filled by those who are naturally and by birth set apart for the work.

Ludlow, who for all his earnest belief in the people was a rigid supporter of discipline and unity of command, would only have differed in name from the greater part of Maurice's creed. But he saw that right of birth, so long as it determined difference of function, did not necessarily secure efficiency, while at the same time carrying with it a prerogative and power in other fields than those directly connected with the exercise of its particular duty ; and in the name of brotherhood and equality of opportunity he protested. They were agreed that society is an organism, its members differing ' in office,' but being equal ' in honour.' Maurice, fearing chaos, accepted existing class-distinctions, and strove to transform them from within by the spirit of brotherhood and the conversion of individuals : Ludlow desired to emphasise the other and more neglected characteristic

of organic life; equally disliking anarchy, he realised that
the traditional categories of monarch, aristocrat, and
populace were already breaking down; while opposed to
revolution by violence, he saw that a radical change of
the social structure was inevitable if brotherhood was to
be possible ; the transformation must be wrought ' in
Christ,' but it would not on that account be less drastic
in its results.   Their ideal was the same, the Pauline
doctrine of membership ; they differed only as to the
road by which it might be most safely and completely
attained.

In answering Ludlow's letter from Paris, Maurice had
written admitting that it had awakened earnest thoughts
in his mind, thoughts which ' conspired with some that
had been working there for a long time,' and declaring,
' I see my way but dimly : this, however, I do see, that
there is something to be done, that God himself is speaking
to us, and that if we ask Him what He would have us
do, we shall be shown.' [1] The discussions which he had had
with Ludlow do not seem to have produced any very
tangible programme of action ; and it is by no means
clear what course they would have pursued, had not the
circumstances of the time brought upon the scene a third
member of the group, who for a few days took the initiative and impelled them to vigorous and public activity.
Of the events and their outcome we must speak in the
next chapter, but of Charles Kingsley, whose appearance
was, as it were, the answer to Maurice's prayer for guidance, something must be said first.   For although he was
neither the founder nor the leader of the movement, he
was for a long time its chief spokesman, and in addition
supplied the motive power for its first enterprise.   If

---

[1] *Life of Maurice*, i. p. 458.

Maurice was the man of vision, the Moses of Christian Socialism, Kingsley with his power of tongue and pen can claim to be its Aaron.

Kingsley's reputation has unquestionably suffered, just as Maurice's has been secured, by the quality of his biography. Beautiful as is Mrs. Kingsley's book, and noble as is the portrait which it paints for us, we cannot but be conscious that it is transfigured by the writer's love, and that its hero is presented to us, not as he was, but as his wife wished and believed him to be. We cannot help comparing it with the man as he is revealed in those episodes of his career on which she is silent, in those aspects of his character to which she was blind. And the reaction has carried us too far. Take, for example, his historical novels. Ever since the defects of his scholarship were disclosed by his professorial utterances at Cambridge and the violence of his prejudices by his attack upon Newman, it has been the fashion for the critics, most of whom are quite incapable of estimating the truth of the matter, to write down his pictures of Alexandrian clergy or Elizabethan seamen as the products of a vivid and biassed imagination. No doubt, like everything else he wrote, they are controversial, sermons in the guise of stories, and as such unsuited to a taste which allows the novel to be used only for providing amusement or preaching vice ; but they need not on that account be untrue, and the signal vindication of *Hypatia* in its attitude towards Cyril and his monks, by the discovery of the ' Bazaar of Heracleides,' should give us pause before we condemn unexamined the work of one who combined considerable power of research with something of the poet's insight and sympathy.

So too with the other sides of his work. ' Muscular Christianity,' that noble and very necessary protest against the mawkishness of the Evangelicals and the affectation of the Tractarians, has in these days, when we all in fact accept it, become a term of reproach. We think of Kingsley as the last and most vocal of the ' squarsons,' as one who exercised himself in oratory on Sundays and in fly-fishing and fox-hunting during the rest of the week, one whose vocation meant to him little more than unlimited opportunity to indulge in field sports. And that is quite monstrously unjust.

Similarly of his social work. So much stress has been laid upon his conservative tendencies, both by those like Hughes, who wished to save him from the reproach of being thought ultra-revolutionary, and by those like Holyoake, who insinuated that his reforming ardour was a sham, an aristocrat's device for riveting fresh fetters upon the people, that we are in danger here too of mis-representing him. It is so easy to set down his Christian Socialism as a youthful outburst of neurotic enthusiasm of which, when he had used it to achieve popularity, he found it expedient to repent. The roseate colours in which he afterwards painted the improvement in social conditions seem so plainly the reflection of the change in his own circumstances; his virtual withdrawal from the movement might arise so naturally from the worldly wisdom of advancing years ; his devotion to sanitary reform may become a mere concession to con-sistency, an attempt to conceal the fact that he had broken with the past. Are these ideas true ? Is he nothing but a ' lost leader '—or a returned prodigal ?

Such doubts arise so naturally and have been so often expressed that they deserve careful consideration. Carlyle warned him [1] early in his literary career that he

---

[1] In his letter of criticism upon *Alton Locke*, cf. *Life of Kingsley*, i. p. 244.

must learn to 'temper his fire.' It is probably true, in view of his temperament and health and of the pressure of his work and domestic responsibilities, to believe that his passion burnt itself out in the white heat of those three years of fierce and ceaseless energy. Between 1848 and 1851 he had not only thrown himself heart and soul into the activities of the Christian Socialists, planning and advising and. discussing, preaching and lecturing and writing for them, but he had also produced *Yeast* and *Alton Locke,*—and all this in addition to the care of a difficult parish, the teaching of the pupils whose fees made possible the support of his family, the burden of voluminous letter-writing, the preparation of the material for *Hypatia,* and a breakdown which meant six months inaction and increased financial anxieties. He was never robust ; he had the artist's acute sensibilities ; and he was working under intense pressure, and literally night and day. It is not surprising that he could not ' stand the pace,' that he exhausted himself by devoting to a few fervid months the energies of half a lifetime, and that after the vigour of his start there should come a steadying-down which might look like the abandonment of the race.

But as we read his protests [1] that it is through no lack of will that he cannot do more for the cause, and his complaints that at Eversley he is being shut out of the work, and his fears that the others will think him in-different when he longs to be with them in the thick of the battle of which he has already felt the burden and heat, we cannot question his sincerity. He was faced with a difficult alternative. Either his duties to his parishioners must be scamped and his literary career sacrificed, with all that this would mean of financial

[1] Cf. Hughes, *Prefatory Memoir* (in Eversley Edition of *Alton Locke*), pp. 37, 69, 70.

worry and wasted powers ; or he must leave ever more and more to others the tasks which they were better able than he to carry on, and to which ' the proper impulse had been given,' at the cost, it might be, of being accounted a man of Laodicea or of Ephesus. That he should have to choose at a time when the movement was threatened with failure only added to his difficulties and to the risk of misunderstanding—though in fact his choice was virtually made before the movement had reached the zenith of its success.

And so through no fault of his own, when once the enterprise had been undertaken and had secured its position, he left its conduct to others, husbanded his strength, and turned to his special province of educative work as preacher and writer, a man in some respects worn out, and certainly having given to Christian Socialism the best of his vitality and of his talents. We must not underestimate the value of his contribution because it was given quickly and at first. Without him the movement might never have been started at all : without him it could never have achieved its speedy recognition or its lasting influence.

And for the business of opening the campaign Kingsley was admirably qualified. He had a love of nature as pure if not as profound as Wordsworth's ; and might have said with him [1]

> ' she can so inform
> The mind that is within us, so impress
> With quietness and beauty, and so feed
> With lofty thoughts, that neither evil tongues,
> Rash judgments, nor the sneers of selfish men,
> Nor greetings where no kindness is, nor all
> The dreary intercourse of daily life,
> Shall e'er prevail against us, or disturb
> Our cheerful faith, that all which we behold
> Is full of blessings.'

[1] *Lines above Tintern Abbey.*

From his love of her he had been led through the struggles of his early manhood to build up a theology as all-embracing as Maurice's, and in Maurice he had found years ago his prophet. The Evangelical, with his awful indictment of the world as a mass of corruption, and the Tractarian, with his narrow mechanism of ecclesiastical orthodoxy, seemed alike blasphemers to one who had found God amid the beauties of the undrained fens and of the coast of northern Devon. He, like Maurice, was akin in spirit to the great Greek Platonists, to Justin and Clement and Origen, who saw Christ against a background of eternity and the world as the continuous unfolding of the self-revelation of the divine, who dare not gainsay goodness wherever they might find it, and who hailed all men as sons of God by reason of their birthright in His image. Hence, if we take the influence of Darwinism as the great dividing line between yesterday and to-day, he too like Maurice is of the moderns—witness his comment upon the critics of the *Origin of Species* in 1863 : ' they find now that they have got rid of an interfering God—a master-magician as I call it—they have to choose between the absolute empire of accident, and a living, immanent ever-working God.' [1]   Hence too, though the two men had reached their goal by different roads, comes the intimate sympathy between him and the great teacher from whom he learned how to give his convictions articulate expression ; or, as Ludlow puts it,[2] ' Charles Kingsley could not help being a genius, and he would have been one had he never heard of Mr. Maurice. But his whole theology is drawn from Mr. Maurice, and his chief mission was to be a populariser of the principles set forth by Mr. Maurice.' He himself expresses his obligation

---

[1] *Life of Kingsley*, ii. p. 171.   [2] In *Economic Review*. iii. p. 499.

with warmth and generosity in his earliest letter in 1844, when he says,[1] ' To your works I am indebted for the foundation of any coherent view of the word of God, the meaning of the Church of England, and the spiritual phenomena of the present and past ages.'

And if his sympathy with Maurice and the similarity of their outlook conditioned his usefulness in the movement, this was increased by the differences between them. Ludlow has summed them up in one of his most brilliant sayings : ' Kingsley's genius is essentially masculine; Maurice's is essentially human, and thereby more Christlike.'[2] For Kingsley, despite his love of nature, was utterly unlike the conventional mystic. There was in him a vigour, an impetuous and unresting virility, which contrasts strongly with the prim and placid quietism of Wordsworth and with Maurice's deep spirituality and self-effacing saintliness. Like Browning he was ' ever a fighter,'[3] often rash, often mistaken, often smitten with penitence and despondency, yet never consciously unjust, never insincere, never afraid to give or to receive hard knocks, never resorting to subterfuge or secret methods or poisoned weapons, a great lover and a good hater, not a saint, but a man singularly warm-blooded, large-hearted, high-souled.

As such he was ideally fitted to take the lead at the commencement. Ludlow had neither the self-confidence nor the dramatic instinct ; he was a leader but not a figure-head. Maurice had neither the pugnacity nor the incisiveness to make an effective protest ; he saw both sides of a question too clearly, and was more concerned to do justice to the merits than to denounce the errors of an opponent.

---

[1] *Life of Kingsley*, i. p. 127.   [2] *Economic Review*, iii. p. 494.
[3] ' Berserkerwuth ' is Brentano's term (l.c. p. 26).

' Parson Lot,' with his vigorous and arresting personality, could supply just what the others lacked; and if his gifts had much less permanent value, if he was rather the dashing cavalry leader than the strategist or organiser of victory, he had a place of immense importance at the outset of their enterprise.

Afterwards, when once they had settled down to the arduous business of their warfare and had learned that ' shock tactics ' alone would not force the enemy to surrender, his peculiar qualities were less useful, were indeed often embarrassing. Patient thought, careful calculation of resources, nice adaptation of means to ends, deliberate and sustained action, for these he was ill-suited either in temperament or in talents. No one can read his contributions to the *Christian Socialist* without feeling that he is sadly lacking in balance and judgment, that his love of argument often leads him into quite untenable positions, and that his recklessness and dogmatism might easily have done irreparable damage to the cause. We have said that he is of the moderns ; but it must be admitted that his ' Bible Politics ' as an attempt to ' justify God to the people ' would nowadays do more harm than good, and we gravely doubt whether this was not its effect at the time.[1] His exegesis shows how far he had failed to understand the historical method and is at once shallow and unsound ; his arguments are clever and sometimes suggestive, but their ingenuity does not conceal their want of foundation, and their rather blatant self-assertion is in painful contrast to the humility of his teacher. They are Kingsley at his worst, patronising and didactic, impatient and often insolent to his opponents, and constantly exposing himself to

---

[1] His other series ' The Church *versus* Malthus ' is less bad.

well-earned and unanswerable retort. They reveal in him just those faults which his subsequent career made so notorious ; and in view of them we cannot altogether regret the fact that he dropped out of the movement before he found a Newman to bring destruction upon him and it together.

With Kingsley there came into the movement the fourth and last of its original members, Charles Blachford Mansfield. They were of the same age and had been friends at Cambridge.[1] Of his short and pathetic life and radiant character a brief account has been given by Kingsley in a *Memoir* of five pages prefixed to the volume of his letters written from South America during the years 1852 and 1853 and published after his death with the title ' Paraguay, Brazil, and the Plate.' It can be supplemented by the remarks in Ludlow's second article on ' The Christian Socialists of 1848 ' in the *Economic Review* ; [2] and a few further details emerge from the study of the literature of the movement to which he made frequent contributions, and from his other published papers.

The impression derived from them is that of a man singularly lovable—' the man I have loved best of any I have ever met in this life,' says Ludlow, and adds that others who knew him must have felt the same affection for him,—modest and unassuming despite his brilliant ability and general popularity, devoted to the service of the poor and starving himself in order to save something for stealthy acts of kindness, deeply interested in the work of the group and bringing to its counsels the resourcefulness and hope of the trained scientist, above all utterly self-sacrificing, alike for his friends and for the cause, and

---

[1] Mansfield had been at Clare College.

[2] Ludlow's preface to the posthumous *Aerial Navigation* is also suggestive.

showing in all the actions of his life the spirit of heroism which brought him to his death. The portrait accompanying the *Memoir* bears out the testimonies to his personal comeliness : it is a remarkably handsome face, thoughtful and winning, full of vitality, sympathy and power : and he was as lithe and active as a deer. Such a man would be invaluable in smoothing down the inevitable differences between men of varying temperaments, and helping them to see the best in one another and to sacrifice their particular whims for the common good.

His mind was gifted with real originality, and this appears not only in his professional work where amongst other matters he paid much attention to the possibilities of aerial navigation,[1] but in his activities as a Christian Socialist. Sometimes it degenerated, and he becomes almost a crank. He was a rigid vegetarian ; and this led him not only to the publication of a cheap and meatless dietary[2] but to the advocacy for the associated shoemakers of a form of prepared cloth or rubber in place of leather.[3] He was also like several of the others a strict teetotaler ; and contributing to a long correspondence in the *Christian Socialist*[4] maintained that the wine recommended by St. Paul to Timothy and sanctioned for use elsewhere in Scripture was unfermented and non-intoxicating grape-juice,—a proposition which Ludlow for all his affection rejects on linguistic grounds. But these and similar foibles, fantastic as they may seem even in these days of

[1] His unfinished work on the subject edited by his brother Robert, with a preface by Ludlow, was published in 1874.

[2] *Christian Socialist*, i. p. 239. He prints two tables, one at 5½d. a day, the other at just under 4d. And on these he had lived for months !

[3] *Christian Socialist*, i. p. 229. The cloth was called Pannus corium and was treated with linseed oil : the rubber was a kind of gutta-percha.

[4] Vol. i. p. 221.

Garden Suburbs, were less extravagant in a student of the physical sciences in that heyday of discovery, when one marvel was following another and our whole outlook towards nature was being revolutionised by men like him who were not afraid to attempt the impossible or to risk a fall from the sublime to the ridiculous.[1] Ingenuity and a scientific training were assets of great value to the group. And Mansfield, though he took little public part in the work, is lovingly remembered by them all as one of their noblest and during his short life most devoted adherents.

If he had done nothing else, his name would be worthy of a large place in their annals by reason of the perfect description he has given us of the weekly Bible-reading at Maurice's which Ludlow always declared to have been, while it lasted, ' the very heart of the movement.'[2] Himself a man who had struggled through doubt to faith, Mansfield in these pages reveals the beauty and sympathy of his own nature no less than the splendid frankness and unashamed spirituality of his colleagues. In the whole length of the *Life of Maurice* there is no more touching tribute to the ' Prophet,' no more illuminating revelation of the source from which he and his followers drew their strength. Such a piece of writing enables us to understand the quality of its author and to appreciate Kingsley's declaration that Mansfield when he died in February 1855 had won ' faith, popularity, place as a scientist, and the prospect of wealth.' Indeed he had done more : a man so lovable, so beloved, had found heaven and was ready to die. Thackeray, who knew the group through

---

[1] Cf. also his efforts on behalf of ' Weston's Nova motive,' the invention of a working mechanic for propelling carriages by compressed air : (*Christian Socialist*, i. p. 118).

[2] *Atlantic Monthly*, lxxvii. p. 112.

Cuthbert Ellison, spoke truth in jest, when he said that ' Charles Mansfield must have the rudiments of wings under his waistcoat.'

It is a striking testimony to the quality of his spirit and of his significance to the group that for years on the anniversary of his death his friends used to meet together in the chapel of Lincoln's Inn and receive the Communion. ' We had therefore,' as Maurice says,[1] ' the best kind of intercourse.'

[1] *Life of Maurice*, ii. p. 259.

CHAPTER III

THE BEGINNING OF THE MOVEMENT

WHATEVER was to be its future the birthday of Christian Socialism could hardly have been more dramatic. The year of revolutions saw thrones tottering and constitutions remade all over Europe. Everywhere the people were throwing off their rulers and when once France had given the lead each nation followed as if in concert with her. Mansfield afterwards asked the question which many then and later have puzzled over, 'What would have happened in England if a king had been her monarch?' and, as it was, rumour was busy and no man could foresee when an outbreak might not come. Maurice's sermons on the Lord's Prayer that spring at Lincoln's Inn show how conscious he was of the crisis and in what spirit he would meet it; and Kingsley also devoted his eloquence to the same theme.

At a time of such tension old grievances and old hopes revived. The workers, who had been led to expect great things from the Reform Bill, had felt ever since its passage into law that they had been tricked, that they had been delivered over to the tyranny of the very classes, the commercial magnates and the small shopkeepers, who were their worst oppressors; and the Chartist movement had been their protest. That had been in the previous decade, and the effort had spent itself in a few local riots and much ill-directed violence. But now encouraged by the news from the continent Chartism reasserted itself. The Monster Petition was signed; and it was announced that on April 10th after a mass meeting on Kennington Common it would be presented to Parliament, and that, if it was refused admittance with its escort to the floor of the House, other and less legal steps would be taken to secure it a hearing.   London was stirred almost to panic. Wild threats had been uttered, wilder stories found credence.   Troops were held in readiness and legions of special constables were enrolled.   Even Ludlow, good democrat though he was, wondered whether he should not enlist to defend the city against an orgy of bloodshed. None knew what the day might not bring forth.   If in all other respects it was fruitless, at least it gave birth to Christian Socialism.   The scoffer will murmur '*parturiunt montes.*' [1]

On the morning of the 10th Kingsley, impatient of his exile at Eversley, came up to London with his friend John Parker, son of the publisher of West Strand, moved thereto as much by curiosity as by anxiety for his father at Chelsea.   On his arrival he went to see Maurice at Queen Square and found him indoors with a cold.   He was given a letter of introduction to Ludlow, whose Paris letter he had seen but whom he had never met.   He found him in his chambers ; and the two spent the rest of the day together.   By the end of it they were firm friends. In the afternoon they set off to Kennington, got as far as Waterloo Bridge, and there met the remnants of the mass meeting trudging homewards disconsolately through the rain.   Having heard the news of the fiasco they returned with it to Maurice and discussed the situation with him.

[1] For an excellent summary of the 'hungry forties' and the 'shaking of the earth' see Masterman, *F. D. Maurice*, pp. 55-61.

That night they determined to act. Kingsley wrote next day,[1] 'Maurice is in great excitement. He has sent me to Ludlow, the barrister who wrote those letters from France, and we are getting out placards for the walls, to speak a word for God with . . . I am helping in a glorious work ; I feel we may do something.' And on the same evening he adds, ' I was up till four this morning, writing posting placards under Maurice's auspices, one of which is to be got out to-morrow morning, the rest when we can get money. . . . Maurice has given me the highest proof of confidence. . . . We are to bring out a new set of real " Tracts for the Times," addressed to the higher orders. Maurice is determined to make a decisive move. He says, " If the Oxford Tracts did wonders, why should not we ? " '

And so the placard addressed to the ' Workmen of England ' and signed by ' A Working Parson ' was written, and posted up next day.[2] It assured the workers that ' almost all men who have heads and hearts ' know their wrongs and the patience with which they have been borne : it warns them that though ' the Charter is not bad *if the men who use it are not bad* ' it will not of itself make them free : it implores them not to ' mean licence when you cry for liberty,' since ' The Almighty God, and Jesus Christ, the poor Man who died for poor men, will bring freedom for you, though all the Mammonites on earth were against you ' : and it concludes, ' There will be no true freedom without virtue, no true science without religion, no true industry without the fear of God and love to your fellow-citizens. Workers of England, be wise, and then you *must* be free, for you will be *fit* to be free.'

It is the first manifesto of the Church of England, her

[1] *Life of Kingsley*, i. pp. 155, 156.   [2] Brentano l.c. p. 28.

first public act of atonement for a half-century of apostasy, of class-prejudice and political sycophancy.   And as such, quite irrespective of its contents, it may fairly be described by that much abused word epoch-making.

On the next day, April 12th, Maurice, Kingsley, Ludlow and Mansfield, with Maurice's brother-in-law Archdeacon Hare and a friend the Rev. Alexander J. Scott,[1] met and decided, largely upon Ludlow's advice, to ' start a new periodical—A Penny Peoples' Friend.'   Since his return from Paris Ludlow had already tried to use the press and had actually been offered space by Charles Knight in his short-lived magazine, *The Voice of the People*: but the offer had been withdrawn when it was explained that the articles would deal with social subjects and would take a strong line.[2]   Maurice himself demurred to the suggestion from his dislike of the anonymity and irresponsibility of journalism, and expressed his preference for a series of tracts in which each author could take his own line without seeming to concur in views to which he might object.   The general opinion of the meeting was in favour of both schemes, a paper for people of the middle and working classes, and tracts more especially addressed to the clergy and definite Christians. This was accordingly resolved upon : but, when practical details of authorship and expenses came to be discussed, it was agreed to leave the second half of the programme untouched for the present and to concentrate their resources upon the periodical.   Maurice and Ludlow were asked and consented to act as joint editors.   The next morning Kingsley returned to Eversley worn out with

---

[1] He was at this time at Woolwich and had met Maurice through their mutual affection for T. Erskine of Linlathen.   For an account of him cf. *Letters of T. Erskine*, ii. pp. 381-386.

[2] For the influences upon Knight in this withdrawal cf. Harriet Martineau, *Autobiography*, ii. p. 298.

work and excitement. The country parson had made full use of his visit to town. He had not only seen the formation of the group of Christian Socialists and helped them to discuss and develop their plans, but he had himself composed their first proclamation and entered upon his career as their spokesman, the noblest episode in his life.

The others set to work upon the production of their paper, which they decided to call ' Politics for the People.' Fortunately they had as yet no great difficulty in finding a publisher.   John Parker, junior, son of the head of the West Strand firm that published *Fraser's Magazine*, was a friend of Kingsley, and persuaded his father to undertake it.   But contributors were less easy to find, and many questions of method and scope had to be settled before the preliminary prospectus could be drawn up. This was speedily issued in the form of a couple of leaflets. The earlier of these contained two paragraphs, one by Kingsley headed 'Workmen of England,' the second by Ludlow and headed ' Gentlemen of England.' [1]   In the later version, these two were reprinted with a preface by Maurice.   The date of issue was fixed for May 6th, and on that day it duly appeared.

Each of the weekly numbers consisted of sixteen octavo pages with two columns to a page. Every month an extra supplementary issue was published, in order to enable the editors to include stories and articles too long to be contained in an ordinary number and unsuited to serial production.   Seventeen numbers, comprising 284 pages, were printed, four and a supplement in May, the same in June, and five and two supplements in July.

[1] Neither paragraph is signed, but the names are preserved on copies of the leaflets in the first volume of the Ludlow Tracts.   When this prospectus appeared in the first number of *Politics*, Ludlow's paragraph was omitted.

Although the names of nineteen contributors have been preserved,[1] most of the articles, if signed at all, bore only an initial, and the vast majority of them were written by the four founders of the movement. Ludlow himself over the signature ' John Townsend,' or more generally ' J.T.', which he used all through his Christian Socialist journalism, was responsible for more than a third of the total contents ; seldom less than two and frequently as many as four separate items from his pen appear in a number, and he deals with a large variety of topics, mainly political, legal, or historical, and always in essay form. Maurice, whose work is either unsigned or signed 'A Clergyman,' wrote the introductory article ' Fraternity,' several dialogues (always a favourite form of his), a long story filling two of the supplements, and a few other papers on the principles of social life. Kingsley sent several contributions on the value of Museums and Picture Galleries, the three ' Letters of Parson Lot,' several short poems, and a tale, ' The Nun's Pool,' which Maurice refused to accept and which afterwards appeared in the *Christian Socialist*.[2] Nearly all his work is signed with his famous *nom-de-plume*, the origin of which Hughes has narrated, with a slight inaccuracy of date,[3] in his Memoir. Mansfield, as ' Will Willow-wren,' is much less prominent, and supplied articles of a kind and style rather

[1] A complete list of authors and contents will be found in Appendix A, pp. 371-375.

[2] This was actually set up in type to be issued as the first Supplement (for May, No. 5), its full title being *Tales of Whitford Priory. No. 1. The Nun's Pool.* When it was suppressed, the ordinary number for the following week was issued as a Supplement ; but its paging was not altered. Hence in the published copies of *Politics*, pages 65-80 are missing. Part of the Tale was incorporated in *Yeast*. The references in the *Christian Socialist* are vol. ii. pp. 13, 29, 46, 78, 94, 125, 142.

[3] He dates his first meeting with Kingsley and the group 1847 instead of 1848. Cf. *Life of Kingsley*, i. pp. 159, 160 ; *Prefatory Memoir*, p. 5. In this error he is copied by Kaufmann, *Charles Kingsley*, p. 146.

resembling some of Kingsley's. Of the others something
will be said hereafter. Most of them were either colleagues of Maurice at King's College, or members of his
congregation at Lincoln's Inn. William Lovett, formerly
the leader of the ' moral force ' party among the Chartists,
sent an address,[1] which Maurice reviewed. One or two
working men sent letters, but their number was dis-
appointingly small.

The first number contained six articles, a poem, and a
report of a lecture. Its purpose was explained in the
prospectus which was printed at its head, and of which
certain sentences are worth quoting. ' Politics have
been separated from Christianity ; religious men have
supposed that their only business was with the world to
come ; political men have declared that the present world
is governed on entirely different principles from that.
So long as politics are regarded as the conflicts between
Whig and Tory and Radical ; so long as Christianity
is regarded as a means of securing selfish rewards, they
will never be united. But Politics for the People cannot
be separated from Religion. They must start from
Atheism or from the acknowledgment that a Living and
Righteous God is ruling in human society not less than
in the natural world. . . . The world is governed by God ;
this is the rich man's warning ; this is the poor man's
comfort ; this is the real hope in the consideration of all
questions, let them be as hard of solution as they may ;
this is the pledge that Liberty, Fraternity, Unity, under
some conditions or other, are intended for every people
under heaven.' The object of the paper is declared to be
' to consider the questions which are most occupying our
countrymen at the present moment, such as the Extension

[1] Probably that ' to the People of London,' printed in *Life and
Struggles of William Lovett*, pp. 342-9.

of the Franchise ; the relation of the Capitalist to the
Labourer ; what a Government can or cannot do to find
work or pay for the Poor.'

Maurice in his article on ' Fraternity ' [1] explained the
method by which the paper was to serve this purpose.
' We do not exact uniformity,' he says, ' we promise and
desire a conflict of opinions.' They aimed rather at the
ventilation of grievances, the discussion of problems,
the expression of individual views, and the exposition of
general principles than at detailed statements or a clear-
cut policy of reform. Only incidentally do actual facts
as to the condition of the workers or definite proposals
for their betterment appear, perhaps because the paper
was professedly intended for those who might be supposed
to know their own sufferings only too well. Yet if more
attention had been directed towards obtaining evidence
of the evils which it desired to cure, *Politics* might have
created the sensation that the *Morning Chronicle* revelations produced twelve months later. As it was, the
enterprise suffered from the very variety and scope of its
contents, which were partly educative, partly controversial, and partly literary. No doubt the attempt to cover
so much ground, to provide material suited to such
different tastes was, from the point of view of large circulation, a mistake. Had they concentrated more
precisely upon one or two chief matters they might have
attracted more notice. But their efforts were conditioned
by their circumstances. They were conscious of the wide
divergence between their own opinions ; except Ludlow
they had almost no acquaintance with schemes of social
reorganisation ; except the clergy and doctors none of
them had any intimate knowledge of the workers or their

---

[1] *Politics for the People*, p. 4.

needs ; above all they were as yet altogether out of touch with the leaders of those whose cause they desired to defend, and were in consequence regarded by them with inevitable suspicion. Hence this first publication could not be more than tentative. It was valuable chiefly as a proclamation of sympathy and an earnest of its practical expression. By it men who were sensible of the iniquity of the existing order or who had suffered as its victims were drawn towards the little circle, and Maurice as their recognised leader was gradually led into a position from which for all his diffidence he could not but go forward. When that had been done, *Politics* had served its purpose.

To the modern reader who is at all familiar with the horrors described so vividly in *Alton Locke*, or in Engels' *Condition of the Working-classes in England*, or in Marx's *Capital*, or in the recent books of Mr. and Mrs. Hammond, the most striking characteristic of the paper is its studied moderation. Though Chartism is discussed with some fulness, the tenour of all the articles is to warn the workers continually against any appearance of violent or hasty action. 'Parson Lot,' whose three letters were generally reckoned the most advanced and dangerous utterances in the paper, is almost wholly occupied in emphasising the peril of mistaking false for true freedom, and of preferring material to ultimate well-being. Though avowing himself a ' radical reformer ' he is bent much more upon individual than upon political reform ; and in this he speaks for them all.[1]   Monster meetings, physical

---

[1] *E.g.* in his ' First Letter ' he had written ' God will only reform society on condition of our reforming every man his own self—while the devil is quite ready to help us to mend the laws and the parliament, earth and heaven, without ever starting such an impertinent and "personal" request' (*Politics*, p. 29). For Ludlow's parallel utterance, cf. below p. 187.

violence, hasty judgments, the tendency to disregard the real goodwill of the more fortunate classes and to condemn them as hostile when they are in fact only ignorant, all these symptoms of impatience are frequently and faithfully rebuked. Even Ludlow, the best informed and the most progressive of them all, is cautious, detached, almost academic, in his treatment of controversial topics. The whole paper breathes a lofty idealism and it is hard to find anything in it which could nowadays be called revolutionary. We are tempted to wonder what novelty there was in its attitude. In face of the evils of the time we feel that they could scarcely say less, that they would have been justified in saying very much more.

This is just the charge that is most frequently brought against them by those who think that no Christian can be anything but a reactionary, however much he may disguise the fact. And it was the charge which at the time bred suspicion among the workers, until at last the evidence of deeds prevailed and refuted it. Yet if it be admitted that the facts on which it is based are true, that *Politics* and indeed all their utterances opposed the violence of the professional agitator and the appeal to overt action, it must be admitted too that, whatever may be the case to-day and whatever we may think of ' unconstitutional methods ' in the abstract, at that period the Christian Socialists were wise in their policy. They were well advised to resist and condemn practices which could only have produced outbreaks of civil strife, discredited the cause of the people, and denied those principles of brotherhood and mutual service upon which all hope of progress was dependent. Maurice was right in preaching love not hate, in invoking the goodness already present both in individuals and in society ; and his powerful influence is due chiefly to his consistent belief that growth must be continuous, that construction, not destruction, is the reformer's true duty, and that there exists boundless capacity for development in all persons and in all classes if only this could be realised. Just as in theology he was bent upon proving that the truth as he saw it was implicit in Creeds and Articles, so in social matters he maintained that God who was guiding every effort after righteousness in the present had also inspired all that was good in the past, that truth here as in theology was already present and only needed to be seen and explained. He has often been accused of being unpractical: at least he was practical enough to realise that it is more consistent and reasonable to preach brotherhood in the sphere in which it can be exercised, in the thousand unremembered acts of daily life and in those social reforms which can here and now be made effective, than to proclaim it along with bloodshed and hatred on the hustings. There were plenty of prophets like Feargus O'Connor crying for red revolution, stirring up passions, and stimulating the forces of reaction : those men with all their easy clamour did not effect, and did not deserve to effect, one tenth of the lasting improvement which the steadier and less theatrical methods of the Christian Socialists achieved.

Moreover, what seems almost insipid to us seemed startlingly dangerous to many of their contemporaries. If proof be wanted of the results of their work and of the change that has come over our outlook, we may find it in the storm of protest which *Politics* produced, not only from opponents but from well-wishers. Archdeacon Hare himself wrote [1] to Maurice strongly deprecating the tone and contents of the second letter of

---

[1] Cf. *Life of Maurice*, i. 475-478.

' Parson Lot,' a plea for the Bible as the true ' Reformers' Guide,' and accusing Kingsley and even Ludlow of conceit, lack of respect for their elders and betters, and excess of zeal : friends and relatives protested against their action, warned them that they were ruining their prospects, and lamented, if not their sympathy with the people, at least the time and method which they had chosen for its utterance [1] : critics and the public at large treated them with an icy scorn or an indifference that was even harder to bear : their fellow-Churchmen responded only with insinuations against their orthodoxy : and worst of all the very workers for whom they were incurring odium met their advances with distrust.

Ludlow, ' that brave spirit,' was unmarried and was living with his mother ; he was ready to sacrifice his professional career if need be, and was never a man afraid of opposition or much regardful of public opinion ; he felt for his friends far more acutely than for himself. Maurice, sensitive to a fault and suffering hideously, had already learned to expect nothing but censure and misunderstanding : ' in all time of our tribulation, in all time of our wealth, good Lord deliver us. It is the Christian soldier's business to receive either as they come, and to seek strength for each '—that is his reply : [2] he could understand, even sympathise with, his persecutors, could accept their rebukes as no more than his deserts and set them aside with a comprehending charity. But Kingsley was younger, as sensitive and much less disciplined, dependent upon the affection of others and by no

---

[1] For example the Rev. S. Clark, one of Maurice's most loyal disciples, lamented bitterly that Maurice and Ludlow by their socialistic writings were ' losing that influence which God formed them to exercise ' : Memorials of Samuel Clark, pp. 268, 269.

[2] Life of Maurice, i. p. 479.

means free from honest ambition, a splendid fighter when upheld by the excitement and comradeship of battle, but less fitted than his colleagues to bear the strain of a lonely struggle. He had at Maurice's advice been a candidate for an appointment at King's College, hoping to combine the work there with that which he was already doing at Queen's. He was rejected, and both he and his supporters recognised that the rejection was due to his connection with *Politics*. He might set his teeth and refuse to surrender, but his letters reveal the passion of his soul. ' I will not be a liar,' he cries,[1] ' I will not flatter myself into a dream that while every man on earth, from Maurice back to Abel, who ever tried to testify against the world, has been laughed at, misunderstood, slandered, and that, bitterest of all, by the very people he loved best, and understood best, I am to escape. My path is clear, and I will follow it.' ' For myself,' he writes to Ludlow,[2] ' chaotic, piecemeal, passionate, "lâche-mar" as I am, I have fears as great as your own. I know the miserable, peevish, lazy, conceited, faithless, prayer-less wretch I am, but I know this too that One is guiding me, and driving me when I will not be guided, who will make me and has made me go His way and do His work. . . . He has made the " Word of the Lord like fire within my bones," giving me no peace till I have spoken out.'

The attitude of the three to one another and to their work as it is revealed during this first trial of their powers is characteristic of their future relationship and worth some study. Kingsley and Ludlow were the firebrands of the movement, impatient of anything ' compromising and half-hearted,' proud of being ' go ahead,' and needing to be reminded that ' this phrase as it is used by young men

---

[1] *Life of Kingsley*, i. p. 178.   [2] *Life of Kingsley*, i. p. 180.

generally implies a recklessness about the moral sense
of their countrymen, a delight in making people start and
look about them.' [1] They might have replied without
injustice that it is the wholesome function of the young to
make their elders jump, and to prevent the world from
settling down into sleepy acquiescence, or the inaction
which excuses itself under much heavy talk of prudence
and order and steady progress. But Ludlow was only
twenty-seven and was gifted with quick sympathies,
fearlessness, and restless energy ; Kingsley, two years
older, was much less balanced, and with his pugnacity,
power of speech, and dramatic instincts might easily
have degenerated into a mere demagogue ; there was
real risk that they might waste themselves by reckless
violence and premature agitation. Maurice realised the
danger and his own responsibility. He answered Hare's
accusation in an apologia for the younger generation of
singular insight and generosity. But none the less he
hardened his heart, in his capacity as chief editor refused
several of their contributions, and in private wrote to
Ludlow a letter of earnest warning. ' We are to reverence
the *conscience* of high as well as low, rich as well as poor.
. . . So far as we wound the conscience of any man
we do a positive injury to him and to ourselves . . . why
spend your time in trampling upon people's corns and
gouty feet, supposing them to be nothing more ? . . .
Kingsley and you have so much real God-given strength
that you have no right to be spasmodic, and I will not
let you be, if I can help it.' If only Kingsley had had such
an adviser beside him all his life !

  Meanwhile if the qualities of the little group were being
tested and tempered, it was becoming clear that *Politics*

----

[1] Cf. *Life of Maurice*, i. pp. 478, 479.

could not be long continued.   In a notice ' to the Reader '
at the beginning of the first number in July it was announced that the paper had not won sufficient support and
did not cover its expenses ; and a hint was given of the
existence of a still more serious difficulty.   Parker had
been growing restless for some time ; had complained that
the publication was damaging his connection ; and had
finally refused to carry on the venture beyond the three
months.   This note is expanded in the survey of their
performance with which the last issue closes.   There it
is admitted that though they have fulfilled some part of
their programme they have failed to deal adequately
with what was their chief subject, Socialism or the relation
of the Capitalist to the Labourer.   Some years later, in
the issue of the *Christian Socialist* for January 4th, 1851,[1]
Ludlow pointed out the full measure of their achievement,
and his words are worth quoting.   ' They failed after
three months' trial.   They had the satisfaction of finding
themselves abused on all sides.   By Chartist contemporaries, clear-sighted enough to see in the writing of a
water-drinking lawyer the handiwork of a jolly parson
over his bottle of port.   By High Church newspapers,
shocked at their dangerous Radicalism.[2]   They failed,—
far be it from me to say that it was not from their own
fault as writers,—even if it were by their misfortune as
men. . . .   Yet their failure had been,—as all failures in
a good cause must be,—a partial success.   They were but
three or four at the first ; they numbered at the last a
goodly band of earnest and willing contributors.   They
had a small but staunch public of two thousand readers

[1] Vol. i. p. 73.

[2] Cf. *Politics*, p. 144. ' We are grateful to *The Commonwealth*
(London Chartist Paper) for its attack upon our aristocratical, clerical,
and mediaeval tendencies ; and to the *Oxford Herald*, for its attack
upon our democratical tendencies.'

even to their long-announced dissolution. Although
distrusted or unheeded by the great bulk of the working
classes, they had begun to reach them by their paper in
Glasgow, in Manchester, and personally, even in London.
And when they parted,—when it was seen that their
attempt was really no rich man's conspiracy to coax or
bully the working-men out of their rights or out of their
hopes, but the sincere endeavour of a few men to see and
to speak the truth, then indeed their true success began,
in the regret manifested by many working men for their
disappearance from the arena of the Press, in the personal
friendship contracted with some. They failed, but with
words of hope upon their lips, encouraging others to take
up the fight in which they had been defeated, and conquer
in it.'

And his next paragraph dwells in more detail upon the
sequel. ' Yet that bond of brotherhood which had been
the very ground of their undertaking could not be dissolved
by its failure. They might cease to see each other's
thoughts side by side in print, week after week. They
could not cease to meet and converse with one another,
whether in writing or in person, for those very ends, and
on those very subjects, which had brought them together.
Their work was not a literary one, but a human one, and
as men they had still to carry it on under God's eye.
And they did carry it on,—how fitfully, how imperfectly,
none so well know as themselves,—losing indeed many
a laggard by the way, but gathering also as they went on
new comrades into their fellowship. They carried it on,
each one according to his opportunities, in schools and
lecture-rooms, in town and country pulpits, in the pages
of periodicals, in the common meditation of the word of
God.'

Indeed *Politics for the People* had been simply the

proclamation of their revolt against aloofness and apathy, the announcement of the existence of some who were prepared when occasion arose to take action. The serious business of the movement had still to be begun. And before we describe it, we must expand the tale of their resources and of the activities to which, pending a clear call to more precise forms of service, they devoted themselves.

The group, as Ludlow has noted, had increased, chiefly at present by the inclusion of personal friends. Of these some account must be given.

Ludlow had himself introduced one whose character and subsequent history make his appearance among them almost startling. Frederick James Furnivall was at this time twenty-three and had come down from Cambridge in 1846. He was reading for the bar in the chambers of Bellenden Ker with whom Ludlow had also worked. He was still a Christian of a somewhat conventional sort, and the violence of tongue and temper which in later life sometimes degenerated into coarseness and brutality and cost him the loss of many friendships [1] had not yet been given full rein. Moreover, then as always, he was interested in social matters and genuinely opposed to class-prejudices and injustice. His acquaintance with Ludlow led to an invitation, and he became one of the most enthusiastic of the Christian Socialists and contributed regularly to their legal and literary work. He was the author in 1850 of a pamphlet entitled ' Association a necessary part of Christianity,' though this was not published under the auspices of the group ; wrote many articles in defence of their work ; and

---

[1] As his biographer more delicately puts it, he was ' devoid of tact or discretion in almost every relation of life.' (Sir Sidney Lee in *Dictionary of National Biography*.)

made a careful and complete collection of their tracts
and leaflets, which is contained in two small volumes
and is now in the library of the British Museum,[1]
being an invaluable source of information as to their
doings.   In the early years of their work he was one
of the most energetic of them all, being always ready
to attend meetings and investigate new openings.   During
Ludlow's tour in the north, in September 1851, he was left
in charge of the *Christian Socialist*, and was the recipient
of the detailed reports and descriptions of co-operative
efforts, that are so prominent a feature of its second
volume.   Later on at the Working Men's College he
took some share in the teaching and a prominent part
in the organising of recreations, and in spite of his quarrels [2]
with the original founders he carried this on for many
years.   Although at first a warm admirer of Maurice,
he disagreed very fiercely with him over the question
of Sunday excursions in 1858 ; [3] and having by this time
passed out of his religious phase, both spoke and wrote [4]
on the subject with a sneering contempt which alienated
from him the feelings of his former associates, and almost
succeeded in driving Maurice to resign.   To his influence
on the Council and with the students may be assigned
the weakening of those religious ideals [5] with which the
College was at first inspired.   Ludlow never forgave him,
and as late as 1904 could only write of him as [6] 'that

---

[1] 08275 e. 33 and 34.

[2] *E.g.* in 1861 there was a strong difference of opinion over the holding
of dances, in which, though he was in a minority of one, he behaved
with violence and impropriety.

[3] *Life of Maurice*, ii. 318-321 ;   *F. J. Furnivall*, pp. xxix-xxxi.

[4] In articles in the *People's Paper*, especially one on Aug. 7th, 1858.

[5] Cf. the Principal's article in *The Working Men's College 1854-1904*,
pp. 250-251.

[6] Letter to Rev. J. Carter.

most wrong-headed of all creatures in human shape now living.' The outrage upon Maurice and the wrecking of Maurice's work was to him the unpardonable sin—and he himself had brought Furnivall into the group.

Mention may next be made of two members whom Mansfield introduced. His cousin, Archibald Mansfield Campbell, was by profession an architect, but had gone into business and in the early days of the movement took an active, though, thanks to his home being at Weybridge, not a specially prominent part in its work. He was quite unacquainted with social problems until he joined his cousin, and suffered from the typical prejudice against anything savouring of Socialism : but he was soon drawn into the fellowship around Maurice, and his series of articles in the early numbers of the *Christian Socialist* on the ' Evils of Competition ' show how fully he entered into their spirit. Like most of the group he managed to combine religion and commonsense with very effective results.

Charles Robert Walsh was considerably more important to them. He was a doctor and for some time shared rooms in the same house, 42 Half Moon Street, with Mansfield. The two men had much in common, in temperament as well as in interests. Ludlow speaks of Walsh as the sweetest-tempered man he had ever met, and like his friend he was always giving proof, by acts of kindliness and self-sacrifice, of the reality of his love for others. They were both keenly interested in the application of science to the public health, worked together in Bermondsey during the cholera outbreak, and strove to direct the attention of the group to this field of effort : Walsh, under the pseudonym of ' Jacob,' contributed several letters on sanitary science to the periodicals of the Christian Socialists. Like Mansfield, he died young, though in his case death was from disease. Ludlow has told how to the end he watched and noted his own symptoms in the hope that the knowledge might be useful, and how gallantly and cheerily he faced his end.

Representing quite a different type was Cuthbert Edward Ellison, the ' swell ' of the movement, who had been at Cambridge with Kingsley and Mansfield, and was a member of that curious ' Young England ' party which Disraeli and Ellison's friend Lord John Manners, afterwards Duke of Rutland, had founded, and which Kingsley introduces in *Yeast*. The ' Young Englanders ' desired to restore the traditions of mediaeval chivalry into social relationships, to remedy the evils of industrialism by reviving the feudal ideal of a contented peasantry and a philanthropic nobility ; they would do for the State what the Tractarians were doing for the Church. Ellison was at this time living in chambers with Thackeray and Tom Taylor, afterwards editor of *Punch*, and despite his faultless dress, perfect manners and conservative views, threw himself keenly into the work of the group. In 1850 he moved to Lincoln's Inn and was thus brought still more closely into touch with them. Ludlow claims that he was the original of Arthur Pendennis.[1]

Another of their earliest recruits was Francis Cranmer Penrose, the architect and astronomer, the youngest son of the lady so famous as ' Mrs. Markham ' in the childhood days of the last generation. He was two years older than Kingsley and Mansfield, but had gone up to Cambridge rather late and had known them both there during his residence at Magdalene. After his degree he had travelled ; but returned from Athens in 1847, and became an active member of the group in the

[1] *Economic Review*, iv. p. 35.

summer of 1848. Though he never seems to have written anything for them, he was one of the original teachers at the night-school and a regular attendant at the Bible-reading : probably the composition of his own elaborate work, *The Principles of Athenian Architecture*, which was published in 1851, explains the fact that he did not take a more prominent part in their later activities. In 1852, after his appointment as Surveyor of St. Paul's cathedral, his professional skill was placed at their disposal for the designing of the Hall of Association.

An older man, who though never a member of the Society of Promoters took a keen and life-long interest in their work, was the Rev. John Sherren Brewer, at this time classical lecturer at King's College and chaplain of the Bloomsbury workhouse. His sympathies were largely with the Oxford Movement whose leaders he had known at the University ; but his friendship for Maurice, whom he succeeded as Professor, was intimate and loyal. He was one of the first to ' fraternise ' : but his devotion to research and his scholarly and literary tastes left him little leisure, and he was never closely connected with the practical business of the Associations. In 1854, when the Working Men's College had been proposed, he felt that he could be of greater service. Thanks to his journalism he got the scheme very favourably noticed in the *Morning Herald*, and when the syllabus was constructed joined the teaching staff. Although the commencement of his colossal task upon the state papers of Henry VIII. interrupted his work for the College, he continued to serve it until he left London in 1877.

Among the others who took part in the work at this stage were John William Parker, junior, the friend of Kingsley, who taught at the night-school ; Matthew Inglett Brickdale, a barrister and member of the Bible-reading and a teacher at the school, who broke a lance with Parson Lot under the *nom-de-guerre* of ' Tory Bill ' in the columns of the *Christian Socialist*; Frederick Daniel Dyster, a retired doctor who contributed several articles to it on popular science ; the Rev. Alfred Baker Strettell, a colleague of Maurice at Queen's College ; Viscount Goderich, afterwards the first Marquis of Ripon, who joined them at this time, although he took little part in their work until the winter of 1851-52 ; David Masson, then doing journalistic work in London ; Arthur Hugh Clough, the poet, a friend of Masson's and his predecessor at University College ; Alfred Nicholson, famous in his day as a player on the oboe and one of the most devoted of the Promoters ; and finally the two brothers, Daniel and Alexander Macmillan, the former of whom was almost the first [1] to draw Maurice's attention to social problems, and who both took a keen interest in the group. These last were particularly important because from their influence with the undergraduates of Cambridge they were able to introduce many of the ablest of them to Christian Socialism. One of the earliest of these was Fenton J. A. Hort, whose letters contain a most valuable impression of the Movement and who admits that he swallowed *Politics* readily.[2] He never actually joined them, or indeed accepted their socialism : but others were converted more completely, and supplied a steady stream of new recruits to the later stages of the work. The enthusiasm of the Macmillans bore fruit in Llewelyn Davies, Litchfield, Westlake, Vernon Lushington, and many another.[3]

[1] In a letter written in 1840 cf. *Life of Maurice*, i. p. 329.

[2] Cf. *Life and Letters of F. J. A. Hort*, i. pp. 70-276. For the Macmillans' influence, cf. *Memoir of Daniel Macmillan*, pp. 211-215 and 230.

[3] A complete list of the members of the Society in 1852 is given in the *First Report* and reproduced in Appendix B, pp. 378, 379.

In addition to these actual members there had also been collected a body of sympathisers whose influence and powers were even more notable. The list of contributors to *Politics* contains such well-known names as those of Richard Whately, the Archbishop of Dublin, a pioneer of social science; Richard C. Trench, then a colleague of Maurice at King's College and afterwards also Archbishop of Dublin; Arthur P. Stanley, afterwards Dean of Westminster; S. G. Osborne, Kingsley's brother-in-law, author of the 'lay-sermons' signed S.G.O. in the *Times* and afterwards Lord Sydney Godolphin; Edward Strachey, a pupil of Maurice in 1836 and afterwards a baronet; Arthur Helps, author of *Friends in Counsel*, afterwards knighted and Clerk to the Privy Council; James Spedding, editor of the works and author of the *Life and Letters* of Bacon, who lived in Lincoln's Inn Fields; John Conington, afterwards Professor of Latin at Oxford, who sent some rather heavy verse, and whose interest in the working classes was said to be due to the conversation of his 'scout'; and William A. Guy, dean of the medical faculty at King's College and a contributor to the first number. Even though these were not officially connected with the movement, their interest in it was a real encouragement to a group the members of which were nearly all young and as yet quite without recognised position. And several of them continued their support throughout the history of the movement.

There was therefore some foundation for Ludlow's praise of the 'goodly band' which had been gathered by the issue of *Politics*. He himself with Mansfield was responsible for most of the recruits and was indefatigable in collecting likely members and bringing them to meet Maurice, and then, if they passed the scrutiny successfully, drawing them into definite connection with the work.

When *Politics* ceased, it was clear that the interest aroused by it must not be dissipated, and there was now abundance of material for the launching of some fresh enterprise. What this should be was by no means plain ; and Ludlow's mind turned towards the fulfilment of his old scheme for the betterment of the district around Lincoln's Inn. In 1846 the difficulty had been lack of workers prepared to give the necessary time to the task. Now these were available and were anxious to be used. Nevertheless a new obstacle had arisen. The group already consisted of marked men. Maurice would not engage in any activity without the sanction of the incumbent of the parish ; and he was not welcome everywhere. So there was a brief spell of uncertainty. In the summer, however, the way was opened by a suggestion made by the Rev. William Short, the rector of St. George the Martyr's, Bloomsbury, that they should try to civilise the inhabitants of Little Ormond Yard, a court quite near Maurice's house, which at the time neither clergy nor police dared to enter. They agreed to make an attempt by starting a night-school for the men of the place. A house was taken, and evenings were allotted to most of the group, Campbell, who was an ardent champion of phonetic spelling and wished to try his theories upon untutored minds, being ruthlessly refused entry. Desks and benches were brought in and the school opened on September 21st, Ludlow, Campbell, Penrose, Furnivall and Parker being present and a short service of dedication being conducted by the curate, a fellow of Christ's College, Cambridge, the Rev. Joseph Clark. It was provided that Maurice, who was never a strong disciplinarian, should always be accompanied on the nights when he took classes ; and in the early days, when the yard was really dangerous, the teachers generally went there in couples.

The work was at first often exciting, but, when once they had gained a footing, success was rapid.   It was thoroughly educative—for masters and pupils alike, particularly the former.   Hitherto most of them had only a second-hand knowledge of poverty and its needs ; here they gained experience for themselves and laid the foundations of the Working Men's College, the last and in a sense the most permanent of their enter-prises.   Before the men's classes had been going long, the lads were anxious to come in, and special arrange-ments had to be made for them.   Then the women began to claim attention, and though the group had not the courage to supply teachers for them out of their own number, they engaged a lady to take a class and also to look after the wives and families of their male pupils. Amongst their other innovations in social reform may perhaps be reckoned the provision of a day in the country —the forerunner of the activities of the Fresh Air Fund. It was a great occasion when first on June 27th, 1849, they packed the inhabitants of the yard into vans, men, women, and children huddled in as tight as possible, and carried them off for a day in Epping Forest.

It was at this time that the group gained one of its most devoted and best known members, one moreover ideally suited to work of this description.   The story of his coming is familiar,[1] but will bear retelling.   As has been said, Ludlow and Mansfield had been doing most of the enlisting of newcomers ; and it was therefore with some pride that Maurice announced one evening that he had got hold of a man who might join and be useful at the night-school. His words seem to have roused mirth ; and there was a general request for the candidate's name.   When Maurice

---

[1] Cf. *Life of Maurice*, i. p. 483, and Ludlow in *Economic Review*, **vi.** pp. 298, 299.

replied 'Thomas Hughes,' the laughter increased ; for the reputation of the old Rugbeian who had only just come down from Oxford was as yet solely athletic. 'We're not going to start a cricket club ! ' said one : ' let's have a look at him !' said another : and in he came, and to Maurice's huge delight proved an immediate success. Thenceforward the group must never mock at their leader's powers of selection ; for had he not alone and unaided secured for them Hughes, ' the man of childlike heart, of knightly loyalty, of the most humane geniality, and of the simplest Christian faith,' [1] Hughes the type of all that is finest in our race ?

He was an asset of quite incalculable value in his effect both upon his fellow members and upon the public. A movement for reform inevitably attracts to it all the available freaks in the community. Socialism, as anyone who has ever been to a Fabian Society meeting will know, has been especially cursed by its fatal fascination for the degenerate and the eccentric. And the group was not immune. There was Mansfield with his cotton-cloth shoes, and Campbell with his 'fonetic nuts,' and Furnivall, vegetarian and non-smoker and teetotaler, with a spelling all his own ; [2] and there was the unnamed with the blue plush gloves who was so repulsive to the sensibilities of Kingsley ; and even the leaders were a couple of parsons and a strange fellow who had spent half his life in France. They were admittedly on their own showing a queer collection ; even Alexander Macmillan, who loved them dearly, called them the ' Crotchet Club ' [3] ; an outsider

---

[1] J. Llewelyn Davies in *The Working Men's College, 1854-1904*, p. 10.

[2] He kept throughout life the habit of mutilating past participles and perfects (' raisd,' ' askt,' ' walkt,' etc.)—a habit apparently first introduced by Julius Hare, and fashionable for a few years about 1845.

[3] So Hort relates (*Life*, i. p. 153). Cf. *Times* 27 Jan. 1852, ' mustachioed and long-haired individuals . . . Socialists or foreigners or both.'

might be pardoned if he thought them simply cranks, —or lunatics not yet proved to be harmless. And to them had come Tom Hughes, the ' blue,' with the healthy mind and the healthy body, whom no one could accuse of madness or vice, who was the ideal hero of the British public and the sporting press. He had come, he shared their life, and loved it, and they loved him. Here was something to give their critics pause : Tom Hughes had joined them ; they could not be so bad after all if a man like that was among them.

But the new member was much more than a guarantee of respectability. Most of us, thank God, have known men of his stamp, built on a large scale spiritually as well as physically, and combining the disciplined strength of the athlete with the simplicity and unselfconsciousness of the child ; men full of comradeship, of breezy and unaffected friendliness ; men of healthy instincts, lovers of the open air, clean-minded, frank of speech, devoid of guile ; men utterly reliable, incapable of envy, unspoiled by popularity, who could do nothing mean or false or selfish ; men not cursed with intellectualism, unperplexed with doubts, often seeming dull and stupid until they startle us by proof of their power, as Hughes startled Ludlow by the production of *Tom Brown*.[1] We may laugh at them, and sharpen our wits upon them ; we may gibe at schoolboy heroes and at the system which has made them what they are ; but in our hearts we love and revere them, and know that they are greater than ourselves ; and when we are lonely or in trouble it is to them first that we would turn.

And Hughes when he had thrown in his lot with the movement became in a sense its centre. Maurice ' had an exquisite joy in the complete sympathy of such a

[1] *Economic Review*, vi. p. 307.

helper.'[1] Ludlow became his most intimate friend, poured out his worries to him and shared with him his plans and hopes. Kingsley found in him a man after his own heart, his chosen companion by the trout-stream and in the cottages of the poor. It was in him that Neale found sympathy and support and a lifetime of partnership when he felt himself a stranger to the rest. They all leaned upon him and loved him ; and if he initiated nothing and never took the lead, he was always there to brighten the way when it was difficult, to give them fresh courage when they wavered, to rejoice in their successes, and to face their failures undismayed. In every team there must be someone ' to do the donkey-work,' to rally the forwards for those last five minutes or to pull the side together when batsmen are set and runs coming all too quickly : in Christian Socialism that man was Thomas Hughes.

With Hughes there came a new influx of members into the group, the most prominent of whom was another old Rugbeian, the Rev. Septimus C. H. Hansard. He was at the time curate at St. Mary's, Marylebone, where Hughes was then living; and, although his own work absorbed much of his time, he threw himself actively into Christian Socialism, joined the Bible-reading, and from his knowledge of working men was valuable in getting together the earlier meetings with them. Through his life, and especially as Rector of Bethnal Green, he took the keenest interest in social problems; and from his friendship with William Allan and William Newton, two of the most prominent leaders of the Amalgamated Society of Engineers, exerted a powerful influence over the development of the Labour Movement. Ludlow has described him[2] with his

---

[1] J. Llewelyn Davies, l.c. p. 10.
[2] *Economic Review*, vi. pp. 297-316.

usual skill and vividness in the article which deals also with Hughes, and the two were closely associated in many of the enterprises of the next five years.

Hansard was speedily instrumental in bringing others into the work. George Grove, afterwards knighted and famous for his work in music, was in 1849 a member of the Marylebone congregation. He had started life as a civil engineer, and while engaged on the erection of a lighthouse in Jamaica had received and read with deep interest a copy of *Politics*. Having this link with Hansard he was speedily taken to dine with Ludlow in Cadogan Place, was introduced by him to the group, and joined the Society.[1] He contributed to the *Christian Socialist* and lectured in the early days of the Working Men's College. With him too came his brother-in-law, George Granville Bradley, afterwards Dean of Westminster, at that time at the zenith of his power as a master at Rugby, who joined them as a Corresponding Member.

Soon afterwards George Hughes came up to London to live with his brother, and he also was for a time introduced to the group. In the *Memoir* we have been given a noble picture of him, and the frankness with which his relationship to Christian Socialism is described is very illuminating.[2] George's first difficulty was over the name Socialism ; but his real objection went deeper than this. He realised that if successful the associative principle must involve a radical alteration of the whole system of society ; and from this he shrank, not through lack of sympathy with the ideals of the reformers, but from fear lest they might be fleeing from evils that they knew into others and worse ones which only experience would reveal. So although

[1] Cf. C. L. Graves, *Life of Sir George Grove*, p. 36, where his connection with Christian Socialism is described by Ludlow and Furnivall.

[2] *Memoir of a Brother*, pp. 109-120.

he subscribed to the work and undertook certain tasks in connection with it, his brother's hopes of him as a champion were disappointed ; and after a year or two his only share in it was the purchase of clothes from the Tailors' Association. His attitude was valuable in that it revealed to his brother something of the magnitude of the problems with which they were confronted, and saved him from his first rather thoughtless optimism.

But after all, much as they owed to men like Hughes or Mansfield, the true centre of their fellowship and source of their strength lay, as they were the first to insist, not in the quality of their members so much as in the spiritual basis of their work. The weekly meetings for the reading of the Bible on Mondays at eight o'clock at Maurice's house were begun in December, and were in a real sense the sacrament, the effective symbol of their unity, the means whereby they received their inspiration. To many such a method of preparation for social work will seem unpractical and unreal : we can hardly conceive it being adopted in these days when even at religious gatherings the devotional element and con-fession of faith is often confined to a formal ' opening with prayer.' But no one can read Mansfield's description [1] without recognising that these men felt, and were not ashamed to feel, that the hours spent together in the study of the ancient records, in the effort to understand and interpret them, were the richest and most useful of their lives. And it was not only that so they learnt an intimacy and mutual trust which nothing else could have given, and which was to be severely tested in the storms and conflicts of the next few years; but that, as they listened to the ' Prophet ' bringing out from his treasury things new and

---

[1] *Life of Maurice*, pp. 488-493.

old, they began to share his vision of the reality and nearness of God, his certainty of the ultimate triumph of the Christ, his confidence in the message and the meaning of the Kingdom. They learned on those evenings that religion was part and the greatest part of a true man's life and a true man's work ; that difficulties must be honestly faced and could be honestly answered ; that sincerity and sympathy were the essential conditions of comradeship: and as the experience of God came into their lives the bonds which linked them one to another became holy, and the venture upon which they were embarked was transfigured into the splendour of a crusade.

And on these evenings as they studied together, and Sunday after Sunday as they met at Lincoln's Inn Chapel when the ' Master ' prayed and preached, they learned to feel for him a loyalty and an affection such as has been given to few in all the ages of the Church. Whatever the world might think of him, however much his diffidence and hesitation might perplex his followers and endanger their plans, although at times it seemed scarcely possible to be patient or to accept his verdict without cavil, they were his disciples and would obey him ; and he whom the mass of his contemporaries so completely misunderstood, whom his Church distrusted and scorned, found in them his encouragement and consolation, and through them the means whereby his message might be given in concrete shape to the life of the future.

CHAPTER IV

THE DISCOVERY OF A POLICY

THE work of the Christian Socialists in 1848 had been confessedly lacking in clear and constructive policy. They had made a great and timely protest under the guidance of an impulse which they were not ashamed to call divine. The circumstances of the time and the quality of their great leader's gospel made such an outburst inevitable. They acted under a sense of immediate compulsion : at all hazards they must speak out and speak fearlessly, not waiting to discover a full plan of campaign, but trusting that when once the trumpet was sounded the stages of the attack and the way to victory would be disclosed.

Had Maurice been a man bent upon personal recognition or with less confidence in the capacity of his countrymen to respond to the call of righteousness, he might have been content to prolong this first phase of their work, and to confine himself to what would nowadays be called an educational campaign. Advertisement judiciously used, the creation of a favourable public opinion, the value of an elaborate propaganda, these things are to-day recognised as part of the preparation for any forward movement. Politicians are past masters in such arts ; and Churchmen have not always hesitated to make use of them. No doubt there is a certain wisdom in securing the existence of a demand before we proceed to supply it : it is easier

136

and more exciting to court publicity with committees and speechifying than to settle down and work. But Maurice's tastes did not lie in that direction. He hated and feared above all things whatever savoured of notoriety or ' push.' ' Hot air ' was an atmosphere in which he could not breathe, and his sincerity gave him an instinct for its detection. To be regarded as a public character or the leader of a movement was a fate from which he shrank throughout his life. But he had been forced by his love of righteousness to come forward and make his protest, and knew that something more definite must be done to justify it.

Kingsley was clearly prepared to go on preaching and writing. At Eversley this was all that he could do, and his gifts enabled him to do it singularly well. The stimulation of the public conscience could safely be left in his hands. As a regular member of the group he practically ceased to be available ; for he had been obliged to give up his work at Queen's College ; and his literary tasks with the burden of correspondence which they involved left him little leisure for journeys to London. But for several years more his voice and pen were devoted to the cause, and he was always anxious to keep in touch with its leaders, to follow its new developments, and to contribute lectures and articles in its service.

The immediate practical problem of the next steps to be taken was left to Ludlow to solve ; and when his editorial duties came to an end he set himself to follow up the threads that had come into his hands. Thanks perhaps to his French education, he was entirely free from all class-prejudice. *Politics* had brought him into touch with a certain number of ex-Chartists and other working-class leaders, and the school in Little Ormond Yard gave him access to others. Before long an opening came. His friend, Self, the Scripture reader, introduced him to Walter Cooper,[1] a tailor at that time working in Fetter Lane, a lecturer on Strauss, a Scotchman, and a prominent Chartist, a man of marked ability as a speaker and at this time unquestionably sincere. The acquaintance was carefully fostered. Cooper, though he had lost all faith in the narrow Calvinism of his boyhood, admitted that he had been impressed by *Politics* and was persuaded to go to Lincoln's Inn Chapel to hear Maurice preach ; and after four visits declared that now he had managed to understand him. Soon afterwards he agreed with Ludlow to get together a meeting, at which members of the group could discuss social problems with a few picked representatives of the workers. Neutral ground, the ' Cranbourne ' Coffee Tavern, was chosen ; and there on April 23rd, 1849, the experiment was tried,—with such success that it was determined to repeat it weekly. All through the year these meetings were continued, though the programme varied greatly. Sometimes lectures or addresses were given, sometimes a debate was arranged, often there was no definite business except discussion. Frankness and a spirit of fellowship quickly became characteristic of the gathering, and some valuable recruits were collected. Ludlow's skill in drawing out the shy and winning the confidence of the suspicious, Hughes' geniality and transparent honesty, and Maurice's sympathy and insight could not fail to produce a favourable impression. And when the plunge had been made, the group was enabled to gain firsthand knowledge of the needs and aspirations of the poor, and to discuss with them the practicability of various proposals for reform.

[1] Cf. *Atlantic Monthly*, lxxvii. p. 113.   Cf. Gammage, *History of the Chartist Movement* (2nd edition) p. 354 ; T. Cooper, *Life*, p. 313.

It was apparently on the occasion of the first [1] of these
meetings that an event memorable to all students of the
life of Kingsley took place. The discussion began in a
somewhat frigid fashion. Maurice, who was in the chair,
was nervous and shy ; the rest of the group did not wish
to push themselves forward for fear of frightening their
working friends, very few of whom they knew. The
general embarrassment was not diminished by the first
speakers, who were men with grievances that they were
glad to be able to air. They said many hard things of
their social superiors, and made the group feel distinctly
uncomfortable. The clergy especially came in, as usual,
for a good deal of plain speech. Then up rose Charles
Kingsley ; and with the stammer which marked his
utterance until he lost himself in his subject blurted out
' I am a Church of England clergyman,' and then, after a
pause, and with folded arms, ' And I am a Chartist.'
After which he also spoke with some frankness, and the
meeting became friendly. For when the ice was once
broken, the two sides came together and the situation was
saved.

Later on we have an interesting picture of another of
these occasions from two opposite standpoints. On
June 12th Maurice describes himself [2] as having ' spoken
last night for, I suppose, twenty minutes or half an
hour—not as I might have wished, but much better than
I had a right to expect, or than any preparation of mine
would have enabled me to do.' Kingsley who happened
to be present at the same time says,[3] ' Last night will
never be forgotten by many many men. Maurice was—

---

[1] So Hughes in his *Prefatory Memoir*, p. 14.   From Maurice's letters
(*Life*, i. pp. 538, 542) it appears that it cannot have been actually the
first.   Probably it was the meeting on May 7th.   Hughes' dates are
often confused, cf. p. 110.

[2] *Life of Maurice*, i. p. 547.   [3] *Life of Kingsley*, i. p. 206.

I cannot describe it . . . The man was inspired—gigantic
. . . He stunned us.'

Out of these meetings several of the staunchest
champions of Christian Socialism were secured.
Ludlow has described how at one of their early
conferences ' there rose up to speak a man still
young, with an intelligent face, and with a remarkable
gift of easy, perspicuous, argumentative speech,
evidently well-educated, professedly an Owenite Socialist,
a master-tailor in Oxford Street, and editor of a
weekly newspaper;'[1] and how this man, Lloyd
Jones, despite his sceptical views and the bitter
experience of Christianity which had come to him as
the most prominent of Owen's lecturers, threw himself
wholeheartedly into the plans of the Christian Socialists.
This was an event at once interesting and important.
Hitherto the group's whole knowledge of Socialism had
been derived through Ludlow from the French, from
Fourier and Leroux, Proudhon and Louis Blanc [2]; the
newcomer might be said to represent those English
Socialists of the twenties and thirties, whose work has
been rescued from oblivion by the patient researches of
Professor Foxwell. And on the practical side his connection with them was an asset of the greatest value. Not
only was he a cogent and effective speaker and a

[1] *Economic Review*, iv. p. 39. Cf. also a short memoir by his son William
Cairns Jones, prefixed to the 2nd edition of his *Life of Robert Owen.*
The paper was *The Spirit of the Age*, cf. Holyoake, *History of Co-opera-
tion*, ii. p. 559 (1906 edition).

[2] Louis Blanc actually spoke at the group's meetings and sent to them
his friend Nadaud : cf. *Report* pp. 63, 64 and Ludlow, ' Two Dialogues
on Socialism,' *Economic Review*, iv. p. 343, where their debt to the
French is clearly acknowledged. In Ludlow's large collection of tracts
and pamphlets the only traces of the early English Socialists are copies
of Gray's ' Lecture on Human Happiness,' Minter Morgan's scheme
for a village community, and a number of papers, etc. by Robert
Owen.

journalist of brilliant parts,[1] but he had for some time conducted a co-operative store at Salford, and thus could contribute to the work of his new colleagues a firsthand knowledge of the distributive side of the movement and also of the industrial life of the North of England. In addition he was loyal and straightforward, full of courage and patience, devoted heart and soul to the ideals of Association : neither the difficulties which daunted so many of his new friends, nor the sneers of those like Holyoake who flung his past in his face, could shake his resolve.

Among other recruits from these meetings were the watch-finishers Joseph Millbank and Thomas Shorter, who had been fellow-apprentices and fellow-Chartists, and from the first took an active part in the conduct of the conferences. Ludlow has given vivid pictures of the two friends,[2] Millbank quick-witted and ready of speech, Shorter slow and shrewd but capable when moved of remarkable outbursts of eloquence. They were men of sterling honesty and high principles, and as joint secretaries of the Society of Promoters did a vast amount of solid and efficient work. Millbank emigrated with his family in 1851, and died in Australia in 1860, but Shorter acted for some years as secretary to the Working Men's College until forced by approaching blindness to resign.

Finally there was Walter Cooper himself who for some years played a chief part among the working-class members of the group. Ludlow was strongly attracted to him and recognising his hold upon his fellow workmen selected

[1] Nowhere is his brilliancy in argument and literary skill better displayed than in a letter to the *Reasoner*, defending himself against Holyoake's charge of inconsistency, *Reasoner*, x. pp. 331, 332.

[2] *Economic Review*, iv. p. 38 ; for Millbank, *Working Men's College Magazine*, iii. p. 11, and Shorter, T. Cooper, *Life*, pp. 313, 321.

him for tasks of great responsibility.   In the performance
of these he received unreserved confidence and support,
and was reckoned by the Promoters as their close personal
friend.   Although difficulties arose [1] at an early stage
involving grave charges of mismanagement and even
dishonesty, he was able to explain matters satisfactorily,
and, if actually guilty, succeeded in concealing the fact
for the next eight or nine years.   Probably he was genuine
enough at the start, but too weak to remain loyal when
the cause had lost its novelty and he had himself become
respectable and outwardly prosperous.   Temptation to
abuse his position came upon him while there was still
abundant opportunity : proofs of his fraud were eventually discovered, and ' he passed out of sight disgraced.' [2]
Maurice's gospel bade him place an almost boundless trust
in the inherent goodness of his fellows.   Such trust is
necessarily a searching test of character ; to the rogue
it would seem almost to invite deception.   Yet in spite of
the miscellaneous quality of his following and his lack of
precautions and supervision he was seldom betrayed.
That Cooper's case was exceptional speaks volumes for
his influence and for human nature : and, so far as the
evidence goes, the man did not fall until that influence
had been virtually removed.

During the summer, and while these conferences were
still being held, two further events gave a definite direction
to the plans of the group.   Ludlow spent the vacation in
Paris and while there made it his business to study the
various experiments in social reform which had arisen
out of the turmoil of the previous year.   Louis Blanc's
scheme for *Ateliers Nationaux* had been taken up by the

---

[1] Cf. *Christian Socialist*, i. pp. 62, 69.

[2] This is all that Ludlow will say of him.   Cf. *Econ. Review*, iv. p. 36,
and he is equally brief in *Atlantic Monthly*, l.c. pp. 113, 115 : cf. below
p. 313.

Government, placed under the supervision of Marie, the minister of the Interior, and by him deliberately wrecked. But in spite of the scandal and subsequent official hostility the movement had been carried on by many *Associations Ouvrières* privately organised upon Buchez'[1] original system. Ludlow's attention was specially attracted by this 'then really magnificent work which,' as he wrote, ' seemed to meet the very mischiefs we were anxious to deal with.' [2] He took pains to get a clear understanding of these Associations, inspected several of their workshops personally, and collected a large bundle of papers containing their constitutions, conditions of membership, and regulations. A full account of the results of his research was published in 1850 as the fourth in the series of *Tracts on Christian Socialism,* and he modelled upon it his own plan for Working Associations. When he returned to London the scheme was already plain to him ; all that was necessary was an opportunity to put it into practice.

Another recruit strengthened the links with France. A. L. Jules Le Chevalier, who in May 1850 adopted the name St. André,[3] professed to be a follower of St. Simon, a refugee who ' for twenty years had been mixed up with every socialistic thing.' [4] He was expelled from France in June 1849, and met Ludlow and the group in November. His plausible address, wide knowledge, and ready enthusiasm gave him at once a prominent position in their counsels. At the beginning possibly he was sincere—

---

[1] Cf. Valleroux, *Associations co-opératives en France et à l'étranger,* pp. 2-30.

[2] Letter quoted in *Life of Maurice,* ii. p. 13.

[3] His style varies : at first it is Le Chevalier ; in 1851 it becomes Lechevalier ; in the *Report* it is Lechevalier *(St. Andre)* ; as author of the scheme for a Consumers' Protection Institution he signs himself A. L. J. Lechevalier St. André !

[4] *Life of Maurice,* ii. p. 47.

so far as his ulterior motives and desire to give satisfaction permitted any sincerity.   At any rate the group accepted him.   But after a time their suspicions were aroused ; his dexterous optimism no longer carried conviction ; and in March 1852, he severed his connection with the Society and resigned his position in the Agency.   In 1854 he published a defence of his conduct, *Five Years in the Land of Exile*,[1] valuable chiefly for the documents in its Appendix : but Maurice, the most charitable of men, refers to him, years afterwards and not unjustly, in a letter to Ludlow as a ' clever sharper.' [2]   After the fall of the French Empire and the exposure of Napoleon's intrigues ' Le Chevalier ' was discovered to have served for some years as a paid secret agent ! [3]

Furthermore during the same summer a tremendous impetus was given to the cause of reform by the publication of the articles on *London Labour and the London Poor*, by Henry Mayhew and his coadjutors in the *Morning Chronicle*.   Mayhew, a professional journalist, had been commissioned by the editor to investigate the condition of the sweated workers and the slum-dwellers, and his descriptions of the tragedy and horror of their lives were illustrated with abundant examples of actual cases and were written with poignancy and power.   The country was thrilled.   Attempts to excuse the position were futile.   The evidence was never seriously challenged. And as if to underline his indictment there was an outbreak of cholera during August and September.   Even the politicians became terrified.   Sydney Herbert, who was then temporarily out of office and was financially

---

[1] See below p. 258, and Appendix C, p. 381.

[2] *Life of Maurice*, ii. p. 550, and Huber, *Reisebriefe*, ii. pp. 163-170.

[3] So M'Cabe, *Life of Holyoake*, i. 191-192—pages which contain a racy description of the rotund and genial impostor.

interested in the *Morning Chronicle*, was so moved by its
revelations of the sweating of needle-women that he began
to agitate for schemes of wholesale emigration. Maurice's
followers were not slow to recognise the change of atmosphere. Mayhew's catalogue of iniquities had succeeded
where the calmer appeal of *Politics* had failed. The
Chartist agitation was still fresh in the public mind, and
this demonstration of the sufferings of the poor found
the national conscience already half-awake, and stirred
it for a time into something like activity.

The members of the group plunged into practical
relief-work. Mansfield with his scientific training went
down to investigate sanitary conditions in the plague-
areas. Walsh lost the support of his wealthy patients by
accepting a post as inspector in Bermondsey. Kingsley [1]
came up from Eversley to join the crusade, and from his
experiences on Jacob's Island got the material for one of
the most lurid chapters in Alton Locke. All through the
autumn they struggled without funds or adequate support
to stay the epidemic, and among the dens and hovels of
the river-side disclosed an inferno beside which even
Mayhew's descriptions seemed almost colourless. It
was during these weeks that Kingsley's imagination was
first impressed by the grimly dramatic ironies of the
tailoring trade. The contrast between the squalor of
the workers and the grandeur of their materials, and the
hideous possibilities of retribution upon those who were
content to wear plague-infected garments rather than to
secure decent conditions for their makers, appealed alike
to the artist and the prophet. The plate-glass palaces
with their crowds of well-dressed customers, and the
verminous attics swarming with human sufferers,
supplied him with pictures whose message would enlist

[1] Cf. *Life of Kingsley*, i. pp. 216, 217.

the self-interest not less than the sympathies of the public. He returned to his parish with his soul ablaze with righteous indignation, and within a few weeks had composed his first and most famous pamphlet *Cheap Clothes and Nasty* which was submitted to Maurice in December and published by William Pickering in January. By it the attention of the group was focussed definitely upon the tailoring trade.

Ludlow meanwhile had returned from France busy with schemes for co-operative production, and spent several months in trying to convince the group of the necessity for a practical experiment in this direction. 'Week after week,' as Furnivall has related,[1] 'did Mr. Ludlow press these subjects on our consideration and say " we must no longer be accomplices in this state of things, we *must* get an honest middle-man between us and some working-men at least ; we must have an Association like the French Working Men's Associations that I have known succeed so well, in which the manager shall be appointed by the men and by us, and be a bond between us instead of a division." ' Such methods were obviously appropriate to the case of the journeymen tailors as had been fully shown in Paris, and everything seemed to point to this as the best sphere for the first venture. Walter Cooper's presence was a great asset ; for he could speak of the ' slop system ' from firsthand knowledge, and could get into touch with working members of the trade. With him and one or two others Ludlow began to formulate concrete plans for a Co-operative Association.

But this was not the only proposal before the group.

[1] In an article in *The Working Men's College Magazine*, ii. p. 145 (for Sept. 1860). It is important to notice that their scheme for co-operative production was wholly French in origin. In all the Christian Socialist literature there does not seem to be a single reference to William Thompson or any other of the English writers who had suggested similar methods, whereas French socialists are very freely quoted.

Mansfield, fresh from the horrors of the cholera, conceived a scheme for a Health League, and with Ludlow and Walsh drew up a programme for it. Its object was ' For uniting all classes of society in the promotion of the Public Health, and the removal of all causes of disease which unnecessarily abridge man's right to live ' ; and this was to be accomplished ' by collecting and diffusing information, by furthering the due execution and where necessary the amendment of the law, and by stimulating and assisting all public bodies and private persons in the performance of their respective duties in reference to the Public Health.' [1] Ludlow, who admits that the scheme would probably have been premature, thought at the time that it was the most immediately useful work that they could undertake. He and Mansfield were both men of restless energy who felt the challenge of the time and did not mean to refuse it. They were getting impatient for action. Discussion and study had been well enough as a preparation until they could discover what to do. Now that their plans were made, delay might easily be fatal. They must strike while the public interest in social matters was still keen.

But Maurice hesitated from motives admirably described by his biographer and expressed in burning words by himself. ' I could go mad too,' he wrote to Ludlow in December,[2] ' and these bewildering charges and countercharges and protests and objections upset my head and heart more even than the evils which upon such terms can never be remedied. "Ten grains of calomel." "No, Bleed! Bleed!" "Fool! Mesmerism is the only thing." "How dare you say so?" "There is Hydropathy; there is Homoeopathy." "Thank you,

---

[1] For details cf. *Economic Review*, iv. pp. 30, 31.

[2] *Life of Maurice*, ii. p. 29.

doctors, one and all. You may draw the curtain. The patient is gone!" Poor England!' He agreed readily enough that emigration was no proper solution of the problem, and approved the letter which Mansfield had sent to the *Morning Chronicle* criticising Herbert's proposals and advocating Association as the truer remedy. But he refused kindly but firmly to countenance the Health League—' the dread of societies, clubs, leagues, has grown up in me ' [1]—and seemed disposed to postpone indefinitely the starting of a co-operative workshop. He would suggest nothing more definite than night-schooling and individual visiting of the poor. A programme of social reconstruction seemed to him a dangerous companion, and a fatal substitute, for a gospel of personal reformation.

Slowly his convictions altered and hardened—how slowly may seem strange to us to-day. But we have to remember not only his almost morbid diffidence and dread of becoming in any sense the leader of a party, but also the peculiar difficulty of the methods which he was asked to adopt. Ludlow with his French education knew that the Socialism of that day was in no single instance professedly anti-religious or atheistic [2] : but to his colleagues and to English Churchmen generally co-operation was a term of evil significance : for it inevitably suggested either the bloodshed and barricades of revolutionary Paris, or the communism for which Marx and Engels had lately issued their *Manifesto*,[3] or at best the Rochdale experiment of the Owenites. Tennyson's perpetual sneers at ' the blind

---

[1] *Life of Maurice*, ii. p. 23. Cf. Ludlow in *Spectator*, 11th Oct. 1884, ' On Maurice the word " system " acted as a red rag upon a bull ' ; and below, p.186.

[2] Cf. his defence of the early French Socialists in *Atlantic Monthly*, lxxvii. p. 109.

[3] In 1847. It is the most violent of Marx' many violent utterances

hysterics of the Celt ' are enough to show how the educated Englishman of the period regarded his French neighbours : the Communists' programme combined crude violence and blatant atheism : followers of Owen were reckoned foes alike to religion and morality. A man could only discover co-operative movements at all by plunging into regions where no self-respecting Christian would naturally be found. It is the glory of the Christian Socialists that to them nothing was common or unclean, that they dared to follow Christ in believing that a man was not necessarily accursed because universally reviled and persecuted, and that, like St. Paul, they could take a much-abused term from a disreputable source and transfigure it.

Nevertheless, pending their leader's decision, the loyalty of the group was severely strained. Old doubts of his practicality were reviving. In his desire not to thrust himself forward he gave them the impression that he was out of sympathy with their project. Ludlow actually determined to relieve him of the responsibility of a decision, and with this object invited seven members of the group and two working men to dinner late in December.[1] Maurice was deliberately left out, but at the last minute to the surprise and delight of his friends asked to be allowed to join them. That night's discussion marked the crisis. Plans for the starting of co-operative workshops were fully discussed, and it was unanimously decided to make a beginning at once. Maurice himself entered heartily into the venture and on January 2nd wrote to Kingsley the confession of his faith.[2] ' I do not see any further than this. Competition is put forth as the law of the universe. That is a lie. The time is come for us to declare that it is a lie by word and deed. I see no way but associating for work instead of for strikes. I do not

---

[1] Brentano, l.c. p. 40.   [2] *Life of Maurice*, ii. p. 32.

say, or think we feel, that the relation of employer and employed is not a true relation. I do not determine that wages may not be a righteous mode of expressing that relation. But at present it is clear that that relation is destroyed, that the payment of wages is nothing but a deception. We may restore the whole state of things : we may bring in a new one. God will decide that. His voice has gone forth clearly bidding us come forward to fight against the present state of things ; to call men to repentance first of all, but then also, as it seems to me, to give them an opportunity of showing their repentance and bringing forth fruits worthy of it. This is my notion of a Tailors' Association.'

On January 8th, 1850, a meeting of the promoters of the scheme with several working-men and one or two master-tailors was held at Maurice's house. Practical details were discussed from various points of view, and a skeleton constitution,[1] based upon those of the Paris Associations and very similar to that afterwards embodied in the laws of the Society, was adopted. It was further decided to secure premises and enroll associates as soon as possible, Walter Cooper being appointed manager at a fixed salary of two pounds a week, and the initial expenses being guaranteed by the group.[2] Shortly afterwards a shop and workrooms were found at 34 Castle Street in a very suitable neighbourhood, and a lease for three years was signed on January 18th. Meanwhile a public meeting of journeymen tailors was held at the Mechanics' Institute, Chancery Lane, and a strong motion

---

[1] It is given in full by Hughes, *Tracts on Christian Socialism*, ii.

[2] Furnivall's diary for Jan. 8th contained this entry ' Little Ormond Yard School from 7.30 till 9.15 ; meeting at Maurice's about starting an Association of Tailors—about twenty there—talked till 12 ; appointed a committee, etc. ; £300 wanted ' (*Working Men's College Magazine*, ii. p. 145).

was passed declaring that 'individual selfishness, as embodied in the competitive system, lies at the root of the evils under which English industry now suffers : the remedy for the evils of competition lies in the brotherly and Christian principle of Co-operation—that is, of joint work, with shared or common profits : this principle might be widely and readily applied in the formation of Tailors' Working Associations.' Twelve men eventually undertook to join on February 5th ; work was begun on February 11th ; and two months later the number of men employed had risen to two dozen.

Among these first Associates was one of the most remarkable figures connected with the movement. Maurice writing to Kingsley on February 28th says : [1] 'Has Ludlow told you of our Chartist poet in Castle Street ? He is not quite a Locke, but has I think some real stuff in him.' This was Gerald Massey. Although at this time only twenty-two, Massey had been connected with the Chartists for some years, and in conjunction with his friend Leno, afterwards a member of the Working Printers' Association, had in 1849 edited a journal written entirely by working-men and called the *Spirit of Freedom*.[2] He had already printed a slim volume ' Poems and Chansons ' at Tring, his birthplace, and had contributed several lyrics to the *Leader* and other papers. In November 1850 appeared his first poem in the *Christian Socialist* [3] inscribed ' to a worker and sufferer for humanity,' and reprinted in 1850 in his first book of poems *Voices of Freedom and Lyrics of Love* with Maurice's name added to the inscription. His work appears frequently in both volumes of the *Christian Socialist*,

[1] *Life of Maurice*, ii. p. 36.
[2] Cf. Gammage, *Chartist Movement*, p. 346.
[3] Vol. i. p. 16.

and on 1st May, 1852, he undertook the co-operative columns in the *Star of Freedom ;* [1] but he seems to have remained as secretary to the Tailors' Association until 1854,[2] when the success of his collected poems, *The Ballad of Babe Christabel,* which went through five editions in one year and were greeted with universal praise by the critics, encouraged him to devote himself entirely to literature. Massey's early life was freely quoted by Samuel Smiles, and supplied many features in George Eliot's *Felix Holt.*[3] After 1869, when his *Tales of Eternity* was published, he wrote hardly any poetry. From that date till his death in 1907 he gave himself up to the study of Egyptian mythology and the practice of spiritualism, fields in which his vivid imagination untrained in scholarship and unfettered by accurate knowledge led him into strange and extravagant theorising.[4] A complete edition of his poems, entitled *My Lyrical Life,* was published in two volumes in 1889.

An account of the start of this first Association was written by Hughes and published in the spring as the second of the *Tracts on Christian Socialism ;* and a letter of Maurice's of February 7th to Daniel Macmillan refers to the same topic and also introduces another favourite scheme of his which had been revived at this time. He writes : ' Those *Morning Chronicle*

---

[1] *Journal of Association,* p. 33. Massey's reports in it are freely quoted in the *Transactions of the Co-operative League.* Cf. Gammage, l.c. p. 385.

[2] Of this I am uncertain : he wrote to the *Christian Socialist* (ii. p. 235) as secretary in October 1851, and there is no mention of his leaving in any of their publications.

[3] A *Memoir* was prefixed to the first edition of *Babe Christabel,* its place being taken in the third edition by an article by Smiles, originally published in *Eliza Cook's Journal* on April 12th, 1851. A biography of him by Sir Sidney Lee appears in the *Dictionary of National Biography,* second supplement.

[4] He published four large volumes, two entitled *A Book of the Beginnings,* and two *The Natural Genesis.*

letters have set us all grieving, thinking, and I hope in some measure acting. One association of tailors in which the working-men are to receive the profits has been started, I hope with a real prospect of co-operation and success : it begins operations on Monday in Castle Street, Oxford Street. We shall send you a list of prices ; pray make it known in Cambridge . . . I hope also that a Needlewomen's Association on the same principle, only with more superintendence from ladies, will be begun shortly. It is but a first start ; perhaps we shall fail utterly ; but the principle I think is sound, and will spread and bear fruit hereafter. Our great desire is to Christianise Socialism. We wish to begin working on a small scale, but also to explain what we mean by a series of tracts. I have written the first, which is a dialogue. The series we have called boldly "Tracts on Christian Socialism." Is there any chance of circulation ? It is what we have talked of so often coming to some expression.' [1]

The mention of these tracts introduces us to the literary activities of the movement, and these require a chapter to themselves.

---

[1] *Life of Maurice*, ii. pp. 35, 36. It is interesting to find that Hort, then at Cambridge, reported the contents of this letter to his friend John Ellerton on Feb. 8th. Macmillan was an admirable propagandist. (*Life of Hort*, i. p. 130.)

CHAPTER V

LITERARY ACTIVITIES

WE have already recorded Maurice's desire for the issue of new ' Tracts for the Times.' While *Politics* was being produced, his plan was left in abeyance. Now when the group was launching its bold experiment, it found itself without any organ of publicity. Ludlow as a preparation for the venture had written a strong article on ' Labour and the Poor ' which appeared in *Fraser's Magazine* for January 1850. Taking his text from the *Morning Chronicle* revelations he produced a very searching series of proposals for reform. He covered a wide field : education, politics, legislation, social problems and industry all receive attention : but in the forefront of his constructive programme he placed industry, drawing attention to the *Associations Ouvrières*, and urging that all those whose consciences had been stirred should band themselves together to adopt this or some similar method of co-operative production. But, although the article was inserted and the editor, who had already printed the earlier version of *Yeast*, was by no means unfriendly, he made it clear in a prefatory note that he could not identify himself with Ludlow's proposals; and evidently, if the movement was to be supported by literature, its promoters could not afford to be dependent upon the hospitality of casual journals.

Ludlow himself strongly advocated the issue of a

periodical and in this received enthusiastic support from Kingsley.[1] But for the present this was not found to be practicable, and to remedy the defect the suggestion of a series of tracts was accepted. The question of the title 'Christian Socialism' has from the first been matter of acute debate.[2] The *Reasoner*[3] and the *Record* were equally offended at it. In the second number of the *Christian Socialist*[4] there is a letter of vehement protest. Hughes has left an interesting account of his brother George's objections to it;[5] and his case is very typical. Even Neale, one of the movement's most devoted champions, has recorded that he never liked it.[6] Yet Maurice stoutly defended it, and his letter to Ludlow on the subject is one of the most freely quoted of his utterances. 'I see it clearly,' he writes,[7] 'We must not beat about the bush. What right have we to address the English people? We must have something special to tell them, or we ought not to speak. "Tracts on Christian Socialism" is, it seems to me, the only title which will define our object, and will commit us at once to the conflict we must engage in sooner or later with the unsocial Christians and the unchristian Socialists. It is a great thing not to leave people to poke out our object and proclaim it with infinite triumph. "Why you are Socialists in disguise." "In disguise, not a bit of it. There it is staring you in the face on the titlepage." "You want to thrust in ever so much priestcraft under a good revolutionary name." "Well did not we warn you of it? Did we not profess

---

[1] Cf. *Life of Kingsley*, i. p. 235.
[2] Huber summarises it admirably, *Reisebriefe*, ii. pp. 165, 166.
[3] Cf. Holyoake in *Reasoner*, x. pp. 265, 266. (15th Jan. 1851.)
[4] P. 13.   [5] *Memoir of a Brother*, pp. 113, 114.
[6] In the *Co-operative News*; cf. Holyoake, *History of Co-operation*, ii. pp. 538-9.
[7] *Life of Maurice*, ii. pp. 34, 35.

that our intended something was quite different from what your Owenish lecturers meant ? '' This is the fair play which English people like, and which will save us from a number of long prefaces, paraphrases, apologetical statements which waste time when one wants to be getting to business.' His own introductory tract followed a similar line and contained the famous definition of Socialism as the attempt to bring God's government into the corporate life : ' The watchword of the Socialist is co-operation ; the watchword of the anti-Socialist is competition. Anyone who recognises the principle of co-operation as a stronger and truer principle than that of competition has a right to the honour or the disgrace of being called a Socialist.' [1] Ludlow in the opening article of the first number of the *Christian Socialist* develops the same theme : he concludes a noble essay with the words,[2] ' If it be given to us to vindicate for Christianity its true authority over the realms of industry and trade ; for Socialism its true character as the great Christian revolution of the nineteenth century, so that the title of '' Socialist '' shall be only a bugbear to the idle and to the wicked, and society, from the highest rank to the lowest, shall avowedly regulate itself upon the principle of co-operation, and not drift rudderless upon the sea of competition, as our let-alone political economists would have it do ; then indeed we shall have achieved our task ; and, in the meanwhile, we trust in God that no amount of obloquy, ridicule, calumny, neglect, shall make us desert it, so long as we have strength and means to carry on the fight. For a fight it is, and a long one, and a deadly one, a fight against all the armies of Mammon. Will the working-men of England stand by us ? We have no fear of the issue if they will.'

[1] *Dialogue*, p. 1.   [2] Vol. i. p. 2.

Of the tracts thus named Maurice's *Dialogue between Somebody (a person of respectability) and Nobody (the writer)*, quoted above, was the first, and set out the general ideals and meaning of Christian Socialism. It was published by George Bell on February 19th and during the next nine months was followed by six others. These are :—II. *History of the Working Tailors Association* by Hughes ; III. *What Christian Socialism has to do with the question at present agitating the Church* (the ' Gorham controversy' on baptismal regeneration) by Maurice ; IV. *The Working Associations of Paris* by Ludlow ; V. *The Society for promoting Working-men's Associations* by Ludlow and Sully ; VI. *Prevailing idolatries or hints for political economists* by Ludlow ; [1] VII. *Dialogue between A. and B., two clergymen, on the doctrine of circumstances* (important from its reference to Robert Owen's ideas) by Maurice.[2] Number VIII. *A Clergyman's answer to the question ' on what grounds can you associate with men generally ? '* [3] also by Maurice, was added to the series after a year's interval. Ludlow writing of them in January 1851 says [4]—' The Tracts have been circulated to the extent of thousands, and have been favourably noticed in the most unforeseen quarters by men perhaps whose candour their authors were presumptuous enough to distrust.'

These earlier tracts were all definitely topical in scope, written in order to give publicity to their proceedings and taking the place of a periodical. As a substitute for this

[1] No. vi. is dated Oct. 1850.

[2] No. vii. was published after the appearance of the *Christian Socialist* in December 1850.

[3] Published November 1851, cf. below pp. 268, 269 for circumstances. All these Tracts are to be found among Furnivall's papers in the British Museum (vol. i. Nos. 2-8), except No. viii. Of this there is a copy in the library of the Working Men's College.

[4] *Christian Socialist*, i. p. 74.

they could not be really satisfactory, and when the Movement developed and the Society got into touch with co-operative experiments in different parts of the country, the need of a regular means of communication became more and more urgent. Ludlow, upon whom devolved most of the supervision of the Associations, was anxious to persuade Kingsley to act as editor : but the breakdown in health which had compelled his absence from Eversley for a long rest during the previous year, and the impossibility of undertaking the work unless he was prepared to spend much time in London, obliged him to refuse. He declined the responsibility, but promised to contribute regularly if he were told what was required.[1] Failing him Ludlow was obliged to do the editorial work himself, and on Saturday, November 2nd, the first number of *The Christian Socialist, a Journal of Association, conducted by several of the Promoters of the London Working Men's Associations* appeared. Each weekly issue consisted of eight quarto-size pages, divided into three columns, and like *Politics* its price was a penny. It was printed by the Working Printers' Association and published by John Tupling, 320 Strand. As the organ of the Promoters its general object was ' to diffuse the principles of co-operation as the practical application of Christianity to the purposes of trade and industry,' but its programme was a wide one and shows a vastly more developed and coherent policy than was possible in their previous venture. The economics of trade, education, land-tenure, poverty and the poor-laws, social legislation, sanitation, finance, and Church reform, these are the chief subjects with which Ludlow proposes to deal ; [2] and co-operation is to be the principle in the light

---

[1] *Life of Kingsley*, i. p. 241.

[2] Cf. article on ' Our Principles,' pp. 2, 3.

of which they are to be considered. Each week there was inserted a *Gazette* containing a record of the doings of the Society and news of the various Associations in London, the provinces and abroad. This was the only portion of the paper for which the Society was officially responsible, and it was supplied by its joint secretaries, Millbank and Shorter, who had succeeded Sully the first holder of the position a few months previously. The circulation reached fifteen hundred copies almost at once,[1] and this total was doubled during the next year. Though Ludlow himself still did the bulk of the writing, he secured a large number of contributors, several of whom, notably Dyster, Furnivall, Hughes, Kingsley, Mansfield, Maurice, Shorter, Walsh and latterly Neale, were regular and reliable. Ludlow in his private copy[2] of the thirty-five numbers which make up the first volume has preserved a list of the names of forty-three writers and correspondents whose work appears in it, and this is not quite complete. Kingsley (' Parson Lot ') amply fulfilled his promise of support, his most important contribution being a long series of papers on *Bible Politics* whose aim was to demonstrate the falsehood of the belief that ' the Bible is the book which, above all others, supports priestcraft, superstition and tyranny.'[3] Maurice contributed almost as largely, a serial ' The Experiences of Thomas Bradfoot, schoolmaster ' being his longest piece of work. Mrs. Gaskell, who was an acquaintance of the Maurices, and whom they recognised as a powerful ally, allowed them to use two short tales ;[4] J. A. Froude

[1] So Kingsley in a letter of Dec. 4th, *Life* i. p. 246.

[2] Kindly lent to me by the Rev. J. Carter. Cf. Appendix A.

[3] *Christian Socialist*, i. p. 9.

[4] ' The Sexton's Hero ' and ' Christmas Storms and Sunshine,' already printed elsewhere : for her meeting with Maurice cf. Mrs. Chadwick, *Mrs. Gaskell*, p. 172.

an essay on the socialistic principles of the Essenes ; [1] Massey and a number of working-men wrote essays and poems, some of them showing distinct ability. Not the least interesting items in the paper are to be found in the *Free Correspondence* columns which cover a very wide range of subjects, varying from ' A Plea for Cursing '[2]— in rhyme—to ' The Admission of Clergymen to Parliament ' : [3] among others there are two letters from Alexander Campbell, the disciple and editor of the ' sacred socialist ' John Pierrepont Greaves. A marked feature of the contents is the defence of the movement and its members against misrepresentation and calumny in the secular and religious press : the barristers Ludlow, Hughes, and Furnivall, who were responsible for these replies, write with crushing candour and great power ; but their task did not grow lighter as their cause grew in influence. Finally there was an admirable *résumé* given in weekly instalments in Numbers 2-24, of the evidence and report of Mr. Slaney's Committee of the House of Commons which will be largely quoted hereafter.

The second volume was commenced on July 15th, 1851, the format being altered to sixteen octavo pages with two columns to a page. The publisher was changed at the beginning of August, and thereafter was John James Bezer,[4] the one-eyed Chartist bookseller of 183 Fleet Street whom the group nicknamed ' Monops.' The general scope and contents remained unchanged,

---

[1] P. 14. Froude had been taken in by the Kingsleys when his father disowned him after the publication of his *Nemesis of Faith*. He lived with them for some months, thereby bringing fresh suspicion on his host's orthodoxy (cf. H. Paul, *Life of Froude*, p. 51.)

[2] P. 30 by J. B. Leno.   [3] P. 62 by the Rev. Ph. Bland.

[4] The change is announced on p. 72. Tupling's last number is that of Aug. 2nd. Bezer had been released from prison on 30th April : cf. Gammage, *History of the Chartist Movement*, pp. 338, 353, 380.

several new contributors appearing, one of the most interesting of these being Robert Owen, who wrote from Spring Grove, Hounslow, a long letter [1] in defence of his determinist philosophy in its application to social reform. A tale of Kingsley's, 'The Nun's Pool,' which had originally been sent to *Politics* but had been rejected by Maurice,[2] and a series of articles on the poetry of Tennyson by Gerald Massey [3] are among the most interesting of the literary papers now published. On the technical side the development of co-operative distribution and the efforts of the Promoters to bring the two methods into harmony supply many items of the greatest importance. Towards the end of the year it became clear that the periodical must secure a circulation of at least five thousand if it was to pay its way, and a strong appeal backed up by abundant testimony to the value of the paper was sent out. Hitherto the group had been content to run their production at a loss, recognising that the hostility of newsagents, reviewers, and respectable persons generally could not be overcome at once ; but they were not in a position to carry on the sacrifice indefinitely, and though the paper had made a secure position for itself and been accepted as the recognised organ of the co-operative movement, it was necessary to cut down expenses before the next volume was commenced.

So at the close of the year Ludlow announced that the size must be diminished to eight octavo pages weekly, which would allow them to print a leading article and the *Gazette* and perhaps one other short essay or poem. This

[1] Pp. 90-92, and 107, 108.

[2] *Life of Maurice*, i. p. 478.

[3] Vol. ii. pp. 140, 155, 187, 204, 220, 236, 246, 284. They show admiration, but also judgment. He afterwards received a warm letter of praise from Tennyson to whom he had sent a copy of his poems, *The Ballad of Babe Christabel*, and to whose metrical skill much of his work owes its form : cf. *Memoir*, i. p. 405.

would involve confining the paper to matters directly concerned with the Associations, and therefore the first half of its title would be dropped and it would appear as *The Journal of Association*. He proposed to hand over the editorship to Hughes and actually did so for some four months,[1] after which when Hughes proposed to suspend publication he resumed control on April 12th,[2] and carried on until the close of the volume. The last number appeared on June 28th and containing a hopeful and inspiring ' Farewell ' by the indomitable ' J.T.' and in addition ' Parson Lot's Last Words ' and an ' Epicedium ' of six verses signed Charles Kingsley.[3] This final volume, shorn though it is of its literary pretensions, contains many important articles upon the progress of co-operative methods, upon the great lock-out in the iron-trades, and upon the passage through Parliament of the Industrial and Provident Societies' Bill. When publication ceased the Promoters, however disappointed they might feel at the lack of support which their venture had received, could not fail to be vastly encouraged by the immense advance of their cause during the twenty months in which they had been its public champions. They had seen the principle of co-operation applied both to production and to distribution with what appeared to be ever-increasing success ; they had seen it sanctioned by legislation as the result of their own almost unaided efforts ; they had seen the summoning of a great Co-operative Conference, ' a true Labour-Parliament '[4] to meet in

---

[1] *Economic Review*, vi. p. 302. Cf. Brentano, *Chr-soz. Bewegung*, p. 77.

[2] Cf. *Journal of Association*, p. 121.

[3] The conclusion of this poem bears a close resemblance to the third quatrain of Clough's famous ' Say not the struggle nought availeth,' apparently written some three years earlier. This is interesting in view of the fact that Clough had joined the group, though he appears to have taken little part in their work.

[4] Ludlow, ' Farewell,' *Journal of Association*, p. 209.

their own hall in London during the coming month. Against results like this what did their own failure matter ? They were instruments, feeble instruments, in the hands of God, and the purpose for which He had used them was being fulfilled before their eyes. They had done what they could, giving lavishly of their time and talents and losing some £400 over the three volumes.[1] If proof was wanted that their effort had been worth the sacrifice, they could find it in the chorus of protest from co-operators all over the country, when it was announced that publication must be suspended, and in the warmth of the speeches on the subject, summarised in the *First Report*. Ludlow could lay down his task without bitterness, humbly grateful for the measure of his achievement and with words of kindly warning and good cheer. It is with no desire to mitigate difficulties or exaggerate success, but in a spirit of faith and hope that ' Parson Lot ' concludes his paper : [2]—' Let us say little, and work the more. We shall be the more respected, and the more feared too, for it. People will begin to think that we really know what we want, and really do intend to get it, and really believe in its righteousness. And the spectacle of silent working faith is one at once so rare and so noble, that it tells more, even on opponents, than ten thousand platform pyrotechnics. In the meantime it will be no bad thing for *us* if we are beaten sometimes. . . . The return-match will come off, and many who are now our foes will then be our friends ; and in the meantime,

> "The proper impulse has been given,
>   Wait a little longer." '

The appearance of the periodical whose vicissitudes

---

[1] So Ludlow in his speech at the Conference : *Report*, p. 70.

[2] *Journal of Association*, p. 212. Cf. *Life of Kingsley*, i. p. 330.

we have thus described ' fulfilled many of the purposes
to which the tracts were originally devoted ' ; and in an
advertisement prefixed to the first of the new series
(wrongly described by a printer's error as number VIII.)
it was announced that ' henceforth our tracts may pass
over many topics in which Christian Socialists take an
interest.' The title of the issue was *Tracts by Christian
Socialists*, a difference designed to mark their wider and
less topical character. The first of them was issued in
May 1851 [1] and planned as Number One in a *Series on
English History by a Clergyman*, the author being Maurice
and the series being never in fact continued. It was introductory in scope and complete in itself, dealing with the
writer's relation to the three established parties, Tory,
Whig, and Radical, and containing a developed statement of his political ideals. As its successor, *Cheap
Clothes and Nasty*, previously issued as an isolated pamphlet, was reprinted, this ' second edition ' being priced at
twopence instead of fourpence. The third and fourth
contained another reprint, Ludlow's article on *Labour
and the Poor*, which had originally appeared in *Fraser's*
and was now extended, brought up to date, and issued
in two parts. And there the series ended. Ludlow was
too absorbed in the *Christian Socialist* to write anything
else or to urge others to do more than contribute to its
pages : Maurice and Kingsley both had books on hand :
Hughes may well have been secretly engaged upon *Tom
Brown*. For nearly eight months the *Tracts* were suspended, though their place was to some extent filled by
the issue of the lectures given at the monthly meetings
of the Society of Promoters. Then in August 1852
further publication definitely ceased, and ceased in a

---

[1] Cf. *Christian Socialist*, i. p. 230.

sufficiently dramatic fashion.[1] It had always been the practice of the Society to submit all the tracts before acceptance to a publishing committee consisting of Maurice who had the right to veto anything on his own responsibility, Kingsley, Ludlow and Hughes. During Maurice's absence the manuscript of a tract entitled *The Duty of the Age*, written by Lord Goderich, was sent in for approval. It was a strong plea for democracy and universal suffrage. Ludlow and Hughes passed it ; Kingsley, who thought none the worse of its author for being a lord, sent it back ' with a perfect song of triumph ' ; Hughes, unable to get into touch with Maurice and well aware of the value which such a profession of faith would possess, sent it to the press at once. Maurice returned when the printing had just been completed, saw a finished copy, recognised that its whole treatment of democracy was contrary to his own belief, decided that a matter of principle was involved, and asked that the whole edition be suppressed. The ensuing correspondence [2] has been already quoted to illustrate the difference between his conception of society and that of Ludlow. Its result was a splendid testimony alike to the courage of the leader and to the loyalty of his following. But it put an end to the issue of the *Tracts*, so far as Christian Socialism is concerned. The final series to which members of the group contributed, the *Tracts for Priests and People*,[3] was first mooted in January 1854, and when it appeared was almost wholly confined to religious and theological subjects.

In addition to these tracts and periodicals there was issued a large number of other pamphlets. Most of these contained the lectures already mentioned, or the sermons

---

[1] Cf. Hughes' account of this in *Life of Maurice*, ii. pp. 126, 127.

[2] *Life of Maurice*, ii. pp. 127-138. Cf. above pp. 90-2.

[3] Cf. *Life of Maurice*, ii. p. 231.

and addresses of Maurice and Kingsley; and the more important will be described hereafter. The latest of them seems to have been issued in 1853, its title being *Strikes Superseded by Self-employment*. Of these casual papers far the most valuable is the *First Report of the Society*,[1] a document of 106 pages, dated July 26th, 1852, and priced at eighteenpence. Only the first 35 pages deal with the actual report, the remainder being devoted to a full account of the Co-operative Conference for which it had been prepared. As a summary of the ideals and difficulties, the failures, the lessons and the results of their work, the *Report* represents the only complete account that has been composed. It was the work of a committee, Ludlow being responsible for the majority of its contents.

These smaller publications are after all of little interest save to the student of social history. The greatest of the literary achievements of Christian Socialism has a much more secure title to fame. Kingsley writing years afterwards to Hughes [2] could truthfully complain that the Movement, while it had brought to the others nothing but calumny and loss and to Maurice something like actual persecution, had given him, without a tenth of the sacrifice that they had made, reputation and an assured position, and as he frankly adds £150 from his publishers.

'Alton Locke' had been commenced in the winter of 1848–1849 as 'the Autobiography of a Cockney Poet.'

---

[1] A copy is in the Ludlow tracts at the Goldsmiths' Library (vol. i. No. 17.). A *Report of the Co-operative Conference at Manchester, Aug. 1853*, was also issued, largely under Christian Socialist influence : it is invaluable as a source of information as to their work : cf. Ludlow tracts vol. i. No. 24. Both these reports were published by Edward Lumley : for Bezer had emigrated to Australia (Gammage, l.c., p 402).

[2] In May, 1856, cf. *Life of Kingsley*, i. p. 277.

Thomas Cooper, author of the striking poem called *The Purgatory of Suicides*, whose career made a powerful impression on Kingsley and with whom he had been in touch since the previous summer,[1] seems to have been the model from whom this earliest Alton was drawn. From the first, as he writes,[2] ' the book revealed itself to me so rapidly and methodically that I feel it comes down from above and that only my folly can spoil it.' The general outline and much of the actual writing were completed during the rest consequent upon the nervous breakdown which compelled him to spend the whole summer at Ilfracombe. His visit to Jacob's Island and the composition of *Cheap Clothes and Nasty* were responsible for turning the hero into a tailor, and by January the manuscript was sufficiently finished to be sent to Ludlow for criticism. How far his verdict and suggestions involved alterations is not clear. In acknowledging them Kingsley writes,[3] ' A thousand thanks for your letter, though it only shows me what I have long suspected, that I know hardly enough yet to make the book what it should be. As you have made a hole, you must help to fill it. . . . I will alter, as far as I can, all you dislike.' Finally, before the end of the next month, a fair copy of the whole work was made by his wife and submitted to Parker for publication.[4]

Then for a time there was delay. The senior member of the firm, the father of their friend, although he had produced *Politics* and *Yeast* when it appeared in *Fraser's*, decided that he had suffered enough commercially and

---

[1] His first letter to Cooper was written on June 19th, 1848. Cf. *Life of Kingsley*, i. p. 183.

[2] To Ludlow, *Life of Kingsley*, i. p. 197.

[3] Quoted by Hughes, *Prefatory Memoir*, p. 27.

[4] Cf. *Life of Kingsley*, i. p. 233.

in reputation from his connection with ' Parson Lot,' and refused to be mixed up with any more revolutionary literature.   Such an obstruction was no new thing to the Christian Socialists : they had set up their own printing-press to avoid this kind of difficulty.   But Kingsley was seriously perplexed.   A periodical might be produced by an Association of four working printers and circulated by a small bookseller : a full-length novel was far beyond their powers.   So he applied for help to Carlyle,[1] received an introductory letter to his own publishers, Chapman and Hall, and eventually heard that they had considered the book and were willing to accept it.   It appeared in August 1850 in two volumes, of 306 and 300 pages respectively, without any preface, being published anonymously as *Alton Locke, Tailor and Poet.   An Autobiography.*

Its publication created something of a sensation.   The national conscience after the events of the past two years at home and abroad was highly sensitive, and the book was a challenge which could not be passed over.   The measure of its influence and therefore of its success may be gauged by the speed, violence and length of the attacks upon it.   From reviewers of all shades burst out a chorus of condemnation.   The lordly *Edinburgh*, the most influential of all periodicals, devoted the first thirty-three pages of its issue for January 1851 to an article by William Rathbone Greg on ' English Socialism and Communistic Associations,' [2] in which *Alton Locke* was made the text for a defence of the orthodox political economists.   Its author was taken severely to task for his use of fiction

---

[1] Cf. *Life of Kingsley*, i. p. 234.

[2] xciii. pp. 1-33 : reprinted in Greg's *Essays in Political and Social Science*, i. pp. 458-504.   The *Christian Socialist* contained four articles on it (vol. i. pp. 107, 114, 122, 131) and Ludlow dealt at length with it in his lecture on ' Christian Socialism and its opponents.'   For Greg's chief criticism see below pp. 168-9.

as a vehicle of propaganda, as well as for his incontinent and indiscriminate violence : but nevertheless, while condemning it, Greg gave up several pages to a description of Christian Socialism and the Castle Street Association—an advertisement to the cause of which they were not slow to take advantage. The tone of the *Edinburgh*, though severe, was by no means offensive : Ludlow reckoned it 'far more favourable on the whole than might have been expected,' and admitted that 'with such a writer we have much in common ' : and in this respect its criticism compares favourably with its rivals. *Fraser's*[1] whose editor must have known the identity of its author and recognised its resemblance to *Yeast*, while admitting the power and value of several of its descriptive passages and quoting from it extensively and not unfairly, decided that 'if the book is to be regarded as a protest against society, we are bound to say that society has no great reason to be uneasy.'[2] *Blackwood's*[3] declared it roundly to be 'a barefaced and impudent assumption of a specific profession by a person who knows no more about tailoring or 'slop-selling' than he has learnt from certain letters in the *Morning Chronicle*'[4]; but nevertheless found it necessary to devote thirty-six columns to the discussion of what it sums up as 'a book which exhibits in many passages marks of genius, but which, as a whole, is so preposterously absurd, as rather to excite ridicule than to move sympathy.'[5] Nor was this the worst. The *Quarterly*, which at that time shared with the *Edinburgh* the premier

---

[1] xlii. pp. 576-585.   [2] L.c. p. 578.   [3] Vol. lxviii. p. 593.

[4] Kingsley answered this charge in a letter of Jan. 13th, 1851, *Life*, i. p. 249 ; and in *Yeast*, ch. viii. pp. 133, 134 (Eversley ed.) there is an allusion to it.

[5] P. 609.

position among periodicals, at first kept silence, but in September 1851,[1] when Kingsley's authorship of the ' Autobiography ' had been avowed, produced a ferocious attack upon him and Maurice in an article by J. Wilson Croker, entitled ' Revolutionary Literature.' *Alton Locke* was reviewed in company with a selection of inflammatory French pamphlets and its author was accused of preaching similar doctrines under the specious guise of Christian Socialism.[2]

Yet the very violence and weight of the attack was not without its value to the cause. Hitherto they had been sorely hindered in their propaganda by the refusal of newsvendors to stock their tracts and papers, by the refusal of editors to insert their advertisements, by the refusal of reviewers to notice their work. Forty-five copies of the first number of the *Christian Socialist* [3] had been distributed amongst the London Press : hardly a single reference to it had been made. Constantly their efforts were frustrated by their inability to secure a fair hearing. Attacks were made upon them freely and publicly ; they were answered with courage and candour ; but the general public could not hear the arguments of the defence ; and in the eyes of men the case seemed to go by default. To the majority of those to whom they were trying to appeal they were entirely unknown, or known only as a little group of cranks whose experiments need not be taken seriously. Under such circumstances the publication of *Alton Locke* marked a triumph which no amount of hostile criticism could impair. Now at last it was made plain that if the great Reviews thought the

[1] Vol. lxxxix. pp. 491-543.

[2] For a candid account of Croker cf. Harriet Martineau, *Biographical Sketches*, pp. 376-385 (4th edition).

[3] Cf. *Christian Socialist*, i. p. 74.

matter worthy of such lengthy and powerful assaults it could no longer be dismissed by educated persons as unimportant. And here the evidence could be studied without restriction, and men could read for themselves what this new and much-abused sect had to say. Henceforth they might hate it still ; they must at least give it their attention. They did so :—and the book sold. Three editions had appeared within little over a year ; and when the name of its author was announced he sprang at once into fame.

And he deserved his position. Though nowadays few of us would agree with Sir Leslie Stephen that '*Alton Locke* may fairly be regarded as his best piece of work,' it remains a book of eminent literary merit as well as of surpassing social importance. Its contents lack the grandeur, richness and variety of his great romances ; its style has not yet attained the inimitable rhythm which long wrestling with English hexameters gave to his later prose. The justice of Carlyle's judgment upon it [1]— ' the book is *crude* ; by no manner of means the best we expect from you '—was amply confirmed by the appearance of *Hypatia* eighteen months later. The monotony of its effect unrelieved by humour or change of key, the incessant denunciation which, despite its general eloquence and sincerity, grows wearisome through sheer repetition and occasionally lapses into shrillness and hysteria, the rhapsodies and sermonisings whose want of restraint robs their appeal of power,—such faults are obvious enough. In addition it suffers from weakness of construction and, with the splendid exception of Sandy Mackaye, of characterisation. If it is to be judged as a work of art, such blemishes would expose it to serious

---

[1] *Life of Kingsley*, i. p. 244.

criticism, even when full allowance is made for the change in taste during the past half-century. But its author had a higher object in view than the creation of a literary masterpiece. ' Charles Kingsley was not professed novelist, nor professed man of letters. He was novelist, poet, essayist, and historian, almost by accident, or with ulterior aims. Essentially he was a moralist, a preacher, a socialist, a reformer, and a theologian ' [1]: that verdict, true as it is of all his work, is doubly true of *Alton Locke*, ' his noblest and most characteristic book—at once his greatest poem and his grandest sermon.' [2] Indeed it is hardly to be judged as a novel at all, but as a tract writ large, an expansion of *Cheap Clothes and Nasty*, an outburst of righteous indignation against enthroned and self-satisfied Mammon. And as such its literary qualities are of the highest order. Kingsley's supreme gift is his power of description. No single writer among the masters of English speech is his equal as a painter of scenery ; whether it be the splendour of the tropic forest or the squalor of the sweater's den, the thronging life of the quays of Alexandria or the futile frenzy of a riot in the Fens, his pictures live before us. With the imagination of a poet he can visualise the myriad details of their atmosphere, with the eloquence of an orator he can reproduce in us their every tone and hue. We share his acute sensibility to sights and sounds and smells ; our souls respond with his to the impression which they combine to create. And this supreme gift is nowhere put to nobler use than when he is leading us into contact with social evil, when he is forcing us to enter the haunts of vice and heroism, of sordid misery and patient martyrdom, to whose existence we would fain be blind. It is

[1] Mr. Frederic Harrison, *Studies in Early Victorian Literature*, p. 179.
[2] J. Martineau, quoted in *Life of Kingsley*, i. p. 306.

to this that *Alton Locke* owes its greatness. What the authors of *Politics* had not attempted, what Mayhew had done in part, Kingsley does with unrivalled skill. Many in recent years have described scenes of even greater physical horror with a more exact knowledge of the facts and as deep a sympathy with the victims : none of them has achieved a result of such haunting poignancy. Much as his critics might declaim over the fallacies of his economics and the injustice of his strictures upon society, they could not deny the pathos and the passion, nor, save in trivial details, the truth of his pictures. He tore away the veil from the eyes of the prudish and pharisaical : he revealed to them the horror of competitive industrialism in all its nakedness : they might shudder and protest ; but they could not wholly forget. Though they might refuse to accept his remedy without enquiry, they could hardly refuse to notice and investigate it.

And the influence of the book was proportionately immense. Men might shut their eyes and remain obstinately self-engrossed : but England could never again be quite the same. The social conscience, sluggish as it still is, has never relapsed into complete torpor. When we marvel at the acquiescence in manifest iniquity of good men like Wilberforce or Pusey and give thanks for the change that has come over politics and religion since their day, we must grant to Charles Kingsley a place in the front rank with Dickens[1] and Shaftesbury among those to whom, under God, the awakening is due. *Alton Locke* is much more than a piece of literature ; it is one

---

[1] It is in Dickens that the best side of the reforming work of Bentham, and particularly his attack upon the abuses of the law, finds its most popular exponent. For the value of his work, especially of *Hard Times*, as a factor in the movement for reform cf. Ruskin, *Unto this Last*, pp. 14, 15.

of the great formative elements in the history of the English people. Its influence may well be over-emphasised by one whose whole sympathies are with its creator ; so, lest we be thought too enthusiastic, we will conclude our account of it with the words of a detached and exacting critic, whose creed and outlook were to Kingsley a thing abhorrent and whom none can accuse of partiality. Mr. Frederic Harrison seldom resists the temptation to sneer at a faith which he neither understands nor would hesitate to destroy : yet he has written [1]—' It is possible that the genteeler taste of our age may prevent the young of to-day from caring for *Alton Locke*. But I can assure them that five and forty years ago the book had a great effect and came home to the heart of many. And the effect was permanent and creative. We may see to-day in England widespread results of that potent social movement which was called Christian Socialism, a movement of which Kingsley was neither the founder nor the chief leader, but of which his early books were the main popular exponents.'

Next year his other Christian Socialist novel *Yeast* was published in book form. As originally written it had appeared serially in *Fraser's Magazine*, running through the monthly numbers of volume thirty-eight from July to December, 1848 ; and now Parker, encouraged by the success of *Alton Locke*, decided to undertake its reissue. Certain additions, notably in the last chapter and epilogue, were made and the whole was carefully revised, but the entire substance of the story and the great mass of its contents remained unaltered. It was published anonymously in March 1851 as a single volume, the title-page of the original edition bearing the

[1] L.c. pp. 194, 195.

words *Yeast : a problem. Reprinted with corrections and additions from Fraser's Magazine.*

In a survey of the work of the Christian Socialists we are not specially concerned with the agricultural problems so prominent in *Yeast*. Kingsley himself knew them far more intimately than the problems of industrialism ; and in many respects the condition of the rural population deserved attention even more urgently. A book like this, reviving the warnings of the Luddite riots and revealing the total absence of decent housing and sanitation and of all save the most demoralising recreations, was sorely needed, and may well have contributed to bring about those improvements which its author noted in his later and more optimistic years. But when it was written he had no very definite proposals to make for remedying the state of affairs, and confined himself to the task of criticising the value of spasmodic charity and of describing the activities of good and bad landlords. Even when he put forward more elaborate proposals for extending the principle of association to rural areas, he found no one in the group able to support him or put his scheme into practice. Their work and interests were wholly in the towns.

And *Yeast* is vastly more than a study of the farm labourer. It is interesting mainly as a diagnosis of the unsettlement in the minds of the younger people of the educated classes at this time. Much of ' the Thoughts, Sayings and Doings of Lancelot Smith, Gentleman ' [1] is plainly autobiography—a record of those stormy years which Kingsley had spent at Cambridge and before his ordination. As such it possesses not only a permanent historical value, but when compared with *Alton Locke*

[1] The original sub-title prefixed to the first three instalments in *Fraser's*.

an astonishing modernity of outlook. There may be still reproductions among us of the struggling tailor-poet —though the Education Act has materially altered their situation. But Lancelot Smiths abound everywhere, and their prototype need hardly be modified at all. ' Yeast ' is recognisable as a stage in the evolution of nearly all of us, and is a fairer title than ' Sinister Street ' for the period of our adolescence. As a portrait-study of the youthful male its psychology is far more universally truthful than the priggishness and pruriency of Mr. Compton Mackenzie, or the sensuality of Mr. H. G. Wells, or the coarseness of Mr. Arnold Bennett.   The doubts and the idealism, the alternations of self-satisfaction and self-contempt, the revolt against accepted beliefs, the restlessness and yearning for fixity of conviction, the awakening of social conscience, the humbling contact with lives nobler than our own, the guidance of human affections, the shocks of circumstance, the vision afar off of the Christ whom we have too hurriedly caricatured and denounced, the gradual formation of a Christ-centred philosophy —these are well-marked stages in the journey of thinking Christians of our generation.   The skill and truthfulness with which they are described give the book a freshness and vitality that are wanting in the strained propagandism of *Alton Locke*. A speculative detachment which regards life itself primarily as a problem to be solved, and a wide toleration of divergent solutions may not be wholly admirable qualities : at least they are characteristic of the present age. Cut-and-dried programmes whether of social reform or of doctrinal theology, such as Kingsley apologises for failing to produce, arouse nowadays nothing but distrust.   It may be that we lack faith—so our elders often warn us—or it may be, as we think ourselves, that we are exercising the responsibility of

liberty : a study of Lancelot Smith would even now help
to make our difficulties intelligible.

The fact is that the book is far more an autobiography
than a sociological treatise. The preacher and the
partisan are much less in evidence—though Kingsley
never loses the opportunity for a sermon or a fight.
But in the main he is here concerned rather with
the record of his own spiritual development and the
exposition in dramatic form of the philosophy and
theology of his great teacher. ' I think this will explain
a good deal of Maurice,' [1] was his only remark to his
pupil John Martineau when *Yeast* was finished ; and the
work owes much of its modernity to the fidelity with
which the disciple has fulfilled his purpose. It is no
small testimony to the abiding merit and present influence
of ' the Prophet ' that the thoughts of Lancelot Smith
are so consonant with the spirit of the present day.

Apart from this the book contains many obvious
blemishes. The conclusion, though its abruptness may
be partially excused by the nervous breakdown of its
author, strikes the taste of to-day as at once clumsy and
unnecessary. Literary convention no longer forbids the
asking of unanswered questions. Kingsley's method is
too realistic for allegory and not realistic enough for
verisimilitude. He is preaching again, and will not leave
us to follow his clues unaided. Further, the irrelevant and
crudely-argued controversy over Roman Catholicism
forces upon us that side of his activities which his admirers
would most gladly forget. The feminine portraits and
philosophy of sex in the book are definitely Victorian and
prepare us for his later attitude towards the movement
for Women's Suffrage. Even the pictures of social

---

[1] *Life of Kingsley*, p. 305.

evil, though they were based upon a far wider experience, lack just that *saeva indignatio* which sears the souls of readers of *Alton Locke* : he feels deeply and describes faithfully, but his passion has not yet blazed up to white heat, and by comparison its influence leaves us almost cold.

The book from its less didactic character was received with dislike rather than hostility. Some of the reviewers even commended it for calling attention to a sphere where reform was urgently required. Maurice expressed the fear that *Yeast* was ' going to be rather too popular and respectable.' [1] It was left for the *Guardian*, the recently founded organ of the 'high' Churchmen, which had praised *Alton Locke* and shown no antagonism to the Christian Socialists,[2] to take it as the text for a scathing denunciation of the ' latest and most philosophical phase of Christianity.' [3] They had previously devoted a long article to the work of the group and had expressed approval of the method of association. Kingsley had written a friendly reply to this article which they had inserted, and Maurice had examined it at length in the *Christian Socialist*.[4] So the attack in their issue of May 21st was wholly unexpected. The reviewer had little to say of the social or economic tendencies of *Yeast*, but concentrated upon its theology and upon its morals. Sheltering himself behind the supposed anonymity of the author, he accused him roundly not only of heretical opinions but of directly condoning if not encouraging ' youthful profligacy.' The charge was so monstrously unfair in view of the whole tone of the book that it might have been safely left unanswered. But Kingsley was stung to the heart,

---

[1] *Life of Maurice*, ii. p. 59.

[2] *Guardian*, 16th Oct. 1850, 19th and 26th Feb., 5th March, 1851.

[3] *Guardian*, 7th May, 1851.   [4] Vol. i. pp. 161, 162, 178.

and in an outburst of indignation acknowledged his authorship and accused his critic of shameless lying. Such violence was, as Ludlow pointed out,[1] not less unwise because it happened to be justifiable. The reviewer replied with a clever mixture of grovelling and insinuation ; Kingsley was left with his sensibilities wounded and sore ; and a beginning had been made of that campaign of studied calumny and misrepresentation with which the so-called religious press strove to overwhelm the efforts of the Christian Socialists during the next few years.

Encouraged by the reception of *Yeast* Kingsley took the opportunity to expand its message in a more concrete form.   On May 28th he gave the monthly lecture for the Society of Promoters, the meeting being held on this occasion at the Concert Room, 71 Mortimer Street.   His subject was ' the application of associative principles and methods to agriculture,' and his discourse, which took nearly two and a half hours to deliver, was published in pamphlet form as well as fully reported in the *Christian Socialist*.[2]   It is a document of some importance, and although its contents lie somewhat outside the scope of our subject we will conclude this chapter with a brief survey of it.

He begins with a protest that his views are to be taken as purely tentative, the result of seven years' thought and experience, but in no other sense authoritative.   Then he explains his relation to the political economists, professing his admiration for their studies where they deal with matters in their own province, but warning them that many of their problems are rather moral than economic in character, and that in these they have no right to dogmatise.   Next he defends himself and his

---

[1] *Christian Socialist*, ii. p. 18.   [2] Vol. i. pp. 252, 253.

friends against the charge of desiring to abolish private property, and explains that personally he has no such desire, although he regards property not as held by absolute right but as a trust from God for the benefit of the common-weal. So he turns to his subject, and as his basis refers to ' the portraits of the labouring peasantry as set out without exaggeration in *Alton Locke* and *Yeast.*' He assumes as generally acknowledged the facts of their hideous poverty and the futility of almsgiving as a remedy : he criticises the poor law as ' an ingenious means of keeping a poor man a slave without starving him into revolution ' : he maintains the true Socialist and Bible doctrines of the right to labour and the right to enjoy labour's fruits. Then turning to more practical matters he declares that by scientific farming the output of the land could be increased fourfold, that such scientific farming is mainly a question of manure, that the best manure is sewage, that this is not available so long as the population lives in the towns, and that even when obtainable it is largely wasted by being poured out into the rivers where it breeds pestilence instead of producing crops. ' Why is the country a desert and the city a crowded stye ? ' [1] he asks ; and concludes that ' the problem seems to be how to restore the sewage to the land.' [2] In order to bring back the population to the countryside several methods have been proposed ; and he specially condemns among these the system of peasant-proprietorship with small holdings, which he considers scarcely workable except at the cost of ceaseless and debasing drudgery. Two conditions he describes as essential, firstly the development of new products such as flax or silk which could supplement or take the place of

[1] Page 41.   [2] Page 45.

cereals, and secondly the encouragement of interest on the part of the labourers by some system of association to profits. Two such systems he sketches; in the former he depicts a landlord developing a farm-colony on a basis of profit-sharing, the labourers being grouped in a block of well-built and well-drained houses with a common kitchen and a co-operative store attached to it, and receiving a percentage of the earnings in addition to regular wages; in the latter he suggests that any group of labourers, who could raise enough money to rent a farm, could start as an Association and work together in partnership like the Moravian Socialists—only adding that they ought to choose as superintendent some competent Scot or Yorkshireman and resolve to obey him without question.

The lecture was received by a numerous audience with the closest attention, and when published was warmly welcomed by the press, even the *Guardian* [1] remarking that ' it abounds in that earnest philanthropy which distinguishes the Christian Socialists among the reformers of the day ; and, we must add, in that satisfied dogmatism which distinguishes Mr. Kingsley from other Christian Socialists.' But the group was not able to put its suggestions into practice, and if it produced any results they lie outside the scope of our present subject.

[1] Issue of 8th Oct., 1851.

CHAPTER VI

THE EARLY ASSOCIATIONS FOR CO-OPERATIVE PRODUCTION

In this account of the literary activities of the Christian Socialists we have departed from the strict sequence of events, and must now return to the Associations. Nothing in the whole history of the movement is more remarkable than the rapidity with which the first eight of these succeeded one another,—unless it be the long subsequent interval during which no new ventures were launched. Yet this outburst of enthusiasm and the lull following it, though Ludlow makes full use of it [1] as an incentive and rebuke to the Associates not to let their spirit wax faint, was under the circumstances inevitable. The Promoters desired to test by experiment the soundness and practicality of the principle of co-operative production and to discover the best methods for carrying it into effect. They started without any guidance save the study of the Associations in Paris, and even of these their knowledge was almost exclusively derived from the documents that Ludlow had collected, from brief visits by himself and Neale,[2] and from casual correspondence. In consequence they had little knowledge of the actual difficulties that

[1] *E.g.* in his sixth ' Letter to the Working-men's Associations' *Christian Socialist*, i. pp. 195, 196.

[2] And at a later date by their friend William Coningham whose lecture on the subject was one of their publications : cf. *Christian Socialist*, ii. pp. 52-55. The pamphlet is among Furnivall's papers : vol. i. No. 22.

would occur, when these paper schemes adopted by workers of another nationality were applied to the conditions of business life in England. In order to learn, it was necessary for them to launch a certain number of Associations, if possible in different branches of industry, to watch these with the closest attention, and to be constantly ready to modify their methods and to meet the needs which practice alone would reveal.

Furthermore the original group of Christian Socialists was all young and poor, dependent upon their professional work for their livelihood, and obliged to restrict their financial obligations within narrow limits. With the advent of Neale, of whom we shall speak shortly, they were able to take larger risks. But even then it was manifestly unwise to undertake the charge of more numerous establishments than they could personally supervise, until they had collected and formulated the results obtainable from their first batch of experiments. And, as we shall see, the new method, when applied to men chosen at random and working under managers not always either competent or trustworthy, taxed their time and patience to the uttermost. In the opening pages of the *First Report* [1] it is admitted that at first all was chaos and bewilderment, through which they had to grope their way. Principles that seemed secure one day, had to be revised the next : experiments might succeed brilliantly for a month, only to result in disaster. It is with a sigh of astonishment for their survival that they look back upon those days of peril ; and with an air of justifiable conviction that they recount the conclusions wrung from their three years of effort. If we are to understand the character of their purposed reforms and to

---

[1] It was owing to these difficulties that the *Report*, which was to have been issued annually, did not appear until the summer of 1852.

appreciate the scope and significance of their results, we must survey in some detail the general plan upon which they modelled their Society and the history of the eight Associations in which they tested its merits.

At first, and indeed until after the establishment of the Tailors' Association, the movement had not adopted any definite constitution. The Promoters were a band of friends meeting weekly for the discussion of business and more frequently still for religious and social purposes. Such an informal body might supervise the starting of one or two Associations all the more easily, because they were not bound by any hard and fast rule. But when the number seemed likely to increase and questions of management and policy became more complex, a more business-like organisation became obviously essential. Yet here a somewhat characteristic difficulty arose, largely through tactlessness ; and as it illustrates both the ideals which Maurice had formed for the movement and the consequent obstacles with which Ludlow might find himself confronted, it is worth relating.

Almost the only special provision hitherto made by the group for carrying on its activities had been the engagement of a paid secretary. Charles Sully,[1] formerly a bookbinder, had been employed in Paris and had taken a full share in the revolutionary outbreaks of the two past years. Becoming convinced of the futility of physical force as an instrument of reform, he left France and came to London with a strong recommendation from a friend of Ludlow's. The group were delighted to have found one who knew the French Associations at first hand, and who was honest, energetic, competent, and experienced. Unfortunately he was not at this time a Christian.

---

[1] Cf. *Economic Review*, iv. pp. 36, 37.

The undertaking appealed to him simply as a business concern : its idealism and the religious principles that animated it he did not profess to understand. So in urging upon Maurice the need for proper organisation he blurted out that the workers wanted to make a profit, that they could not expect to compete successfully with individualistic firms unless they were much more scientifically managed, and that the control ought to be vested in the hands of a small body of experienced business men who should form a Central Board. No doubt to Sully's mind the attempt to run a commercial enterprise under the guidance of a middle-aged parson assisted by an assortment of young lawyers, doctors and scientists, whose meetings were more like a bible-class than a board of directors, seemed more ridiculous than sublime. He expressed himself clumsily, but his proposal was sensible enough. At any rate Ludlow had long realised that efficiency must not be disregarded and that some definite scheme of management was necessary. But Maurice saw in it only a relapse into selfishness and into that trust in machinery which he and Ludlow, ever since the days of *Politics*, were agreed in condemning. Hitherto he had accepted the need of more precise and methodical organisation ; now Sully's words caused him to recoil in horror. He wrote a long and for him unusually violent letter to Ludlow, refusing to have anything to do with the proposed Central Board.[1] ' Talk as much as you like about putting the hand to the plough and drawing back. I never did put my hand to *this* plough. I have put my hand to another from which I should draw back at once and for ever if I tolerated by any word or act the maxim which Sully distinctly avows and upon which he rests the necessity of

---

[1] *Life of Maurice*, ii. pp. 42-45.

a central board. Talk as you like about my system-phobia. It is this which I mean by system—the organisation of evil powers for the sake of producing good effects. . . . God's order seems to me more than ever the antagonist of man's systems ; Christian Socialism is in my mind the assertion of God's order. . . . Every attempt to hide it under a great machinery, call it Organisation of Labour, Central Board, or what you like, I must protest against.' It is easy enough to sneer at him,—especially in these days when we all find it so much easier to reconstruct society than to reform our own lives,—but there remains an unpleasant suspicion that after all the dreamer may be right, and that no mechanism of government however elaborate can take the place of a change of heart or supply us with a cheap substitute for unselfishness.

Yet precious as such idealism must always be, it was on this occasion somewhat misplaced. To condemn all organisation on these grounds would be to worship a God of chaos. It was a matter not of selfishness but of commonsense. If Associates were to be enrolled, the duties and conditions of enrolment must be stated ; if managers were to be appointed, their powers and responsibility must be defined ; if the Society was to unite the various groups of workers, its composition and functions must be decided upon. So Ludlow persisted in maintaining, and for a fortnight it seemed as if a breach between the Promoters and their president was inevitable. Eventually after much correspondence and talk Maurice agreed to give way, so far as the existence of the Central Board was concerned : but he insisted that its functions be restricted solely to business matters and even there that the veto of the Council should remain : and in face of strong pressure he refused to join it.

So, early in April, Sully set to work to plan out a constitution for the Society.[1] When his draft was finished Ludlow overhauled it drastically. It was then debated sentence by sentence and approved subject to a few further alterations by the Promoters. In June it was issued as Tract V., containing (*a*) the Organisation of the Society, (*b*) the Constitution of the Union of Associations, (*c*) the model Laws for an Association.

Ludlow, who wrote the introductory paragraph himself, makes an interesting allusion to the peril against which Maurice had protested, and in so doing repeats almost verbally some very striking sentences which had appeared in his leading article in the third number of *Politics for the People*.[2] ' In offering this machinery to others,' he writes, ' we are bound to protest against that idolatry of social mechanism, which imagines society as a mere assemblage of wheels and strings, and not as a partnership of living men ; which takes account of the form only, and not of the spirit which animates it.' With this warning he proceeds to the formal scheme, which we must summarise as briefly as we can, adding details where necessary from other sources.

The Society consisted of all those engaged in the movement whether as Promoters or Associates. It met as a whole, for the discussion of some business topic relative to its objects, on the first Wednesday of each month at the Central Office, which until the autumn of 1850 was at 458 New Oxford Street and then for the next two years at 76 Charlotte Street, and for a lecture and conversazione on the second Wednesday. These meetings were a continuation of the conferences previously held with working-

---

[1] When this was finished, Sully gave up his post, emigrated to the United States, and had some success in promoting co-operative principles there. Reports of his doings appear frequently in the *Christian Socialist*.

[2] Entitled ' Politics,' pp. 33, 34.

men, except that now the general public was not admitted
—a point which called out occasional protests from
readers of the *Christian Socialist*. Many of these monthly
lectures were published.

The executive work of the Society was divided between
two bodies, the Council of Promoters and the Central
Board. The functions of the Council were to transact
all business between the Society and the Associations,
and the Associations and the public, to collect and
administer funds, and ' to diffuse the principles of Co-
operation as the practical application of Christianity to
the purposes of trade and industry.' This latter phrase
is important. It was inserted at the instance of Ludlow
who wished to see the religious basis of the movement
clearly confessed; but, being too strong for certain of those
who sympathised in other respects with the work of the
Society, it became the subject of keen debate when the
constitution was redrafted after the passing of the Industrial and Provident Societies Act in 1852. The
Council was chosen by co-opting any of the Promoters,
and consisted of a President, who was always Maurice,
twelve ordinary and an unlimited number of honorary or
corresponding members. It had a paid secretary or
secretaries, and met weekly on Fridays at the Central
Office. Two of its members were expected to attend at
the office every day, the names being taken in rotation.

The Central Board represented the Associates or
members of the Working Associations recognised by the
Society. It met every Monday evening [1] and was
composed of the managers of all the Associations or
their deputies and in addition a delegate chosen from
each of them by its members, and a secretary appointed

---

[1] Hence Maurice's Bible-reading was held on Tuesdays after this
Constitution came into force.

and paid by the Council. Provision was also made for one more member from each Association to attend and speak but not to vote; and this privilege was extended to all members of the Council and their friends. The duties of the Board were to regulate the relations of the Associations with one another and, subject to the consent of the Council, the relations of the united Associations with the public, to co-operate with the Council in the formation of new Associations, and to see that the provisions of the constitution were duly carried out by the Associations, though here too an appeal to the Council was permitted. At first the meetings of the Council and the Board were separate, but in April 1852 [1] it was agreed to meet jointly.

The Associations themselves were controlled each by its own Council of Administration, consisting of the manager, a chairman, treasurer and secretary and a specified number of Associates. This Council had the right to be consulted by the manager before he made purchases or contracts beyond a fixed amount in value, or gave instructions for conducting the business : it could also fix prices for the goods produced by the Association subject to the control of the Central Board. But the executive authority remained in the manager's hands : he alone took orders, directed the preparation of the material, gave out the work, sold, delivered, and received payment for the goods. The chairman however was recognised as head of the workshop and as such had the right to enforce fines for breach of duty there.

The appointment of new Associates was only to be made after they had served a probationary period. During this probation they were to be paid at the same

---

[1] *Journal of Association*, p. 142.

rates as full members and were to receive in addition a
fixed sum in lieu of profits, but they could take no part
in the control of the Association. The appointment of
the manager was intended to come eventually into the
hands of the Associates, who would thus be entirely self-
governing. But at the start a reservation was made,
and it was provided that, so long as money was owed to
the Promoters, they should retain the right to veto the
manager whom the Association might appoint and also
to define his powers and duties. These rights would lapse
as soon as the loans for initial outlay had been repaid.
At first no arrangements were made for the admission
of apprentices ; but at a later date a scheme for doing so
was drawn up by the Central Board and sanctioned by
the Council.[1]

The most elaborate portion of the Constitution is that
which deals with the allowances paid in lieu of wages,
and with the division of profits.

In the first place the communistic principle of an equal
wage for all is explicitly condemned. A note in the
margin of the Tract says :—' Some French Associations
have agreed to pay equal wages to all ; but this is a grave
error. Our object is the Organisation of Labour, so that
it shall receive its due reward ; and to pay equal wages
would be to take from the talented, the strong, or the
industrious, for the sake of giving to the simple, the weak,
and the idle. The effect would be, in our present state of
society, that the Associations would be in danger of
being filled with indifferent workmen, and that most of
the good workmen would remain with competitive
employers.' The note concluded by pointing out that
there was nothing to prevent the more highly paid, or

---

[1] *Report*, pp. 16, 17.

those with fewer expenses at home, from contributing voluntarily to the support of their comrades. Obviously equal payment for all, even if it be ultimately feasible, cannot be introduced piecemeal or by private experiment. Nevertheless the subject was constantly arising, and about a year later Ludlow returned to it in the *Christian Socialist*.[1] There he points out that while true communism, the holding of all things in common, is and must be the ideal of the Socialist, payment of equal wages to workers irrespective of their responsibilities, needs, and tastes is not communism, is in fact the reverse of it ; for such a system treats the wage-earner not as a living being but as a mere unit. Neale afterwards published some striking remarks upon the same topic in the *Journal of Association*, which were followed by a correspondence running through several numbers.[2]

Setting this aside therefore, the principle followed by most of the Paris groups was accepted, and it was laid down, *firstly*, that an allowance be paid to each Associate, 'which shall be a fair day's remuneration for a fair day's work whether by time or piece according to the custom of the trade,' and that the allowance be in proportion to the skill and energy of the recipient ; and *secondly*, that the net surplus or profit, after deducting current expenses, setting aside a proportion for repaying or paying interest upon loans, and reserving a third of the remainder to increase the capital and extend the business of the Association, be divided every six months between all the Associates 'in proportion to the time they have severally worked.' In this way it was hoped that both talent and industry would be duly rewarded.

Finally certain further regulations deserve notice. All

[1] Vol. i. pp. 234, 235.   [2] Pp. 79, 103, 135.

work was wherever possible to be done on the premises of the Association. There was to be no Sunday work at all ; and the hours on week-days were not to exceed ten daily excluding meal-time, unless with the assent of the Board and the Council. Every Associate was expected to pay one penny weekly towards the upkeep of the Central Office. No Association was to be made an instrument or agent of political agitation, though individual members were at liberty to act as they pleased. All disputes between members or between members and their manager were to be settled by arbitrators chosen by each party, such arbitrators being members of the Society. Quarrels between Associations were adjudicated upon by the Central Board, provided that an appeal could be made to the Council if a third of the members of the Board desired it. In the event of an Association being dissolved, four-fifths of the profits were to be handed over to the Society, the remaining fifth being distributed amongst the late Associates. Every Association admitted to the Society was expected to frame a constitution for itself following the model prescribed in the Tract and to send a copy of it and a list of Associates to the Central Board.

This Constitution had been drawn up with the greatest care, the Promoters meeting morning after morning at 6 a.m. at their office, 458 New Oxford Street, and going through it clause by clause.[1] In consequence, few alterations had to be made in it, and it remained in force until the passing of the Industrial and Provident Societies Act in June, 1852. Indeed the only modifications afterwards found desirable arose firstly from the lack of any

___

[1] Cf. *Life of Maurice*, ii. p. 75. An interesting description of a visit to the group just at this time is given by Hort in letters to his friend John Ellerton, afterwards well-known as a writer of hymns, who on his recommendation became a ' corresponding ' member of the Society (*Life of Hort*, i. pp. 149-163) : cf. Housman, *John Ellerton*, pp. 32, 33.

central fund ;—and here, as we shall see, though the Promoters strongly urged the pooling of profits by all the Associations, the proposed change was not accepted ; —and secondly, from the need to exclude half-hearted or unsuitable Associates, a need which was met by requiring all applicants to serve for a definite period on probation, or pay a contribution in money to the Association.

Excellent as the scheme was, it could not, under the condition of the law at the time, be legally enforced. The Associations were neither private partnerships, in those days limited to twenty-five members and involving other grave difficulties, nor joint-stock companies; and these were the only forms of combination recognised at that time for purposes of trade. So the constitution had to remain a private compact, dependent for its observance upon the loyalty and honesty of the members of the Society. That there were hardly any instances of its deliberate infringement is proof of the goodwill of all parties to it. But the lack of legal support promoted a sense of insecurity which had its bad effects upon the morale of the workers.

It was on the financial side that the absence of legal protection created the most perplexing problem. And here the arrangements of the Promoters must be briefly stated.

The money raised by the Society had first to be secured against involving its lenders in unlimited liability. Their experiment was a precarious one : they were not rich men : and though willing to risk the loss of the sums actually contributed they could not involve themselves more heavily. So they arranged that it should be given as a loan to the manager of the Association on the security of a bill of sale on the premises and stock given under his hand.   As a set-off this was of course totally inadequate ; and, in fact, they were entirely dependent for the repayment or safety of their money upon the honesty of the manager.   It is not surprising that, under the circumstances, they had inserted in the rules the condition that so long as the debt was owing they should have the right of veto upon his appointment and of defining his powers and duties.   The persons who actually advanced the money were represented by trustees in whom the whole property of the Society was vested and in whose names loans were made to the managers.   These trustees were Neale, Hughes, and Neale's cousin Vansittart.

Such was the constitution which the practical experience of Sully, the legal knowledge of Ludlow, and the idealism of Maurice devised upon the basis of the French schemes. Its merits are sufficiently approved by the fact that scarcely any important modifications had to be made in it, and that such difficulties as arose were in all cases due not to the system, but to the human agents responsible for its working.   What these difficulties were will be best disclosed as we study the history of the various Associations.

The Castle Street Working Tailors, whose beginning we have already recorded, were fortunate in possessing excellently fitted and ventilated premises with large and airy workrooms, and in receiving from the Promoters a loan, entrusted personally to Walter Cooper, of some £300 to meet their initial outlay.   In other respects, too, their start could hardly have been more propitious. At this stage, the only newspaper to attack them with any ferocity was the *Daily News*.   Kingsley's pamphlet sold better than any of the other tracts and reached prospective customers in many quarters.   ' Three copies of *Cheap Clothes and Nasty* are lying on the Guards'

Club table ! Percy Fielding (captain in the Guards) went to Castle Street and ordered a coat, and I met two men at dinner yesterday with Castle Street coats on,' [1] —that kind of news must have been vastly encouraging. And *Alton Locke* was already being written. Furthermore, bachelors' wardrobes always need some replenishing ; and the Promoters took the opportunity to overhaul their garments and order a refit. Additional customers from very different social circles were attracted by an 'Address to the Public,' a circular letter signed by Cooper and printed at the end of *Cheap Clothes*, and by a list of prices, issued by the Associates themselves and circulated in Labour quarters and among ex-Chartist friends.

So business was brisk enough. Cooper in his evidence before Slaney's Commission in May [2] declared that during these first three months of their existence the number of Associates had risen from twelve to thirty-four, that they had done business to the value of £250, and that they had made a clear profit of £77, a third of which had gone to repay part of the loan, a third to increase their stock, while the remainder had been divided. Besides their wealthier customers, whose clothes were made to measure, they had found a large demand from their fellow artisans for ready-made goods, and it was hoped that by turning attention to these in the slack seasons they could keep their members fully employed all the year round. Wages were being paid at an average rate of 24s. a week, the skilled workmen getting as much as 33s.—rates which compared favourably with those paid elsewhere in the best houses in the trade. Yet,

[1] Letter to Mrs Kingsley, June, 1850, cf. *Life of Kingsley*, i. p. 236.

[2] Cf. *Christian Socialist*, i. pp. 132, 147.

even so, as a letter of Kingsley's to Ludlow warns us,[1] there were already signs of ' tribulation,' and his advice, ' Toko, my friend, toko is necessary,' was soon to be justified.

Unfortunately, as was freely admitted in the *First Report* of the Society issued in 1852, the members of this earliest Association were chosen with scarcely any enquiry into their previous record or character : ' we called together large bodies of tailors, and told them what we intended to do, and then accepted the first that put down their names.' [2] Unfortunately too, Walter Cooper was not prepared to devote his whole time to the duties of the shop. He had tasted the joys of public oratory in his Chartist days, and now conceived it to be his mission to act as an apostle of co-operation, and to tour the country with that object. Such work was, in fact, one of the most useful activities of the Christian Socialists, and paved the way for the spread of their methods and the formation of the Co-operative Union. But it could scarcely be combined with the duties of a manager.

In September [3] Cooper went off on a lecturing visit to Bury and other manufacturing towns. In his absence the Tailors' Council of Administration had to take over his work, and among other things investigated the accounts and found them in a state of utter confusion. The mistakes may well have been due to his complete ignorance of book-keeping—a disadvantage which he shared with several of the other managers first appointed—and no definite charge of dishonesty was alleged ; but the Council wrote to him on September 12th urging him to return,

---

[1] Letter of August, 1850. (*Life of Kingsley*, i. p. 240.)

[2] *Report*, p. 6.

[3] For this dispute cf. *Christian Socialist*, i. pp. 5, 62, 69 and ii. pp 36-38 ; *Journal of Association*, p. 29.

and commenting on his ledgers in a way that he regarded as insulting. He came back and demanded the immediate withdrawal of the letter. The Council refused. He discharged them. They defied him and were supported by the whole body of Associates. At this stage the Promoters intervened unofficially, and after hearing both sides suggested that the offensive remarks at least might be withdrawn. This was rejected, and arbitrators, Holyoake and Lloyd Jones, were appointed. Their verdict was unacceptable to the Associates, and they presented a memorandum of their grievances to the Council of the Society. Thereupon a full enquiry was held after both sides had pledged themselves to abide by the decision. The award, dated October 20th, found that the Association was virtually dissolved; that the manager had on occasions broken the laws of the Association, but only through carelessness or desire not to interfere with the members' freedom ; that the mistakes in the books, said to exceed sixty, were all explainable except four, and in these four there was not the slightest ground for suspecting that he intended to garble the accounts ; that therefore the insinuations in the Council's letter were unjustifiable. It further instructed Cooper, with his cutter and two of the offending members, to reconstruct the Association, selecting their comrades by ballot. Eleven of the previous members were refused re-admittance. These eleven resolved to start an independent Association of their own without help from capitalists. They chose one of their number, James Benny, as manager, set up a workroom in Oxford Street, called themselves the London Association of Working Tailors, and proceeded to canvass the customers of Castle Street, informing them that that Association had been broken up and that they were its sole repre-

sentatives. After which they sent a vigorous and somewhat defiant letter to the *Christian Socialist*,[1] and managed
to carry on until the following July, when for 'want
of capital they were compelled to dissolve.' [2]

In spite of this valiant opposition the reconstituted
group at Castle Street overcame its difficulties and entered
upon a period of peace and prosperity. On March 7th,
1851,[3] they held an anniversary gathering, and Cooper
reported that on the year's trading they were in a position
to pay off the whole loan of £300 and still to keep in hand
an additional £300. They were an enterprising and
vigorous body, anxious to make fresh experiments and
apparently free from the discords and suspicions which
had produced the crisis six months before. The quality of
their tailoring may have been indifferent in later years,
when Litchfield [4] declared that you could always recognise
a Christian Socialist by the cut of the co-operative trousers,
but at this time they needed no apologies on this score ;
for the men were keen ; Gerald Massey, their secretary,
was remarkably able, and Field, their cutter, was a good
workman. And their prices were well able to stand
comparison with those of other firms.

In July, 1851, Walter Cooper published a history of the
Association in the *Christian Socialist*.[5] He is mainly
occupied with his own difficulties and searchings of heart,
but when he turns to the position of the business he
discloses a state of affairs even more satisfactory than
it had been in March. They had paid wages at an average
rate of over 30s. ; had spent £20 on improving the work-

[1] I. p. 61.
[2] *Christian Socialist*, pp. 300, 301.
[3] *Christian Socialist*, i. p. 165.
[4] Cf. *Richard Buckley Litchfield : a memoir* (privately printed) p. 25.
So too Hughes *Memoir of a Brother*, p. 117.
[5] II. pp. 36-38.

rooms and fitting a bathroom and water-supply ; had had two days of special holiday ; had set up a library whose shelves were full and well-patronised ; and had actually paid off some £150 or nearly half the loan. He pays an eloquent and well-earned tribute to the loyalty and keenness of the men, to the value of the discipline which they had learnt from their early troubles, and to the spirit which had replaced the songs and enthusiasm of the start with a serious and patient resolution to succeed.   Two days after the appearance of this narrative the annual beanfeast was held, and Shorter has given us a quaint description [1] of how the Association, with wives and families, ' proceeded on a voyage up the Paddington Canal to the pleasant little village of Alperton.'

After this the Association's history becomes uneventful until the end of the year.   Then in January 1852 [2] it was suggested that a branch, specially intended to cater for the needs of the lower and middle classes, and consisting of Associates drawn from those tailors who had been reduced to slop-work, should be established ; and for this purpose an appeal was made for a sum of £500 in £5 shares.   This was an attempt to attack the ready-made clothing business, the stronghold of the sweating system in its vilest form, and the Council realised that it was a serious venture.   The records of subscriptions to the requisite £500 fill a place in nearly every number of the *Journal of Association*, and were evidently watched with much anxiety.   In April [3] a start was able to be made, and a house, 68 Westminster Bridge Road, with a large show-shop and workrooms was taken, fitted up, and stocked.   On May 31st [4] it was announced that the

[1] *Christian Socialist*, ii. p. 71.   [2] *Journal of Association*, p. 35.
[3] *Journal of Association*, p. 121.   [4] *Journal of Association*, p. 179.

premises had definitely been opened, and that it seemed 'likely to answer all the expectations of its friends': its official title was the Borough Branch of the Working Tailors' Association. The Castle Street firm at this time numbered nineteen members, and in the second quarter of this year had transacted business to the value of £700,[1] while its branch had eighteen men at work and took about £70 a week.[2] Twelve months later Castle Street had fifteen members and had done £4000 of business during the year ; the branch still had eighteen members, and during its fourteen months' life had taken £2700.[3]

Of the eight original Associations, three were of Boot and Shoemakers, a business which seemed to lend itself admirably to the methods of the Christian Socialists. Unforeseen difficulties, however, arose, due partly to individual failures, but partly to the circumstances of the trade; and it is notable that of all the Associations none showed results more disappointing.

Two of the three were set up at the same time, in April 1850.[4] One of these,[5] the Ladies' Shoemakers, or, to give it its full title, the Ladies' and Gentlemen's Working Boot and Shoemakers Association, was established in part of a large house and shop—11B—in Tottenham Court Road, and began work with an initial loan of £165. The size and cost of these premises, about £160 per annum, were excessive, and the Association started heavily in debt. During the first two months there were constant troubles, and in June the Association was reconstituted. By this time the summer trade in light shoes had been largely

---

[1] First Report, pp. 28, 29.
[2] First Report, p. 50.
[3] Report of Manchester Conference, pp. 38, 39.
[4] The proposal to start the Tottenham Court Road group was passed on Feb. 14th, 1850.
[5] Cf. Christian Socialist, i. p. 101 and ii. pp. 168, 169.

lost, and though the members worked well and made up all the materials they could procure, they discovered that by that time the goods could not be disposed of. By September, when the busy season for heavier footwear is at its height, the Association found itself with a large and useless stock of light shoes on hand and neither money nor materials. For three weeks they were absolutely without resources of any kind. Then the Promoters came to the rescue with a further loan of £65 ; the men got to work again; and prospects began to improve. By the end of the year they had so far recovered that if the business had been wound up the assets would almost have balanced their debt to the Promoters. They had eleven Associates at work and were proposing to take on one or two probationers. They seemed cheerful, considering the difficulties through which they had passed, and it looked for the moment as if the worst was over. Dissensions, however, broke out afresh. The manager, whose record showed him to be defective in business acumen and judgment, found it impossible to keep the confidence of his Associates. The members were none of them high-class workmen, and newcomers fought shy of joining. It seemed hopeless to carry on under such conditions, or to go on increasing the loans, which were already more than £300.

Meanwhile, the Stout Shoemakers, the ' Gentlemen's Working Boot and Shoe and Strong Shoemakers Association,' had been set up in a similar fashion at 151 High Holborn. Like their colleagues they had many troubles.[1] The trade was so accustomed to the principle of ' home ' work that the best craftsmen would not consent to join an Association which made it a condition of membership

---

[1] Cf. speech by A. H. Louis, *Christian Socialist*, ii. p. 24.

that work should be done on the premises. They also had occasion to change their first manager, and were not very fortunate in their choice of a successor. Cobblers have always had a bad reputation for sociability, and it is possible that the rule of the Society, forbidding speculative arguments in the shops, may have pressed hardly upon them. At any rate, though at one time they seemed to be sufficiently flourishing to propose the opening of a branch in Lambeth,[1] they were never a happy family ; and being unable to arrange for the transfer of some of their more discontented members to another establishment, they too seemed scarcely able to carry on.

So in June[2] the Central Board, recognising that the present position was hopelessly unsatisfactory, recommended that steps should be taken to close the Holborn premises and to amalgamate into a single Association the more reliable members of the two. A committee was appointed to put this resolution into effect, and in July the combined workers were restarted at Tottenham Court .Road. Care was taken to get rid of the men who had been responsible for the disagreements.[3] Henry Jefferies, who had been for some time manager of the Ladies' Shoemakers, was continued in authority, and by December the number of Associates stood at eighteen.[4]

Yet, even so, matters showed no lasting improvement. Early in the spring[5] a number of charges was brought by the members against Jefferies, and a joint committee of the Council and the Central Board, consisting of Lord Goderich, Hansard, Pickard of the North London Builders,· and Jennings of Pimlico, was appointed to investigate the whole position. They recommended that it was useless

[1] *Christian Socialist*, i. p. 134.   [2] *Christian Socialist*, i. p. 270.
[3] *Christian Socialist*, ii. p. 9.   [4] *Christian Socialist*, ii. p. 414.
[5] *Journal of Association*, p. 155.

to carry on the Association in its present form, and that before a new one be recognised there should be a period of probation, during which the members should forfeit all rights of self-government and the business should be carried on by the Council of Promoters, on conditions settled by them. A new manager, John Simmons, was appointed to act under their instructions ; and all the accounts were submitted weekly to two of them. This appeared the only possible means of securing discipline and checking the continuous quarrels which had disgraced the Association's record.

After these tribulations the Association seems to have recovered, and for some time all went well, though it did not return to full self-government. In July 1852 they had twenty-four members and eight women binders at work, and the business of the past quarter amounted to £360.[1]

The third Association of cobblers, the 'West End Working Bootmakers,' which had been founded in June, shortly after the other two, had a still more brief and unsatisfactory existence. The original manager was speedily involved in quarrels with his members, and gave up his position. His successor was no more fortunate. After him the Associates selected a man who could neither read nor write,[2] and drew upon themselves a strong protest from the Central Board. Finally in December [3] the patience of the Promoters was exhausted, and the Association, which from the start had never flourished, was dissolved.

In May, a Working Builders' Association was started, and, in spite of the fact that they had no capital and no office or premises, began work at once. Neale, who

[1] *First Report*, pp. 28, 29, 47.   [2] *Christian Socialist*, i. p. 52.
[3] *Christian Socialist*, i. p. 69.

was having large structural alterations made in his new
house in Hill Street, not only handed over the job to
them, but advanced them a weekly sum to pay wages
and buy materials; and the Society allowed them the
use of their own office in New Oxford Street and later
in Charlotte Street.   Thanks to this, the Association
flourished; and in December was able to take premises
for itself in 4 All Saints Place, Caledonian Road.
Regular employment and the prospect of future contracts enabled them not only to pay off the money lent
to them by the Promoters, but even to show a balance
on the credit side, when the accounts were made up.
Their customers were well satisfied with the quality of
the work done for them, and they seemed to be in a
position to demonstrate the business possibilities of co-
operation by the test of success.

But as the Promoters had always insisted, ' association
is more than the bringing of men together into one workshop.' [1] ' It requires a subordination of self, a humbling
of pride a confidence in each other, a faith in the cause,
which few are found to possess.'   And so despite their
financial prosperity their manager, Joseph Pickard, from
whose report the above sentences are taken, was obliged
to announce early in February that the Associates had
quarrelled violently and had insisted on dissolving the
Association.   The actual matter in dispute arose out of
a small constitutional point.[2]   Men who had joined the
Association without a proper probationary acquaintance
with its spirit were able to exercise a share in its government, even when they were not working for it; and used
this power to thwart the manager's authority.   It was
one more instance of indiscipline.

[1] *Christian Socialist*, i. pp. 142, 143.
[2] Cf. Pickard's speech on March 5th, *Christian Socialist*, i. p. 158.

Nor was this the only disappointment.[1] Their balance-sheet showed a net profit of £235 on the nine months' trading. According to the rules of the Society which should have been accepted by these Builders, four-fifths of this sum ought to have been carried to the funds of the Society. It was expected that those who had experienced the value of co-operative work and the difficulty of developing new Associations without initial capital would have complied with this rule and allowed the major portion of their profits to be devoted to the spreading of the cause. But the Builders thought otherwise. They knew that the Society had no legal hold over them ; they claimed that the money had been earned by their labour ; and so after voting a gift of £15 to their benefactors they proceeded to apportion out the whole of the remainder amongst themselves. Even in the distribution they were false to the whole ideal of Association ; for the skilled workmen who had already been given allowances at rates proportionate to their capacity now insisted upon taking a double share of the dividend, in direct defiance of the laws of the Society, by which profits were to be divided on the basis of hours worked, not of skill.

Yet even here there was a remnant that refused to be discouraged. Five of the Associates agreed to take over the premises, to apply for re-admission into the Society, and to make a fresh start. After three months' probation [2] they were fully recognised by the Promoters, their title being changed to the North London Working Builders' Association. Moreover, like their predecessors, their effort was entirely successful, and twelve months later we find them following the example of their fellows in

---

[1] For this section cf. *Christian Socialist*, i. p. 148.

[2] *Christian Socialist*, i. p. 260.

Pimlico [1] and setting up a Co-operative Store for themselves and their friends at 17 Platt Terrace, King's
Cross. Pickard, of whom a charming incident is told in
the *Life of Octavia Hill*,[2] continued to be their manager
and seems to have had no further trouble. At the end
of 1851 they were employing from twenty to twenty-five
Associates; and working as a plasterer among them
Martin Nadaud, formerly a member of the French
Assembly,[3] and afterwards author of a history of the
working classes in England.[4]

During 1852 they were engaged on the Society's Hall
at Castle Street, where they employed from thirty-five
to forty men. In July Pickard reported that if they were
wound up they would be worth between £800 and £1000
clear.

It was in the building trade that the method of
association met with its greatest success, though the
Society had often to complain that the Builders were
adopting the outlook and policy of a joint-stock company
owing to their expressed desire to admit to Associateship
persons not engaged in the trade, provided they contributed to the funds.[5] The Pimlico Working Builders'
Association was founded on July 4th 1850 as the result of a
local strike, and commenced work in the following October.
Its first manager, Henry Field, though keen, was not
popular, and was removed by the vote of a majority of

[1] *Journal of Association*, p 164.

[2] Pp. 46, 47.

[3] *First Report*, p. 33, and *Transactions of the Co-operative League*,
p. 114. Cf. Introduction to his pamphlet *Les Sociétés Ouvrières*, p. vi.

[4] This is described by Ludlow in his preface to Baernreither's *English
Associations of Working Men* as ' a book of remarkable insight, though
with errors of detail which do not allow it to be relied on as an authority.'

[5] *E.g.* Ludlow's speech reported in *Christian Socialist*, i. p. 158. The
relative success of self-governing association in this trade is interesting
in view of the recent movement towards guildising the Building
Industry.

the Associates [1] within six months. But the Promoters found money to tide them over their early difficulties, and the new manager, Barnabas Jennings, proved himself an honest and on the whole a capable man. They were fortunate in having several energetic Associates who were eager to try experiments and to develop their corporate life. Thus they were the first of the Associations to open a Co-operative Store for their members; [2] they rendered great service in helping to establish a Pimlico People's Institute for education and recreation; [3] they took a large part in the monthly conferences and social gatherings of the Society; and if sometimes their methods seemed rather directed towards the benefit of their own number than to the wider ideals of brotherhood which Maurice and Ludlow were striving to inculcate, they at least escaped those disastrous jealousies and quarrels which wrecked so many of the pioneer attempts at co-operation.

Their business began humbly with an office at 2 Upper Dorset Street, but was moved into premises in Tachbrook Street, off the Vauxhall-bridge Road, at the New Year. On April 16th [4] they were able to celebrate the building of their first entire house, and the owner of it, himself a working man, expressed himself as delighted with the quality of their work. By the end of their first year they had opened a yard and depot at Bridge Row Wharf, and their business flourished. By July, 1852, they had forty-six members, twenty-eight continually at work, had built some twenty houses, and owned property

---

[1] Cf. *Christian Socialist*, i. p. 140.

[2] *Christian Socialist*, i. p. 204. The manager of this was William Stevens, cf. *C. S.* ii. p. 312.

[3] *Christian Socialist*, ii. p. 51.

[4] *Christian Socialist*, i. pp. 204, 205.

of the value of £4,700, and more than a thousand pounds' worth of stock.

The two last of the original eight Associations were both small and unexciting ventures. The Working Printers' Association consisted of a group of four friends who were provided with a printing-press by the Society, and with quarters in a house, 4A in Johnson's Court, Gough Square, at a cost of some £44. Their plant and stock were afterwards largely increased, and in July 1852 were reported to be worth £600.[1] They were capable men; their manager, Richard Isham, took an active part in the various undertakings organised by the Promoters[2]; and John Bedford Leno, one of the Associates, formerly a Chartist printer at Uxbridge, and a friend of Gerald Massey, was a fairly regular contributor of verses to the *Christian Socialist*.[3] But they never did much business outside the printing of the Society's periodicals, tracts, pamphlets and catalogues. With this custom coming in steadily they managed to pay their way, to increase their number to six, and on occasion to employ as many as twelve or fourteen workmen. But as a test of the possibility of associative methods their case is of little importance; for they were never dependent on outside orders or free to undertake much more than the Society sent to them.

In the same way, the Working Bakers' Association of 26 Clipstone Street, Fitzroy Square, founded in April 1850, was never large. At first there were some ten members, and the manager was James Clarkson, who had supplied the initial capital. In June a disagree-

[1] *First Report*, p. 47.

[2] He had previously written *Land, Common Property* (Foxwell in Menger l.c. p. 243) and sent several articles to the *Christian Socialist*.

[3] Leno was a candidate for the Executive of the Chartists in 1850 (Gammage, *History of the Chartist Movement*, p. 358).

ment occurred : Clarkson gave up : and thereafter the Association consisted of only three members and did practically no business except what the Promoters put into its way privately. The four seem to have worked well; their new manager, William Watson, was keen and intelligent ; and we have several reports of their success in supplying teas for various functions of the Society or its Associations.[1] But they failed to secure outside custom, and in August, 1851,[2] some fifteen months after their start, they appear in the weekly advertisement in the *Christian Socialist as* ' a Bakery to the Associations,' after which, though various efforts were made to place them on a more independent footing,[3] their name disappears from the list of the Society's business ventures. Certain of their members had cheated them, and pending re-organisation their constitution was suspended, and all self-government was removed from the members, the manager being given the power of an ordinary master. They did not, however, cease to exist altogether, for in December,[4] when the proposal to open a Co-operative Bazaar for the sale of goods produced by the Associations was being considered, it was suggested that if the Bakers would take in some working pastry-cooks, they might set up a refreshment stall and make it a feature of the place. A meeting of the trade was held soon after in order to arouse fresh interest in association and the abolition of night-work : but seems to have been fruitless. The

[1] There is, for example, an interesting reference to an ' Associated Trades Tea ' held on June 11th, 1851, at St. Martin's Hall in Caroline Fox's *Memories of Old Friends*, ii. pp. 170, 171. On this occasion nearly 300 people sat down, and a special complaint was made that owing to the large numbers the Bakers' Association could not do the catering, and that the quality of the food suffered in consequence : cf. *Christian Socialist*, i. p. 269, and below p. 278.

[2] *Christian Socialist*, ii. p. 80.   [3] *Christian Socialist*, ii. p. 152.

[4] *Christian Socialist*, ii. p. 376 : the meeting to follow up this proposal is described on p. 378.

Bakers appear in the tables of the *First Report*, but not in its list of Associations. Eventually they were absorbed into the service of the co-operative stores, as the London Co-operative Bakery.

Along with these eight Associations there had been founded on February 18th, 1850, an establishment of a somewhat similar kind, the North London Needlewoman's Association,[1] which, though affiliated to the Society, was managed by a separate committee of eight ladies, Mrs. Maurice being its secretary. A large and airy house, 31 Red Lion Square, for the rent of which the Maurices made themselves responsible, was obtained, containing workrooms, a shop, and lodging-rooms. Here were placed some twenty sweated women workers, under the control of a superintendent, Mrs. Harriet Hanson, but otherwise living as a family. Five hundred pounds was collected for the purchase of furniture and materials; an appeal for orders for millinery and dressmaking was sent out; and it was arranged that, when the goods on order were insufficient to keep the women busy, they should spend not more than ten hours a day in making up stock for the shop. Each woman got an allowance proportionate to the work done, and they were charged a small rent for the use of the shop and workrooms. Single women could live in the lodging-rooms at a cost of one shilling and sixpence a week. The superintendent was paid a fixed salary and acted directly under the managing committee, one member of which visited the house every day. It was further provided that a certain sum should be set aside from the profits for the repayment of the loan and of interest on it, and that the remainder should be divided among the needlewomen quarterly.

[1] These particulars are taken from the prospectus of the Association.

There is very little news of this experiment contained in the publications of the Society. It was always rather a charitable institution than a business undertaking. It started with nine members, possessed twenty-six in July 1852, and continued with a fair measure of prosperity until the autumn of 1853, when the numbers dwindled and the Association was wound up. The house was afterwards used for the newly founded Working Men's College.

Two further Associations in connection with the Society were founded about twelve months after the others. One of these, the Working Pianoforte Makers' Association, was founded in February, 1851,[1] first appeared on the Society's list on June 14th,[2] but did not really start in business until the following October,[3] when it opened premises at 5 Charles Street, Drury Lane. These, with the plant and goodwill, had been bought from the men's late employer by Neale. Beyond the facts that there were for some time fourteen associates and three non-associates employed, that they had a market for four or five pianos a week, and that the manager's name was John Locke, little can be collected as to the details of their early history. They had a very hard struggle, as they had taken over a contract from their bankrupt predecessor, and to fulfil this they had to supply goods at less than cost price. Other work was not easy to get, though in July, 1852, Locke reported that he hoped to secure orders from firms in the provinces where he had been touring. In spite of their difficulties this Association is singled out in the Society's *First Report* as one from which they had never had one single complaint.[4]

---

[1] *Christian Socialist*, i. p. 117. The *First Report* gives the date of starting as April 3rd, p. 30 : the *Report of the Manchester Conference* as April 1st, p. 36.

[2] *Christian Socialist*, i. p. 264.   [3] *Christian Socialist*, ii. p. 224.

[4] *First Report*, p. 32. For Locke's report cf. l.c. p. 45.

The second of these later Associations was the City Working Tailors of 23 Cullum Street, Fenchurch Street. This undertaking had been planned since 1850, and originally on a somewhat ambitious scale. As many as seventy-eight men expressed their desire to join, but before a start could be made many of these had fallen away, perhaps, as is suggested by one of them, owing to the evil effect of the quarrels in Castle Street.[1] In June, 1851,[2] when they applied to the Society for provisional admission, there were twenty-five Associates all at work, and the manager was A. J. Brown. They had very little capital and started in a shop at the top of a house. This first effort was a failure, and they had to discontinue. But in May, 1852, they started again with six Associates, Neale advancing them money for their initial expenses, and Charles Bowen becoming manager. In July, 1853, the same six were still at work, but had not yet made any profits. The style of the firm had become Bowen, Brown, and Co., and as an Association it was evidently a failure.[3] It disappeared altogether in 1857.

The final Association to be founded under the direct auspices of the Christian Socialists was that of the Working Smiths. This had been suggested by the example of the Pimlico Builders and had been under discussion for a long time, the moving spirit being Henry Field, the Builders' first manager, who held a meeting to discuss it as early as June, 1851.[4] At first it appeared likely to win considerable support : but difficulties arose, and as the Promoters had now made it their practice not to advance money, unless the workers showed signs of real effort and readiness for personal sacrifice, the number of

[1] *Christian Socialist*, i. p. 165.   [2] *Christian Socialist*, i. p. 253.
[3] *Report of Manchester Conference*, p. 38.
[4] *Christian Socialist*, i. p. 260.

possible members dwindled. A start was made in July, 1852,[1] in premises in Pimlico, several orders having come in, and the Builders having undertaken to employ two of their men regularly. The manager was William Livesey, and though the Association was never large it lasted for some years.

Brief reference may also be made to an Association some-what similar to that of the Needlewomen of Red Lion Square, but run on a different and, as it turned out, very unsatisfactory plan. This was the East London Needle-women's Home and Workshop started in the autumn of 1851 at 51 Wellclose Square, Whitechapel. The scheme was one of Ludlow's, and had a twofold purpose, firstly to help the very poorest and most abject of all the sweated women workers, and then to enlist the sympathies of a fresh group of rich and charitable persons. Lord Shaftes-bury and several other notable philanthropists, male and female, were put on the Committee,[2] together with some of the Promoters, Louis a law student at Lincoln's Inn, who acted as its secretary, Ellison, and one or two of the stalwarts. With this wealthy connection it was hoped that a real educational opening had been found; or at least that the Association would not lack support. Yet, to Ludlow's great disgust, the venture received far less support than any of their own efforts: 'the big folk, with the exception of one City Missionary, took no trouble whatever in the matter[3]': thus, although

---

[1] *Journal of Association*, p. 189, and *First Report*, pp. 30, 31.

[2] Shaftesbury was president, and the notables on the committee included Sidney Herbert, Lord John Manners, Viscount Mandeville, and the Bishop of Oxford (Wilberforce). A prospectus is contained in the Furnivall papers, and was also printed at the end of Hughes' lecture 'on the Slop-system.'

[3] *Life of Maurice*, ii. 65. A similar complaint of lack of support is made by Ludlow in an editorial comment upon the Association's first Annual Report : cf. *Journal of Association*, p. 214.

Miss Dennington, the superintendent, was keen and capable, and the effect of the start upon the victims of sweating in the neighbourhood seemed most propitious, the whole plan speedily proved unworkable. The Home survived until 1853, but was only kept open by advances from the managing committee.[1] ' It was the first and last attempt at this kind of joint work.' Their experience of titled patrons on this occasion may explain their refusal to accept any such folk for the Working Men's College.

Finally among the latest efforts of the Society was an attempt to apply the associative principle to the needs of women of a different class. Maurice through his work at Queen's College had long been familiar with the sufferings of the ' distressed gentlewoman.' And early in 1852, thanks to Neale's energy and generosity, a ' Ladies Guild ' was started at 4 Russell Place, Fitzroy Square. Mrs. Caroline Southwood Hill, whose famous daughter Octavia then thirteen years old had joined it, was appointed manager, and the Guild was presented with the patent rights of a new method of painting on glass. Much time was spent in teaching this to the members ; but by July it was reported that twenty-seven were at work. Apart from a couple of letters in the *Journal* and a number of allusions in the *First Report* the history of this venture is only given in Mr. C. E. Maurice's *Life of Octavia Hill*, the early chapters of which are full of interest to the student of Christian Socialism. By July 1853, though its capital was nearly £2000, a long explanatory document was submitted to the Manchester Conference confessing that the prospects were dark. Mrs. Hill was compelled to resign in 1855, and the Guild seems to have ceased next year. From its influence in introducing Octavia

---

[1] *Report of Manchester Conference*, p. 36.

Hill to the Promoters, it deserves a special place in any account of their work. Years after the great pioneer of housing reform wrote to Ludlow to say that ' it was the early connection with that body of " Christian Socialists," to which much of my present work must owe its spirit ' [1]

In addition to the London Associations, mention must be made of the efforts of the group to spread their principles in the provinces. Indeed, one of the features of Christian Socialism that contributed most largely to its importance in the history of social progress was its definitely missionary character. The Promoters realised at an early stage that, if their movement was to be more than an interesting local experiment, and if their methods were to be fairly tested, they must not be confined to the metropolis. In the great centres of industry, and especially in the north, labour problems were far more widely discussed, and the issues at stake were far more vital than in London. It was essential to the success of their efforts that they should secure the attention of the working-classes in Glasgow and Manchester and the chief manufacturing districts. None of the leaders had any close links with these centres or any personal knowledge of their needs, and their activities hitherto had not seemed to produce any suitable openings. But as soon as Lloyd Jones decided to throw in his lot with them, this defect could be remedied. He had had wide experience of educational campaigning ; he was a fine speaker and a brilliant debater ; and through his connection with Owen and residence at Salford he was in touch with the co-operative movement at Rochdale and in the Lancashire towns. So in the summer of 1850 he was commissioned to undertake propagandist work, and to arrange a programme of lectures and visits for the autumn and winter.

[1] *Life of Octavia Hill*, p. 330.

Reports of his tours in Scotland and the northern counties of England appear frequently in the pages of the *Christian Socialist*, and their results began to be felt almost at once.

In this task he had the assistance of Walter Cooper, who as a Chartist had become acquainted with the chief Labour leaders in the industrial centres, and whose ability as a popular lecturer was recognised by his previous colleagues. He tells how, when first he was invited to act as manager for the Tailors' Association, his friends warned him that his true work was that of a speaker and advocate of reform ; and he was eager to combine missionary touring with his duties at Castle Street. So the Council agreed to set him free, and in September and again in December he carried out a series of engagements in the Midlands and Lancashire. At the New Year his efforts were supplemented by the visit of a deputation from the Promoters : Maurice, Hughes, Mansfield, Campbell, Lloyd Jones and W. Lees were present at a meeting in Manchester, and went to Rochdale and Bury, thus getting into touch with the older experiments in the north.[1]

The fruits of these visits were mainly reaped when through them the whole co-operative movement, distributive and productive, was linked up together : but meanwhile the willingness of the Promoters to extend their sphere of operations led to the formation of two provincial Associations connected with the Society, whose histories are of some importance in illustrating the value of the new method.

The first of these was the Southampton Tailors' Association. The plans for this were first mooted spontaneously in April, 1850, by a group of journeymen who, declining pecuniary help from gentlemen in the town, set themselves

---

[1] *Life of Maurice*, ii. p. 56 ; *Christian Socialist*, i. pp. 96-98.

to raise the necessary funds by means of 5s. shares. In November[1] they reported their intentions to the Society of Promoters, and a few weeks later described to them a novel difficulty with which they had been confronted. As a sample of the kind of antagonism which the Christian Socialists had to face this is well worth recording ; for it threatened not only to ruin the success of their project but to bring the cause into grave discredit.[2] A Jew sweater and slop-seller came to one of their meetings, and having failed to persuade them to give up their undertaking, resolved to turn to his own advantage the sympathies which they had aroused. So he issued a handbill announcing his establishment as a Working Tailors' Association, and appealing to the benevolent to support him with their patronage. When this bill appeared the genuine Associates determined to make enquiries. A deputation from them called upon the Jew, assured him of their willingness to co-operate if they could first see and speak to his workmen, and persisting in their wish to investigate his methods at last discovered that there were no Associates at all except one half-grown lad, and that all the goods were produced by sweated labour at a piece-rate. Having thus discovered that the whole scheme was a fraud, the deputation in its turn issued a bill warning the public that the new Association was only an individual speculation, and a deliberate attempt to rob them of their name and of the fruits of their exertions. In consequence of their promptitude the sham Association only lasted from Monday to Saturday, and the fiasco gave them an excellent advertisement, and brought in a supporter of the greatest value, Dr. William Bullar, who undertook to

[1] *Christian Socialist*, i. p. 13.
[2] For this account cf., *Christian Socialist*, i. p. 28.

canvass for a loan for them, and eventually raised a sum
of £40.[1]

In addition to this local support a visit from Furnivall
during the winter not only ' infused new life into them,'
but put them into touch with several fresh friends in the
neighbourhood.   Sufficient money was raised to enable
them to make a start on March 25th, 1851, in premises
at 18 Bernard Street with six Associates,[2] a number that
was increased to eight in May and ten by the beginning
of June.   Their manager, Henry James Ballard, sent a
report of their history at this time to the *Christian
Socialist*,[3] which contains an interesting classification of
their supporters.   This is worth quoting to illustrate the
scope of their business : it is—Nobility, 2 ; Clergy, 7 ;
Navy Officers, 3 ; Army, 8 ; Professional, 8 ; Independent, 5 ; Steam Company's Officers, 3 ; American Officers,
3 ; Customs' Officers, 4 ; Tradesmen, 21 ; Shopmen, 7 ;
Working Men, 49; Indians, 5.   Their prices, as fixed by
a circular modelled upon that sent out by the Castle
Street firm, were a shilling or two lower for the cheaper
qualities than those of the London house.

They had owed much of the success of their start to
a public lecture delivered by Maurice in the Town Hall
on March 31st, and entitled ' The Reformation of Society
and how all classes may contribute to it.'[4]   This had
served to draw attention to their venture and also to
link them up more closely with the Promoters.   They
were fully recognised as an Association connected with
the Society in June,[5] and expressed themselves as deeply
indebted to it, though not under any financial obligations.

[1] *Christian Socialist*, i. p. 45.
[2] *Christian Socialist*, i. p. 229.   [3] Vol. i. p. 278.
[4] Reported in *Christian Socialist*, i. pp. 189, 190, and printed as a
pamphlet by the Society.
[5] *Christian Socialist*, ii. p. 276.

On July 28th [1] an official return of their position was sent to the Promoters. At this time they had twenty-two paying members, working-men who had bought one or more 5s. shares : they had eight men at work, though it was the slackest part of the season : and they considered that their trade was at least as good as that of any other establishment. By September [2] they had saved £40, the sum necessary to repay the initial loan. They had already taken up and were working allotments on the glebe of St. Mary's Church, and were now proposing to open a co-operative store.[3]

Their second circular, sent out in April 1852, speaks confidently of their 'most unequivocal success'; and indeed hitherto all seemed to have gone. well. But at this very time trouble broke out.[4] Ballard, their manager, quarrelled with them, apparently over the question of his salary which, having regard to the dullness of trade, they regarded as excessive. He not only left the Association, but set up an establishment of his own a few doors off with the intention of securing their custom. Jonas Bannister, who had been their treasurer when the effort to raise money was being made, was appointed manager, and did his best to keep the Association together. But things went badly, and when the Promoters sent two of their number to visit and report [5] they found only five men at work, though in other respects they declare it to be ' in a very flourishing condition.' Their task must sometimes have made heavy demands upon the faith of the Christian Socialists, and the courage with which they refuse to accept defeat or to indulge in complaints is almost heroic.

---

[1] *Christian Socialist*, ii. p. 88.
[2] *Christian Socialist*, ii. p. 201.   [3] *Christian Socialist*, ii. p. 120.
[4] *Journal of Association*, p. 126.   [5] *Journal of Association*, p. 164.

The second provincial Association directly connected with the Society applied for recognition in September 1851,[1] and its early history is fully described by Ludlow in two of the letters which he sent to the *Christian Socialist* [2] during his northern tour that autumn, and in the *First Report*.[3] In March [4] ten working hatters at Salford determined to set up an Association, and invited the help of their Trade Union. This being refused they began to subscribe equally to a fund for the purchase of tools and material and to produce samples of their work. They managed to collect £40, £27 being a loan from certain of their own members. In May they received a visit from Cooper, who advised them as to the starting of a shop, bought one of their hats himself, and ordered two dozen for the Castle Street firm. Other orders were received by sending out circulars to co-operative establishments mentioned in the *Christian Socialist*, and arrangements were made with stores in Glasgow, Bradford, Halifax and London to sell their goods at a commission of 10 per cent. In the middle of July they determined to take a better workshop and to employ some of their members for their whole time. Premises were secured at 12 Broughton Road, a large airy room on the first floor, in rather an out-of-the-way situation. They had no saleroom of their own and were thus unable to develop the local trade, or to store much stock during the slack season. Nevertheless, they had eight Associates and three Probationers at work, and their manager, James Dyson, seems to have had little difficulty in keeping them together.

In January, 1852,[5] when they had been fully at work for six months, they sent a short but encouraging report

---

[1] *Christian Socialist*, ii. p. 168.   [2] Vol. ii. pp. 199, 212, 213.
[3] Speech by Dyson, pp. 45, 46.   [4] *Christian Socialist*, ii. p. 248.
[5] *Journal.of Association*, p. 37.

to the Promoters, and drew special attention to the assistance which they had received in the disposal of their goods from co-operative associations and stores in various localities. They regard the opening of a suitable sale-room as essential if their custom with the public direct is to be increased.

Shortly afterwards they were able to secure what they wanted by joining forces with the Manchester Working Tailors' Association. The two set up a shop at 83 Bridge Street,[1] and business became so brisk that with their very limited amount of capital they were not able to make hats as fast as they could sell them. In June [2] they gave up their old workroom altogether and moved to the premises in Bridge Street where the two Associations worked together amicably and with considerable success. They continued to be recognised by the Society, though their colleagues, the Tailors, were independent of it; and when their premises were changed they became the Manchester Working Hatters' Association. During that summer they had twelve members, of whom six were in continuous employment.

This Association was one of the longest-lived of them all. In 1864 there is a very favourable account of it in the *Westminster Review*,[3] from which it appears that they were still living in harmony with the tailors and had nine members, four being always employed. Their capital, including a reserve fund, was now more than £600, and this had been made up ' entirely by appropriations from profits, which in one instance within the last three years were £67, and in another £39 in six months.' ' All those employed,' adds the writer, ' whether members or not,

[1] *Journal of Association*, p. 156. [2] *Journal of Association*, p. 204.

[3] p. 371, quoted by B. Jones. Many references to them occur in the pages of the *Co-operator*.

share ratably in proportion to their wages in any surplus profits remaining after payment of interest at 5 per cent. on capital. What keeps back both hatters and tailors is want of custom.'

They managed to carry on in spite of this until 1873,[1] and then only ceased their enterprise after the tailors had been compelled, for want of sales, to disband. Dyson had been their manager from first to last.

The histories of these two Associations do not in themselves give any adequate idea of the influence of Christian Socialism upon the development of co-operative efforts. ' We are only a very small stream of the great flood ' says the *First Report*.[2] ' Anyone who has been living at all with working-men during the last three years must have been astonished at the wonderful spread of this idea of fellow-work—by people in general called Socialism — amongst them within that time.' All over the country experiments similar in their method to the Society's Associations were springing up, encouraged by their example and helped by their advice. In the pages of the *Christian Socialist* and the *Journal of Association*, we find a continuous stream of enquiries, proposals, reports and discussions coming in from sympathisers and imitators everywhere. The Silk-weavers of Bethnal Green, the Plush-weavers of Banbury, the Cloth-weavers of Galashiels, the Calico-weavers of Salford, the Saw-makers of Sheffield, the Stone-masons of Sunderland,— these are some of the Associations which, though not formally connected with the Society, yet worked in close contact with it. And in several towns organisations parallel in scope to the Society of Promoters had been set up, such as the General Labour Redemption Society

---

[1] B. Jones, *Co-operative Production*, i. p. 132.
[2] Page 34.

of Bury,[1] whose first object, as set out in its constitution, was to unite labourers ' by forming associations.' This was founded on September 16th, 1850, by the ' Central Committee of the Iron Trades of Bury,' made the *Christian Socialist* its official organ in November,[2] and on New Year's day mustered nearly eight hundred members to meet Maurice, Hughes and Neale when they visited the north. Somewhat similar was the Halifax Working Man's Co-operative Society, founded in January, 1851, which sent its reports and balance-sheets regularly to the *Christian Socialist*, and at its first anniversary meeting made a deputation from the Council of Promoters the guests of the evening. As for Tailors' Associations they grew like mushrooms under the spell of Cooper's eloquence : in Edinburgh, Glasgow, Liverpool and Newcastle-on-Tyne Associations were formed which survived the struggles of their first year, and though nowhere large, seemed able to carry on without actual insolvency : and others were mooted and sometimes even started at Doncaster, Norwich, Sunderland, Aberdeen and Dublin. They may have been unsuccessful ; they may have seemed to perish without fruits : but they served to introduce the ideal of co-operation, to proclaim that all was not well with the existing social order, and to prepare the way for that great movement of industrial and political reform of which the Christian Socialists were the most important pioneers.

The details which we have been discussing in this chapter may seem trivial and unimportant. The reader, as he wades through the record of petty disputes and scanty successes, may be tempted to suppose that these narratives of little wars, these struggles of cobblers and tailors, are sorry material for serious students. In these

---

[1] For this Society cf. B. Jones' *Co-operative Production*, i. pp. 98-100.

[2] *Christian Socialist*, i. p. 28.

days of 'world movements' and 'thinking in millions' it is easy for him to sneer at the importance of a Society that lasted barely five years and never had a capital of more than £1500 or an income of as much as £200.[1] But when he realises the vast change which has come over our social life in the past half-century, and discovers the potency of these trifling and apparently futile experiments, he will become convinced that the men who had the courage to act and, in spite of obvious failures and constant disappointments, to go on acting, deserve a fuller share of praise than they have yet received. Nowadays it is too often the fashion to dismiss their efforts with a shrug of contempt, softened only by a few words of admiration for their intentions—with what justice we shall discuss later. Yet these same Associations, whose puny conflicts seem a mere battle of frogs and mice, were not only the forerunners but the forebears of the great co-operative movement, and of the legislation which has made possible the whole career of organised Labour. We have to trace the expansion of the work of the Christian Socialists and justify our estimate of their importance in the following pages.

[1] *Report*, p. 35.

CHAPTER VII

CO-OPERATIVE PRODUCTION AND THE TRADES
UNIONS

THE opening of the first Association brought into the
Christian Socialist movement one of the very greatest
of its members, Edward Vansittart Neale. Though he
was a barrister and had chambers in Lincoln's Inn,[1] he
was not then personally known to the group. The other
lawyers were young men, Ludlow, twenty-nine years old,
Hughes and Furnivall only twenty-seven, whereas he was
already forty ; they were poor and had still to make their
way in their profession ; he was wealthy, with a house
in Mayfair and a place in Warwickshire ; they were
disciples of Maurice and regular members of his Bible-
reading circle ; he was interested in religion but had no
sympathy for conventional orthodoxy, and like many
good men was not fond of parsons. So he had no contact
with their work, although he was keenly devoted to the
study of social problems and of the various experiments
in Socialism,[2] until he happened to see an advertisement
of the Working Tailors' Association. He then visited
Castle Street, discovered who were responsible for the
venture, got into touch with the Society of Promoters,

[1] For a delightful description of the chambers in Old Square and of
a meeting of their occupants—' a nest of birds of the same plumage '—
see Huber, *Reisebriefe*, ii. pp. 38-40.

[2] In a lecture on ' the characteristic Features of the Principal Systems
of Socialism ' in 1851 he shows much knowledge of Fourier, Owen,
and Pierrepont Greaves, the three that he selects for treatment.

and before many weeks had elapsed was invited to join its Council. Though, as Ludlow puts it,[1] he was always rather in the movement than of it, the very fact that he stood somewhat aloof from the others and approached their work from a different standpoint made his contribution all the more valuable. And his knowledge, resourcefulness, persistence, and generosity were assets of incalculable importance. He not only suggested a mass of new ideas, but was in a position to put them into practice.

The character and work of Neale have been vividly described by Hughes in two articles in the third volume of the *Economic Review*,[2] and more briefly by Ludlow in volume IV. [3] of the same magazine. He was a trained student of the religious and political thought of the continental schools, and a speculative thinker of no mean ability. In the intervals of his social activity he found time to publish several pamphlets on philosophic and theological topics, in addition to a more ambitious treatise, *The Analogy of Thought and Nature*, which Ludlow describes as ' one of the stiffest bits of reading I know.' [4] From these pursuits he gained a singularly clear grasp of principles and a habit of fearless enquiry, which stood him in good stead when he became the master-spirit of the co-operative movement. In addition he possessed a fertility and restlessness of mind and a capacity for strenuous and patient exertion which Ludlow himself could hardly rival. The ingenuity with which he devised new methods, the skill with which he invented expedients for surmounting obstacles, and the vitality with which

[1] *Economic Review*, iv. p. 33.

[2] Pp. 38-49 and 174-189.   [3] Pp. 32-34.

[4] Published in 1863 and consisting of three parts : the Law of Thought : the History of Thought ; the Divination of Thought.

he threw himself into each fresh project were a source of constant inspiration to his colleagues. Impetuous and even rash in temperament, outspoken in praise or criticism, and not too ready to suffer fools gladly, he was at first liable to cause friction and misunderstanding ; and his voice, naturally high and when he was excited rising to shrillness, often exaggerated the appearance of irritation in his speech. But all the time he was learning to curb his feelings, to accept disagreement and opposition without cavil, to endure stupidity and even insolence patiently, and to school himself to make the best of the materials ready to his hands ; and when he died in 1892, Professor Brentano of Munich, the author of the most important study of the Christian Socialists, could write of him to Ludlow as ' a unique man . . . a hero and a saint,' and add ' of the names of the men who have done most to bring the social evolution in England into a peaceful way, his will stand foremost. His practical life has done more for the reconciliation of the classes and the masses than volumes written by others.' [1] Ludlow's own summary of him is worth quoting in view of their close connection in the movement : 'When we were working together,' he writes,[2] ' I not unfrequently felt called upon to oppose schemes which his then over-fertile brain and over-hasty judgment suggested. But a life of such generous, such utter self-devotion, I have scarcely ever known.' Holyoake, when he heard of his death, declared, ' His monument is the Co-operative Movement.' [3]

Having decided to throw in his lot with the Christian Socialists, Neale did so absolutely without reserve. Hitherto they had always had to count the cost with strict caution before embarking on any fresh project.

---

[1] Quoted by Hughes, l.c. p. 38.   [2] *Economic Review*, iv. p. 34.
[3] M'Cabe, *Life of Holyoake*, ii. p. 239.

Parson Lot's handbills, Mansfield's sanitary crusade, the night-school and the tailors' meetings, had all been financed by rigid economies and self-sacrifice, and often their continuance was highly precarious. Now, at last, they had a well-filled purse placed at their disposal with a lavish and unsparing enthusiasm. It would have been quite beyond the power of the others to do more than start the Tailors and such Associations as required hardly any plant or costly materials. The campaign in the provinces would have been impossible. Applicants—and in a few months they were numerous and insistent—would have been inevitably met with unconditional refusals. The movement could never have been more than tentative and local; and the losses of the first few weeks would have put an end to the whole adventure. But Neale was a man of large means, and from the first he made it evident that he was prepared to sacrifice everything for the cause. At his instigation and with his support schemes of far-reaching importance became practicable. If at times he seemed reckless and quixotic, if the magnitude of his plans and his commitments almost horrified his friends, there was a noble and uncomplaining promptitude about his extravagance which not only made it easy for his colleagues to accept his help but won for him and them a position of unique confidence among the workers. Even Hughes, his closest comrade in the movement, never knew the extent of his losses,[1] but only that they involved the sale of his house in Hill Street and of an estate in Warwickshire, and constrained him for many years to live with strict economy and to accept a salary for his work. Yet the money, wasted as it might seem in schemes that ended only in failure, could scarcely have been put to better

[1] Cf. *Economic Review*, iii. p. 48.   Greening says they were £60,000.

use ; and the results of his timely generosity are writ
large upon the history of English social development.
Thanks to it, the group and especially Neale himself
became, as Mr. Sidney Webb somewhat reluctantly
admits,[1] ' the trusted legal experts and political advisers
of the leaders of the Trades Union Movement ' : and
their influence upon co-operation has been larger still.
For forty years and more, with an unfaltering faith and
an unsparing self-sacrifice, Neale held up before the
massing armies of organised Labour the ideals of Christian
Socialism of which his whole life was so signal an example.

Of his attitude towards Maurice and the Society of
Promoters he has given a very interesting account in a
letter written a few months before his death to the Rev.
John Carter,[2] which has not been previously published
and is worth quoting at some length. Speaking of the
need of united action in social matters by persons of
all or no religious beliefs, provided they admit the general
principles on which a better order must be based, he
writes : ' This was, I think, Professor Maurice's idea,
though he did not completely give expression to it.
He did not attempt to found a society of " Christian
Socialists." Though he wrote about Christian Socialism
he founded only a " Society for promoting Working Men's
Associations," . . . managed by a Council of Promoters
from whom no profession of Christian faith was required,
and of whom one of the most active members was not
avowedly a Christian at all.

' The defect of Maurice's scheme was, in my judgment,
that although it laid a broad basis for practical union
in work it reserved the teaching of the principles to
τοῖς περὶ Maurice. In consequence no one who did

[1] *History of Trade Unionism* (1911 edition), p. 229.

[2] From his home Bisham Abbey, Marlow, and dated Dec. 9th, 1891.

not look up to Mr. Maurice as a teacher took any interest in advocating the principles of the union, and the co-operative movement has grown up, to its own serious detriment, without that energetic enforcement of the moral principles of which it is the expression, which would probably have accompanied its growth, if this teaching had been allowed to take its own course freely.'

Such a criticism, written at a time when he was struggling, with increasing lack of success, to keep the co-operative movement true to its ideals, and therefore exaggerated in its account of the group's exclusiveness and in its estimate of that exclusiveness' effects, shows very clearly the cause and scope of his divergence from the others. We have quoted it because this difference of attitude towards the religious basis of the movement was the source of several important discussions and at least one serious disagreement within the Society. Maurice himself was in favour of the widest toleration, and strove to avoid schism at all costs short of an actual betrayal of principle. But Ludlow represented the opposite extreme to that of Neale, and, as we have seen, had secured the insertion in the Constitution of the Society of the clause defining co-operation as 'the practical application of Christianity to the purposes of trade and industry.' Both in the matter of the relation of Neale's Central Co-operative Agency to the Society, and in the discussion of the revised Constitution after the passing of the Industrial and Provident Societies' Act, the difference between them threatened to become acute;[1] and it was only the tact and sympathy of Maurice and the patience and loyalty of Ludlow that averted an open rupture. Neale's point of view was generally adopted, and the movement, even if not quite so broad as he desired,

[1] See below pp. 266-269 and 303-307.

always succeeded in uniting in its service men of widely differing outlook : which would have been in the long run the wisest policy is obviously a question in the answering of which there is room for great divergence of opinion.

After Neale's appearance on the Council the work of the Christian Socialists was extended in two separate directions. We will consider first the development of the principle of co-operative production and the attempts to induce the Trades Unions to take it up—attempts which furnish a curious anticipation of the programme of the modern Guild Socialists—and then will narrate the achievements of the group in the sphere of co-operative distribution, in which Neale was particularly prominent, and which led ultimately to the welding together of all the scattered and local efforts after association into one great Co-operative Union.

It is one of the stock charges brought by their modern socialist critics against the Christian Socialists that they did not devote themselves more energetically to the service of Trades Unionism, or were even actively hostile to its development.[1] Estimating the value of such organisations with the wisdom which we can all display after the event, these writers assume that the development of the Trades Societies of that time along the lines actually followed was at once desirable, and inevitable, and that this must have been apparent : but they also neglect, or are ignorant of, the facts that from the first the Christian Socialists made repeated efforts to solicit the support or at least the sympathy of the organised trades ; that after a short experience they advocated boldly the formation of Associations for production on self-governing lines by the Societies themselves ; and that, when the

---

[1] Cf. *e.g.* Webb, *History of Trade Unionism*, p. 207.

opportunity arose, they assisted them in the attempt to do so. There were already in existence various suggestions for the adoption by the Unions of the principle of self-employment ; and at least one body, the National Association of United Trades for the Protection of Labour had actively championed such a policy. It is at least arguable that this line of progress, whereby the organised Unions should become their own employers and devote their funds to the establishment of co-operative workshops, would have been at once more rapid and less wasteful than the militant policy actually pursued. To attack Capitalism by inducing the Unions to produce from their own resources might well seem, as it did to the Christian Socialists, a truer means to its overthrow than simply to fight a series of defensive engagements by means of strikes and turn-outs. Now that interest in Guild Socialism has rescued such a proposal from contempt, it may be worth while to enter into the subject somewhat fully. At least it will establish the almost prophetic insight, the originality, and the courage of the Christian Socialists.

But first it must be noted that the Trades Societies at that period of their existence were very different from what they have since become. They were in general confined to the skilled trades, and even in them were small and sectional. Until the amalgamation of the engineers, machinists, pattern-makers and millwrights in the Iron Trades in 1851, no successful attempt had been made to combine the little groups of expert workers. In consequence they suffered from all the faults that characterise cliques ; they were exclusive, jealous of their privileges, selfish, and quite unwilling to help their more down-trodden brethren. Indeed, they were more likely to oppose than to support any movement for the improvement of the unskilled worker, lest this should detract from their own prerogatives. As a factor in social progress they were more liable to prove an obstacle than an assistance. Provided they could secure satisfactory conditions for their own members and make it difficult for outsiders to find a place in their ranks, they were not prepared to take any large view of their responsibilities towards Labour as a whole. Such bodies could hardly be expected to regard with favour the proposals for association.

Yet as the *First Report* insists,[1] 'it was one of the most anxious wishes of many members of the Society, from the earliest period of its existence, to convert this organisation to the purpose of co-operation' : and in the autumn of 1850 an attempt was formally made to enlist their help. A circular letter,[2] signed by Lloyd Jones and Cooper, the two members most likely to catch the ears of the workers, was sent out to all the London Trades Societies inviting them to grant an interview. 'We are anxious,' they said, ' to explain to you, as men holding official positions in your trade, the nature of the operations in which we are engaged. We are induced to take this step through a desire to secure, as far as we can, the friendly aid of all those who have the confidence of the bodies to which they belong.' The letter led to two meetings with two societies of Cabinet-makers;[3] but otherwise there seems to have been no response. As a first attempt, it was not very encouraging.

No opportunity for advance along these lines occurred until after the great amalgamation of Trades Societies

[1] P. 12.   [2] Printed in the *Christian Socialist*, i. p. 28.

[3] The East London Cabinet-makers Trade Society appointed a committee in Oct. 1852 to enquire into associative methods, and acting on their report formed an Association at 43 Upper North Place, Gray's Inn Road : cf. *Report of Manchester Conference*, p. 32.

among the engineers and ironworkers.[1] During the year 1850 this proposal was keenly discussed all over the country, and the merits of local or vocational organisation were strenuously canvassed. The policy of amalgamation was not without its critics. At Bury,[2] for example, the local branch of the Steam-Engine Makers' Society attacked the proposal to amalgamate on the ground that it would not free even the engineers from capitalist control, much less effect ' the elevation of the whole working population ' ; so they pleaded for ' a union of all workers ' and the development of the principle of association ; and the General Labour Redemption Society was founded in September 1850 with this object by the Central Committee of the local Iron Trades. In June 1851 a special clubroom was taken for fortnightly lectures and discussions on matters co-operative.[3]

In spite of this opposition the Amalgamated Society of Engineers, or, as it was then usually and incorrectly called, the Amalgamated Iron Trades Society, was constituted in January 1851; and speedily showed itself favourable towards the principle of association. The leaders of the A.S.E. were then, as now, the aristocracy of Labour, intelligent and progressive, ready and able to make experiments for the reform of their industry. And association offered possibilities which they were not slow to grasp.

Their first step was one of great importance for the student of Christian Socialism : for it was nothing less than a definite request to the Society of Promoters for help and advice as to the best employment of the large accumulated funds of the Amalgamated Society.[4] William

[1] For this cf. Webb, *History of Trade Unionism*, pp. 187-195.
[2] Cf. *Christian Socialist*, i. pp. 13, 149. [3] *Christian Socialist*, i. p. 260.
[4] *Journal of Association*, p. 25. As proof of their interest in co-operation, it may be noted that the Reports of the A.S.E. for 1852-4 were printed by Isham of the Working Printers' Association.

Newton, who had been the chief leader in the campaigns for uniting the ironworkers into a single body and was the most remarkable figure in the Trades Union movement of the time, was himself a Londoner and sympathetic towards the Christian Socialists : William Allan, who had been secretary of the Journeymen Steam-Engine Makers, and was now holding the same post in the A.S.E., was already winning a very prominent position in the Labour world and was enthusiastic in his belief in association.[1] These two men may fairly be said to have been the most influential and enlightened representatives of the working classes; and they now came, as delegates from the executive of the A.S.E., to consult the Council of Promoters as to the possibility of devoting some of their surplus to the development of Associations in the engineering trades, and on a large scale. We are often told that the Christian Socialists were out of touch with the real leaders of the industrial world, and never tested their plans in an organised industry. So it is important to notice that after full discussion with the ablest and most practical Trades Union leaders the A.S.E. on their advice resolved to experiment with the formation of Associations, approved the scheme of the Christian Socialists, and looked out for an opportunity to act upon it.

During the same summer an occasion presented itself for the application of the principles of co-operative production upon a very much larger scale than had hitherto been attempted. The Associations, whose foundation we have already recounted, had all been formed in ill-organised trades where the work was done under domestic conditions. The great industries had been

---

[1] For an account of these two men and an estimate of their position in the Labour movement, cf. Webb, *History of Trade Unionism*, pp. 188, 189, 192, 216.

entirely untouched, and the Christian Socialists were fully aware that their new method could not be said to have proved its value until an attempt to run a big business had been essayed. Neale, who was a man used to handling money and thinking on large lines, and Ludlow, who went a long tour with Hughes through the northern counties in September 1851, were both watching the policy of the A.S.E. with interest and hope. A few months before this [1] a foundry in Liverpool, the Windsor Ironworks, had failed owing to reckless speculation during the absence of the leading partner. The property was put up for sale. The attention of the Engineers was drawn to the opportunity thus presented. William Allan, the secretary of the A.S.E., was keenly interested, and under his guidance, with the support of the Christian Socialists, it was proposed to raise sufficient capital to purchase and start the foundry, and then to carry it on upon the basis of a productive and self-governing Association.

A study of the prospectus issued by the proposed Association in September [2] reveals how great a share in the scheme was taken by the Christian Socialists. For not only are Hughes, Ludlow and Neale three out of the six trustees, [3] but the whole constitution on which it is proposed to conduct the business is plainly modelled upon the Rules for Associations contained in Tract V.,

[1] The first mention of the scheme in express terms in the *Christian Socialist* is in vol. ii. p. 105, referring to a meeting in its support on July 2nd, but the Promoters had been privately interested in it earlier than this (cf. *Christian Socialist*, ii. p. 57).

[2] Cf. *Christian Socialist*, ii. pp. 195-198. A copy of the original prospectus is in Furnivall's collection of *Tracts*, etc. in the British Museum (vol. ii. No. 8).

[3] The three others being W. Coningham, a friend of the Promoters, J. Finch, a partner in the former firm, and B. Fothergill of Manchester. The six names are in the *Christian Socialist* : in the prospectus itself Fothergill is not included.

with such modifications as practical experience had since
suggested. Details of the arrangement are as follows.
A partnership was to be formed of a few experienced
business men who should act as managers, one of them
being chosen as general manager of the whole concern.
The capital of the firm should be advanced in the form
of a loan to these managers—a special system rendered
necessary in order to limit the liability of shareholders
to the amount actually subscribed, and to avoid the
other disadvantages which made a Joint Stock Company
unsuitable for purposes of co-operation.[1] The workmen
employed were to be selected from the members of the
A.S.E., and after a probation of at least a year's continuous
service were to be eligible for selection as Associates, it
being provided that not less than forty such Associates
must be appointed within the first seven years. The
shareholders, or contributors, as it is better to call them,
were to be represented by the six trustees, approved in
the first instance by the Executive of the A.S.E. ; vacancies
among the trustees were to be filled by the vote of contributors holding not less than £5 in the stock of the
firm. These trustees, in concert with the managers,
were to select the Associates. They were also to issue an
annual report, visit the works officially twice a year,
investigate any complaints against the managers, and
generally act as directors. The managers were to resign
their position at the end of seven years, and successors,
to hold office also for seven years, were to be chosen
by the Associates with the consent of the trustees. The
profits were to be devoted to the payment of interest
at 5 per cent., to providing an unemployment fund,
to improving the condition of the Associates and other
workers employed, and to extending the business or

[1] Cf. below pp. 287-289.

forming similar establishments elsewhere : thus no part of the profits was divisible except in the shape of educational facilities and unemployment benefit. Wages were to be paid at the standard rates fixed by the A.S.E.

The prospectus was issued in September with a covering letter from the Executive Council of the A.S.E. ; and invited the public, and especially members of the Iron Trades and the co-operative movement, to subscribe towards this object by taking transferable £1 shares to be paid for in monthly instalments. Application was to be made for these to William Allan. Not less than £50,000 was estimated as required if the foundry was to be purchased and set up. The project appeared by no means hopeless and aroused interest in many quarters. But before sufficient had been subscribed to make it possible to begin operations or even to secure the Works, the great lock-out of engineers in the spring of 1852 had been started, and the whole plan fell through.

The attitude of the A.S.E. had encouraged the Christian Socialists to make a further effort to win the assistance of the Trades Societies. In the autumn of 1851 a circular was sent out to the Societies of the kingdom asking their support for the Central Co-operative Agency, a body whose creation by Neale we shall describe shortly ; and soon after a committee was appointed to follow this up. This committee consisted of five officials of the Agency, Neale, Hughes, and the three business partners, ten managers or members of existing Associations mostly from the Pimlico Builders, Stevens manager of the Pimlico store, Newton and Allan of the A.S.E., George Alexander Fleming,[1] president of the National Association of United

---

[1] Cf. Gammage, *History of the Chartist Movement*, pp. 283, 290, 380, where Fleming is accused of ' handing over the Chartist body to the middle-class Reformers ' ; and Holyoake, *History of Co-operation* ii. pp. 577-578 etc.

Trades, Thornton Hunt [1] and Richard Hart,[2] two strong supporters of co-operation, and Thomas Shorter to represent the Society of Promoters : the committee itself delegated the work to an Acting Board of eight members : and these with the trustees and partners of the Agency produced the address printed in the *Christian Socialist* [3] for 15th November, 1851. This commences with the recognition of the fact that the Trades Societies are the only bodies in England acting on behalf of the working man and in defence of the interests of Labour, and therefore ventures to urge upon them the need 'to substitute for a mere defensive organisation the application of the principle of direct association for production, distribution, and consumption.' It is then pointed out that Trades Societies, so long as their sole object is the maintenance of the price of labour at an equitable standard, are met by the master's argument that provided the workers are protected against the risk of losses they cannot expect to share in profits, that wages, and the lowest wages that men can be forced to accept, discharge the master's obligation to them : under associative methods the workers can secure for themselves the whole, or at least the greater part, of the profits, and thus maintain a rate of remuneration fairly proportionate to their efforts. Furthermore, thanks to the competitive system, the

---

[1] The eldest son of Leigh Hunt, a journalist by profession, and at this time a representative of what Maurice calls Chartist Socialism, cf. *Life of Maurice*, ii. p. 60, where Ludlow is warned against alliance with him. Cf. Gammage, *l.c.* pp. 356, 378.

[2] Cf. Gammage, *l.c.* p. 392.

[3] Vol. ii. pp. 310-312, and Le Chevalier (St. André), *Five Years*, App. pp. 21-24. The names of the Acting Board are :—W. Allan of the A.S.E., J. Douthwaite of the Central Agency, G. A. Fleming of the United Trades, R. Hart of the press, H. Jefferies of the Shoemakers, W. Newton of the A.S.E., W. Pond of the Pimlico Builders, and W. Stevens of the Pimlico Co-operative Store.

worker in his capacity of consumer is often deprived of a notable portion of his earnings by fraudulent sales of adulterated goods, and in any case has to pay for the private profits of the middlemen, profits at present multiplied beyond all reasonable need : on the principle of co-operative distribution this wastage can be avoided, and a good article secured at a fair price.

The address concludes with the following concrete proposals, which are submitted to the Societies for their consideration : that in each trade a Model Association be formed to execute orders for the goods produced by that trade, and to employ on these orders any members of the Trade Society who are out of work; that, either in each trade or by combining members of different trades locally, Co-operative Stores should be organised to supply articles of domestic consumption and raw materials for the productive Associations, and to provide a market for the products of these Associations ; that the outlay for the establishment and initial expenses of these enterprises be raised either by contributions from the funds of the Societies or by special subscriptions among their members. The Central Agency offers its assistance in supplying goods and raw material at wholesale prices, in warehousing, showing and selling the products, in advertising and collecting orders on their behalf, in providing means of exchange between the Associations, and in putting them into touch with capitalists and with customers. Finally, it is suggested that the Societies should get into contact with the Society for Promoting Working Men's Associations, though the relations between them and it are left to be settled by mutual agreement.

These proposals, which were warmly received by eulogistic articles in the two working-class papers, the

Leader and the *Northern Star*,[1] were an expression of the
settled policy of the Christian Socialists and the logical
outcome of the attitude of the A.S.E. ; and may well have
owed something to previous attempts of a similar character. In the seething activity of the time of the Reform
Bill several efforts had been made by the Owenites to
arrange a combination of Trades Unions and Co-operative
Societies for the reform of the social order. Mr. Beer
has traced the story of these in the later chapters of his
History of British Socialism : and, though they had hitherto exerted no influence upon Christian Socialism, it is
evident that now, through Fleming, Lloyd Jones, and
Newton, direct connection with them had been established.
Certainly the scheme sketched by William Thompson
in 1827, in his book, *Labour Rewarded*,[2] closely resembles
that now proposed ; and his work would have been familiar
to some members of the committee. In any case, Fleming
was certainly aware of the effort made in 1845 to establish
the National United Trades Association for the Employment of Labour, a body which aimed at providing work
for men on strike, and had the approval and support of
the National Association of United Trades. Clearly
the Christian Socialists had by this time become so well
acquainted with the world of Labour that they cannot
have been unaffected by its history or uninterested in its
literature. If their ideas were originally derived from a
French stock, they had been skilfully grafted upon a
plant of native English growth ; and this development
may be taken as proof that the fusion was complete.

As we shall see later, the sending out of this circular
and address did not commend itself to Ludlow, who
disliked the strong Chartist element on the new committee,

[1] Cf. *Christian Socialist*, ii. p. 345, and *Leader* for Nov. 15th.
[2] Pp. 87-93, cf. Beer, *l.c.* pp. 225-227.

and deplored the purely commercial grounds of the appeal as inconsistent with the professedly religious character of their movement. That he was at one with the others in desiring to extend the method of Association by means of the Trades Societies, was made plain a few months later, when the great lock-out in the engineering trade took place.

It is not within the scope of this work to enter into the details or to estimate the rights and wrongs of that famous dispute, the first industrial contest on a large scale.[1] The A.S.E., conscious of their own strength and of the possession of a fund of £25,000, had taken a vote in August, 1851, on the question of the abolition of overtime and piecework. Out of their 11,800 members only 16 had declared against abolition. A circular was consequently sent out to men and masters stating that the Society will stop overtime and piecework on December 31st. Messrs. Hibbert, Platt and Sons, a Lancashire firm, were already in trouble with their men, and the heads of thirty-four iron-works met and decided that if the men's challenge was left unanswered all discipline would be impossible. Ever since 1834 when the Grand National Consolidated Trades Union had been mooted, employers had realised the danger of a general combination. They had been watching the creation of the Amalgamated Society with the gravest concern, and had evidently determined to fight it on the earliest opportunity, and to resist any attempt at dictation. So on December 17th they issued a notice that if a strike occurred on

---

[1] This summary is mainly derived from Hughes' *Account of the Lock-out of Engineers 1851-2* (Macmillan 1860) and from the files of the press. Cf. also Webb, *History of Trade Unionism*, pp. 196-198. A copy of the employers' *Representation of the Case* dated Jan. 17th and signed by Sidney Smith their secretary is in the Ludlow tracts (vol. 1. no. 18) ; and is the document that the Christian Socialists specially attacked.

December 31st they would lock-out their employees ; an explanatory letter justifying this threat appeared in the *Times* stating that the men wanted not only the abolition of overtime and piecework, but the equalisation of wages and the employment of skilled men instead of unskilled on self-acting machines—neither of which latter statements was, in fact, true. On December 24th a mass meeting of employers rejected the A.S.E.'s proposals, and pledged itself to a general lock-out on January 10th if any strike took place on December 31st. On December 30th, at a public meeting, the leaders of the A.S.E. explained that their proposals referred only to overtime and piecework, two grievances of very long standing, and offered to submit both questions to arbitration. To this there was no response. On January 1st, men who were ordered to stay overtime after their twelve-hours day refused to do so. In consequence the employers' threat was carried out; and on January 10th the lock-out began, and thirty-six firms in Lancashire and the South of England closed their works. Nearly 12,000 unskilled and unorganised workers, as well as 3,500 Engineers,[1] were thus driven from employment.

The A.S.E. entered the fight full of confidence. The difficulty seemed a small one and easily adjustable ; and in any case they had what then appeared ample resources. But the employers had made up their minds that a stand against Trades Union dictatorship must be made, that the issue was not really the small point in dispute, but the whole question of the right of masters to control industry, and that the workers must be forced to capitulate without compromise. They agreed that no men should be admitted back to work unless they signed a declaration pledging themselves not to belong in future

---

[1] *Times*, March 1st, says that counting the unskilled an average of 20,000 had been out of work during the lock-out.

to any Trades Union—a deliberate violation of the statute of 1824 legalising combinations. The struggle went on without faltering on either side until March. Then the funds of the A.S.E. began to get exhausted. One by one the members gave way, and the works reopened. The stalwarts held out for another month, suffering acutely and being reduced to pitiable straits. But at last, by the middle of April, when the men had offered to withdraw their circular and submit to overtime and piecework if the masters would in turn withdraw their declaration, and when this offer had been rejected, resistance collapsed and the lock-out ended in a complete surrender. Faced with the choice between starvation, slavery, or perjury, the A.S.E. not unnaturally chose the last named. The declaration was signed ; the men returned to their employment ; and the A.S.E. continued to exist. From every point of view it was a miserable ending to a miserable business.

For the Christian Socialists the strike was a tremendous challenge and opportunity. Opposed as they had always been to the use of violence, realising the wastage and hardship which such a contest must involve, regretting above all the bitterness which it imported into the whole relationship of Labour to Capital, they nevertheless saw that the righteousness of the men's case was unquestionable, and, seeing it, though the Society could not well act in its corporate capacity, its members threw themselves almost unanimously into the fray.

Their first attempt to secure justice was made through Lord Ashburton who had been named by the A.S.E. as one of their arbitrators. He submitted the case to Lord Cranworth and asked for a legal opinion upon it. Here the result was a great disappointment : for the verdict, published on January 17th, was based solely upon the

Masters' statement of the facts, misrepresented and condemned the men, and contained an orthodox vindication of the doctrine of *laissez-faire*. Lord Goderich, who had been active in support of the mass meeting on January 12th, answered it in a letter to the *Times*:[1] but the group, recognising the hopelessness of outside help, fell back upon the effort to secure publicity for the claims and wrongs of the engineers.

Nowhere was the discussion of the facts and of the moral issues at stake more closely and decisively pursued than in their writings and lectures. Hughes, in the *Journal of Association*, Neale in his lecture on ' Labour and Capital,' and his fine pamphlet, ' May I not do what I will with my own ? ' and Ludlow, in three lectures ' on the relations of Capital and Labour,' delivered by request of the Society of Promoters and published with the title, *The Master Engineers and their Workmen*,[2] set out the men's case with brilliant advocacy, and tore the employers' claims to rags. Fighting against every kind of lie and insinuation, with the public press solidly supporting the masters, their efforts were attended by the very greatest difficulty. The public, to whose justice and humanity they appealed, could hardly hear their voices, even if it was not too prejudiced to listen. But to the men their support was invaluable ; and the principles that they laid down in the course of the dispute have since come to be accepted and adopted, as reflecting the righteous relationship of the partners in industry.

Nor was their task rendered the easier by the differences

---

[1] Issue of Jan. 19th.

[2] These three lectures, with two by Louis and one by Neale, were delivered on successive Friday evenings, Feb. 13th to March 20th, at the Marylebone Literary and Scientific Institution : cf. *Report*, p. 13.

of opinion which inevitably existed within the Society of Promoters. Kingsley,[1] who was busy with *Hypatia*, then appearing serially in *Fraser's*, was definitely in favour of neutrality, and wrote the pamphlet, *Who are the Friends of Order?* nominally in answer to an article on the Christian Socialists, but actually to emphasize their opposition to violent methods and to refute the belief that they were attacking the rights of property— wrote it ' as a lecture to friends as well as enemies, as a *sotto voce* hint to Louis and Ludlow no less than an open admonition to the *Times*, *Chronicle*, *Fraser*, etc.' [2] Maurice, though he was anxious for the younger men to express their views freely, was not prepared to advocate any programme himself, unless it laid stress upon the paramount duty of fellowship and the danger of making commercial success seem more important than moral right : above all he feared ' proclaiming that the war with capitalists was begun ', [3] and though his sympathies were all with the men, he often seemed to be lukewarm in his support of their fight. Louis and Furnivall were extravagant in their zest for partisanship and rejected all attempts at moderation. So it was left to the three to bear the chief part in counselling the men, in presenting their cause, and in advocating a policy for them.

This policy was association. Ludlow had written, submitted to Maurice,[4] and printed in the *Journal of Association* [5] a very powerful appeal to ' the aristocracy of the trades ' to take advantage of the present opportunity to put in force the policy which, as he reminds them, they have now been discussing for some eighteen months.

[1] *Life of Kingsley*, i. pp. 311-313. [2] So Maurice, *Life*, ii. p. 108.
[3] *Life of Maurice*, ii. p. 111. [4] *Life of Maurice*, ii. pp. 104, 105.
[5] Pp. 25, 26.

Let them ' take up the standard of Association ' and rally to their cause all the armies of co-operators and their sympathisers throughout the country. Let them organise their labour on an associative basis, use their funds in order to develop self-governing factories, and so show the masters that a great trade can produce the fruits of its own craft without their aid and as free fellow-workers together. That is the one sure way to end this interminable warfare and to build in our land ' that city of the Future of which only the practised eye can discern a gateway here, and there a bit of wall, and here a watch-tower for the seer, and there the frail huts of the builders, building as they of Jerusalem of old, with one hand only and a weapon in the other, building the temple of Brother-hood on the foundations of Righteousness, and yet accused of rebellion and sneered at for impotency by the Arabian and Ammonite without.'

He followed up this challenge in the three lectures already mentioned. In the first he states the masters' position, giving due stress to their difficulties and resent-ment at the interference with their conduct of business ; follows this up with a terrible and haunting description of the conditions under which masses of the population spend their lives (a wonderful *tour-de-force*) ; and con-cludes with a powerful defence from the standpoint of political economy of the workers' right to combine. In the second he examines the arguments for and against overtime and piecework, compares the statements issued by both sides in the dispute, and denounces with passionate indignation the action of the masters in refusing arbitra-tion and relying solely upon force. In his third he discusses the possible issues of the contest ; shows that a victory on either side would only lead to an embitterment of class-warfare and disaster to both parties ; declares that there were three ways in which the strife might be amicably settled—the recognition by the masters that their duty was ' to set up God's kingdom in their factories,' and as a step towards it to admit their workers to a share in profits, or the submission of the dispute to an impartial tribunal, or ' the absorption of the working-men into the master-class by self-employment through associative labour ' ; and suggests that if none of these ways was at present possible a truce might be made on condition that the men withdraw their circular and the masters their declaration.

Neale's pamphlet follows somewhat similar lines. He commences with a temperate statement of the principles involved in the dispute and a strong criticism of the refusal of arbitration. Then he examines the plea that a man may do what he will with his own, and shows that the claim that the establishments belong absolutely to the masters is itself unjust, since ' the results of the work arising from the union of labour and capital ought to be shared in the proportion in which each has helped to produce that work.' Finally he discusses the remedy, association, in which ' Masters shall be leaders of *men*, not employers of *hands*, shall marshall the thickly forming ranks on their advance to accomplish the task which will lie ever clearer before them as the morning opens ; the glorious task of doing the will of God on earth, by asserting in deeds and not alone in words, the brotherhood of mankind.'

Such utterances, which cannot well be condensed without giving a false impression, were powerfully supported in the *Journal* by Hughes' leading articles and by contributions from Goderich and Furnivall. All of them, despite minor differences of attitude and tone, are agreed in recommending the men to set up associative factories, and to let the A.S.E. take the lead in organising production on a co-operative basis. They believed that the fundamental change in the social order, for which they had been working, might thus be easily initiated. The full scope of their vision was clearly described by Ludlow in a paper on ' Trade Societies and Co-operative Production ' read at the Industrial Partnership's Conference at Manchester in 1867, and is precisely stated in a ' Dialogue on Co-operation ' (a·criticism of Miss Potter's book on *The Co-operative Movement in Great Britain*) published in the *Economic Review* [1] in April, 1892. He writes : ' "I want Trade-Unionism to expand into humanity and finally lose itself in it." "Do you mean then that production should be carried on by the Trade Unions ? " " That has been my ideal for the last forty years, ever since I thoroughly understood what a Trade Union was. That is what we old Christian Socialists preached to the Amalgamated Engineers in 1852." ' Equally striking as an anticipation of modern developments and as a proof that they aimed at nothing less than the eventual abolition of the whole wage-system, is a saying on an earlier page of the same article : ' The condition of the wages-receiver,' he writes, ' is not to me an ideal one for the worker. It is a sort of washed-out slavery.' But for an even more exact and significant statement of their aims we must go to the most redoubtable of their contemporary critics, W. R. Greg. In an article on the ' Progress and Hopes of Socialism ' contributed to the *Economist*,[2] after explaining the present methods of the Christian Socialists as illustrated by the Co-operative Stores and the Working Tailors of Castle Street, he adds, ' They will proceed to complete their undertaking by uniting all the Associations in each trade into one vast *guild*,

[1] Vol. ii. pp. 214-230.   [2] Reprinted in Essays, i. pp. 505-525.

governed by a central committee ; and finally by effecting
a union of these guilds into one gigantic fraternal combination, which shall be directed by delegates from all
the guilds. By this means, the whole of the industrial
arrangements of society will be revolutionised ; and the
noble, Christian, and pacific principle of concert and
co-operation will be substituted for the selfish, mischievous,
and wicked one of competition.' And Guild Socialism
was proclaimed as a new thing some sixty years later !

And if they used the lock-out as an opportunity for
preaching co-operation they used it also to put their
principles into practice. On January 6th [1] the Executive of the A.S.E. had resolved to devote £10,000 to self-
employment, and this sum was to be vested in six trustees
for the formation of Associations. The proposal was
endorsed by the votes of ninety per cent. of the members : [2]
and only the length of the lock-out made it inoperative.
The expense of the struggle from the first to last was
upwards of £40,000 actually spent in strike pay. All
the funds of the A.S.E., including the £10,000,
had been spent,[3] and if Lord Goderich had not
advanced £1000 [4] to them in the last week of the lock-out,
the Society would have become bankrupt and probably
have been dissolved. So there was no possibility of the
fulfilment of the policy which the Christian Socialists
advocated unless they were prepared to act themselves.

In this they were greatly helped by one of their
number who had not previously been specially prominent.

---

[1] *Daily News*, 10th Jan.   [2] So Newton and *Times*, 24th Jan.

[3] Their balance at Christmas '51 was £21,700, in June '52 it was
£1,700 (*Half-yearly Report*, p. 95).

[4] Webb speaks of this as a gift of £500. (*History of Trade Unionism*,
p. 197.) Possibly the remainder is the £500 entered in their balance-
sheet as ' Borrowed of a friend ' : cf. *Half-yearly Report of A.S.E.*,
p. III.

Augustus A. Vansittart, Neale's cousin, and also a man of large means, had joined the movement with him in the spring of 1850, had been put on to the Council of Promoters, and for some time had acted as its treasurer. He was a man of great intellectual gifts and a welcome addition to the group, but easy-going and hitherto by no means distinguished for enthusiasm in the cause. Yet beneath his superficial indifference and hesitation he possessed the capacity, when once he was thoroughly roused, for vigorous and self-sacrificing action. The lock-out stirred him into energy. He went among the engineers; saw how not only the members of the A.S.E., but large numbers of the unskilled and unorganised workers attached to the industry and locked-out with the rest, were suffering; realised that he had the opportunity and the power to do something for them; and after consulting Hughes as to the legal part of the enterprise, agreed to supply funds for an Association, being helped in this by an offer of £100 from another of the Promoters, William Johnson, afterwards Cory, a master at Eton College.

There was already in existence a body of men waiting for just such an offer. On January 9th[1] a meeting had been called by the Greenwich Co-operative Working Engineers' Association[2] at Blackheath, at which John Musto, one of seven brothers, of whom the eldest, Joseph, was president of the A.S.E., and Newton had spoken. Musto, whom Huber describes as a huge man 'as good as three at the anvil,' with 'an honest, intelligent face,

[1] *Daily News*, 10th Jan.

[2] This had been started before the lock-out : cf. *Christian Socialist*, ii. p. 362. Its usual title was the Deptford Ironworks Co., as its shops had been moved from Greenwich. It also had been helped by Neale. It was from this group that twenty-seven men were sent out to Australia by a loan of £1000 from Vansittart—a sum which was repaid in full : cf. *First Report*, pp. 47, 48 and *Economic Review*, iii. p. 47.

but a somewhat defiant expression,'[1] was at that time working for Easton and Amos, an engineering firm in the Borough. On January 12th he gathered his fellow employees, and induced them to form the Southwark Working Engineers' Association : they resolved to raise money by shares, to vest it in three trustees, to appoint John Laing as their manager, and to start work as soon as possible.[2] Laing seems to have refused the position : but Vansittart, who had heard of their project at a meeting in St. Martin's Hall,[3] got into touch with them, and secured for them a factory in Cambridge Road, Mile End.[4] The premises are fully described in the *Journal of Association* : the site was large, but the buildings on it had to be altered and extended. The Associates themselves began at once on the construction of machinery, and the Pimlico Builders consented to erect a chimney at the cost of materials and wages. The Trustees were Vansittart himself,[5] Lord Goderich, Hughes, and a Mr. Brigden.

At first the venture was kept somewhat secret, as Vansittart knew that his cousin had spent all that he could afford on the existing Associations. But when the purchase was completed, Neale's help was asked and a notice published on February 2nd in the *Journal*.[6] The first meeting of shareholders was held at the works on March 6th[7] to discuss the rules and elect officers

---

[1] *Reisebriefe*, ii. pp. 485, 486. See Appendix C.

[2] *Daily News*, 13th Jan. They raised £100 of their own.

[3] *Times*, 13th Jan.

[4] *Journal of Association*, p. 92. *First Report*, p. 49.

[5] Not Neale, as B. Jones, *Co-operative Production*, i. p. 135, states— a mistake due to the error in the Society's *Report*, p. 49. The story is told in full by Hughes in the *Economic Review*, iii. pp. 46, 47, and the name correctly given in *Journal of Association*, p. 45.

[6] P. 45.   [7] *Journal of Association*, p. 92.

for the Association. The Constitution was modelled upon that drafted for the Windsor Iron-works, and was adopted with a few slight alterations, the chief of these being that every Associate should subscribe £5 to the fixed capital of the Association, which he should not be able to withdraw if he left, and on which he should receive no interest. The question of limiting Associateship to members of the A.S.E. was also discussed, but the matter was not decided. Four managers were then appointed by show of hands, but the choice of a General Manager was postponed until a really first-rate candidate could be found. It was reported that orders were coming in excellently, and that all the Associates who were not already working would be employed as soon as the shops could be got ready for them.

The A.S.E. had been represented at this meeting by Newton and by the president of their executive, Joseph Musto, and expressed hearty approval of the scheme. Between forty and fifty Engineers applied for admission and twenty-two of them were set to work within the first two months from the purchase of the premises. After some quarrelling and much talk and waste of time John Musto was eventually selected as General Manager.[1]

Meanwhile, Neale had also realised that the best way to help the strikers was to give them the opportunity of helping themselves, and that, if once they adopted the method of association, the revolution for which he was working would be within measurable distance of accomplishment. The executive of the A.S.E. had already pledged themselves to take up the question of self-employment with all their energies : but although at

[1] Cf. Cogger's statement in *First Report*, p. 49 ; and list of managers, *l.c.* p. 60. The manner of his appointment is told graphically and in his own words by Huber, *Reisebriefe*, ii. p. 489

least two other Associations, at Greenwich and Walworth, had been formed,[1] in their present state of impoverishment and while the strike lasted, they could only carry out their resolution if the outlay necessary for establishing works were found for them. So, although he was already heavily involved with the existing Associations and the Central Agency, he was ready for further sacrifice should occasion arise ; and this was not long in coming.

He found a small factory,[2] the Atlas Works, in Emerson Street at the foot of Southwark Bridge, which seemed ideal for his purpose, since it was within half a mile of the central office of the A.S.E. in 25 Little Alie Street, Whitechapel, and thus could very easily be worked under their supervision, should they follow up their resolutions and take over the place. To secure the site he bought the whole business, informed the Promoters and the A.S.E. of his action, and proposed to set up there an Association closely modelled upon the scheme of the Windsor Ironworks. On March 25th the venture was actually launched. Here, also, the tools and machinery had to be made by the engineers themselves before they could start work, but they were keen and energetic, and a large number of them applied to join. Here also the officials of the A.S.E. gave their support whole-heartedly, and Neale had no reason to suppose that they would fail him.

Indeed it seemed a golden opportunity. Hitherto the Promoters had been struggling to develop their methods among the lowest classes of workers, men downtrodden and ill-educated, inexperienced in any form of combined effort and blind to the issues at stake. Now, at last, they had won the sympathy and support of the

---

[1] *Journal of Association*, p. 45.

[2] Cf. Neale's account quoted by B. Jones, *Co-operative Production*, i. p. 134.

aristocracy of Labour, men who had already been pioneers
in extending the principle of united and corporate action,
and who, thanks to the lock-out, were universally regarded
as the leaders and champions of their class. That the one
great amalgamated Union so soon after its creation
should have accepted the principle of association, and
that circumstances should have impressed upon them the
waste and evil of competition in so signal a fashion, must
have seemed to the Christian Socialists a guarantee of
speedy success. Surely the Engineers would rise superior
to the difficulties which had proved almost insuperable
to tailors and cobblers, and would show to the world the
vindication of the new system. No wonder Neale felt
that his hour had come, and that no personal risk must
prevent him from using it.

And at first the A.S.E. seemed prepared to stand by
him. On April 29th there appeared in the *Times* an
address from their Executive Council to their members
and the trades in general, reporting five resolutions which
had been adopted by them on April 22nd. The last of
these was [1] : ' that in the opinion of this meeting hostile
resistance of Labour against Capital is not calculated to
enhance the condition of the labourer. We therefore
advise that all our future operations should be directed
in promoting the system of self-employment in associative
workshops, as the best means of effectually regulating the
conditions of labour, and that this resolution be submitted
to our next delegate meeting.'

Appended to this resolution a letter,[2] signed by W. Allan
on behalf of the Executive Council and dated April 26th,
was sent to the members. This is worth quoting at length,

---

[1] Quoted in *Journal of Association*, p. 150.

[2] Quoted as its leading article with the title ' The Amalgamated
Society on Co-operation,' in *Journal of Association*, p. 153.

as it represents the official endorsement by the recognised leaders of Labour, enlightened men representing the greatest Union of skilled workers in the country, of the policy advocated by the Christian Socialists, and demonstrates how nearly they achieved their object. The letter runs as follows : ' How shall we set about the work of preparation for a coming time ? There is but one way— we must co-operate for production. The events of the last few months have directed the attention of working men to co-operation, and inclined them to it more decidedly than years of prosperous industry could have done. Perhaps a greater good is to come out of present evil than could have been in any other way brought about. We have learned that it is not sufficient to accumulate funds, that it is necessary also to use them reproductively, and if this lesson does not fail in its effects a few years will see the land studded with workshops belonging to the workers—workshops where the profits shall cheer and not oppress labour, where tyranny cannot post an abominable declaration on the gates ; where the opportunity of working is secured without the sacrifice of all that makes work dignified and honourable. Then, indeed, the artisan may successfully assert his claim to be treated as a man with thoughts and feelings instead of a machine. And if the employers, seeking to wrong him, close the gates of the factories, he will not then stand in forced idleness, consuming the accumulations of the past years, but with double energy he will turn to the factory, and there do the work of the country, without the unneeded help of others. " That is a consummation devoutly to be wished," and if we set about the task with only the same earnestness, good faith, and patience as have been brought to bear upon our past movements, it will be accomplished. . . . We must organise for the future. Assisted as we have been by the advice of men who take a deep interest in the promotion of Working Men's Associations, and have counselled the abandonment of all attempts to deal with capitalists in a spirit of hostility—and given it as their opinion that nothing but creating a new relationship between capital and labour can effectually elevate the condition of the toilers of society, we must progress in these principles, and we hope that our next delegate meeting will lay down the basis of our future permanent prosperity. Immediately on receipt of this circular each secretary is instructed to convene a meeting of the members of his branch, so that its contents may be made generally known to the members.'

It seemed a decisive lead : and when the National Association of United Trades followed it up on June 2nd by declaring that ' the time has come for the entire abandonment of strikes and turn-outs as a means of protecting labour,' and that ' the only thing left is to organise and carry out a self-supporting co-operative reproductive system of employment,'[1] the Christian Socialists could not but feel that the sufferings of the great lock-out had been the birth-pangs of the new order, and that their efforts were being visibly crowned with success. Even now it is by no means certain that they were unduly optimistic. It was a crisis in the history of social development : their cause seemed on the eve of its triumph.

[1] Quoted in *First Report*, p. 14.

CHAPTER VIII

CO-OPERATIVE DISTRIBUTION AND THE
CO-OPERATIVE MOVEMENT

WE have now to consider the part that the Christian
Socialists played in the building up and unifying of the
co-operative movement, and their attempts to combine
productive and distributive associations and so revolu-
tionise the whole industrial system of the country. The
missionary work of Cooper and Lloyd Jones was a potent
factor in establishing mutual understanding between the
local groups of co-operators, in promoting the interchange
of experience and of goods, and in paving the way for
the conferences which were already beginning to be
mooted. The *Christian Socialist* and the *Journal of
Association* exercised an even greater influence in the
same direction. But it was the energy and general-
ship of Neale which made possible this portion of their
campaign.

In June 1850 Le Chevalier, who at this time still
possessed the confidence of the Promoters and was a
member of the Council of the Society, put forward a
scheme for the formation of an establishment ' to be
called the Anti-competitive or the Co-operative Agency.' [1]
His proposal was criticised by Ludlow as being based
upon a fallacy; and in its original form was dropped.

[1] Printed in the Appendix to his book *Five Years in the Land of
Refuge*, pp. 1-6. This Appendix contains a collection of nearly all
the documents mentioned in this chapter.

But as a practical step towards developing the distributive side of their work Neale undertook, with the help of Lloyd Jones, who had had practical experience in Salford, the opening of a Co-operative Store in London. Hitherto co-operative distribution, though it had spread from its birth-place at Rochdale over the northern counties, had always ended in speedy failure when tried in the south. Neale took large premises at 76 Charlotte Street, Fitzroy Square, advanced the necessary capital for commencing business, and instituted there on October 24th the London Co-operative Stores in connection with the Society of Promoters. Lloyd Jones was appointed manager, and Le Chevalier supervisor. A prospectus was issued stating that the object of the Stores was to ' enable members of the Associations and other persons who might desire it, to obtain articles of daily use free from adulteration, of the best quality and at the lowest charge, after defraying the necessary expense of management, distribution, and providing for a reserve fund,' and that subject to these expenses all subscribers of not less than five shillings should receive back the profits upon all their purchases. Special terms were granted to members of Associations even if not subscribers. An address ' to the Wealthier Classes '[1] was written by Neale and submitted to the Promoters in which the object of the stores was said to be ' 1. To remove the opposition of interests between buyer and seller. 2. To destroy the system of petty frauds. 3. To save labour and time in distribution. 4. To facilitate the formation of Associations.' Maurice regarded this as belonging solely to the commercial side of the business, and therefore as outside the scope of the Society—a decision which Le Chevalier whose book reveals that he had no sympathy with the

[1] In *Five Years*, App. pp. 57-59.

moral and educative side of the work or with the principle of self-government by the workers, deeply resented. The address was never issued ; but during the autumn public meetings were held in various parts of London to explain the purpose of the Stores and to draw attention to their existence.

It was after their foundation that Neale brought forward his first proposal for the uniting of all the Associations with the Stores into a single body. In September he had visited Paris at the request of the Council, and while there had been much impressed by the danger of the multiplication of small Associations. At this time there were over a hundred independent groups of Associates at work there, and Berard, who acted as Neale's cicerone and was himself manager of a Tailors' Association, complained that in several trades actual rivalry existed owing to the lack of any central controlling body. On his return he not only submitted a report on what he had seen in France, but prepared and circulated to the Promoters a long and important memorandum, dated October 10th, 1850, ' On the position and prospects of the Associations.' [1] In this he drew attention to the lack of discipline and unity in the existing Associations—a lack emphasised at the moment by the quarrel among the Working Tailors ; suggested that as the number of separate establishments increased and supervision by the Council became more difficult, dis-union among Associates and rivalry between Associations would become almost inevitable unless some change were made ; and proposed that a General Union be set up with full power to control policy, receive and dis-tribute profits, settle the interchange of labour, and unite the whole movement under a single management.

[1] In *Five Years*, App. pp. 59-66.

Finally he laid stress upon the unsatisfactory state of the law, which at that time gave no recognition to Associations numbering more than twenty-five members, and therefore no protection against fraud or embezzlement, and showed that if such a Union was established advantage might be taken of the facilities provided by the Joint Stock Company's Act, under which the Associations, if incorporated into a single body, could be registered ; they would thus secure the legal status which was essential to them if they were to attract support from the wealthier classes.

In March 1851 he embodied the chief points of this memorandum in a ' Scheme for the Formation of the Working Associations into a General Union,' which was printed, circulated with a covering letter from himself among the Associations, and discussed at a special conference of Associates and Promoters held on April 23rd.[1] To this conference Neale submitted the concrete proposals which directly affected the constitution of the Associations. These were actually two, firstly, ' that the profits of all the Associations should form a common fund, some portion [2] of which should be applied to certain general purposes of common utility, another portion being appropriated to a reserve fund, as a guarantee to discharge the obligations of the Society and extend its operations, and the remainder being divided among all the Associates according to the amount of labour performed by each, the rate of profit being the same to all Associates ' ; and secondly,[3] ' that all Associates working in the same

[1] Cf. *Christian Socialist*, i. pp. 212, 213. A copy of the scheme is preserved among Furnivall's pamphlets (vol. ii. No. 4), and in the Ludlow tracts (vol. xx. No. 1).

[2] In the printed scheme these portions are to be thirds of the total. Cf. § i. 24.

[3] § i. 12.

trade should form one Association under a common management, with as many branches as may be necessary, so that they might distribute the work more equally without entering into competition with one another.' The other points, central control and legal protection, were not submitted.

The object of these proposals was plain enough. The Promoters had found that while some of the Associations, for example the Builders, were flourishing and receiving not only large allowances but large dividends from profits, others, like the Shoemakers, were scarcely solvent and had no profits at all. They felt it necessary therefore, in order to increase the remuneration and the stability of the weaker Associations, to ask the stronger ones to make this sacrifice. Further the proposal would facilitate the transference of Associates from a workshop where orders were few, to one which was short of labour, and would prevent that rivalry between Associations in the same trade which had been so disastrous in Paris. Finally, it would simplify the development of new Associations and the provision of benefits for all Associates, if the proportion of the profits devoted to these objects, instead of being kept by each Association separately, was pooled and spent for the common good of all. Some such modifications of the original scheme were inevitable as the result of twelve months' experience. The only question was whether the members of the more prosperous Associations would be willing to accept them. And it was to test this that the Promoters took the bold course of inviting discussion upon them.

The report of the speeches is an interesting comment upon the moral difficulties with which the Promoters were faced. On the whole their tone is remarkably high. Jennings of the Pimlico Builders naturally protested in the interests of his own Association ; but the other speakers all expressed readiness to fall in with the proposals. Lloyd Jones, fresh from the Co-operative Conference held on April 18th at Bury,[1] where forty-four stores had been represented, made an eloquent appeal, telling how the stores had become convinced of the need of a common centre and of concerted action, and stressing the value of a general fund especially in relation to the education of the children of Associates. Neale, in closing the debate, explained that it was not proposed to equalise allowances, and maintained that the few criticisms brought forward all dealt with matters that could be easily adjusted. The scheme was referred to the Central Board.

And there it seems to have been dropped. Although the Board resolved on June 23rd to form themselves into a General Industrial Association and thus secure a legal status, there is no record of any action being taken upon their decision, nor is it again mentioned in the *Christian Socialist*. Probably the prospect of the success of the agitation for a change in the law convinced Ludlow that at present it would be unwise to make any drastic change. Slaney's Bill was already being drafted, and if passed would give them an opportunity of recasting the whole method of their work. And the Associates were evidently not ready for any act of sacrifice at present. The Constitution of the Windsor Ironworks[2] proves how strongly the Promoters felt the value of these changes.

Neale however was not prepared to give up the attempt to federate the movement. Other plans of a more far-reaching character were already under consideration. Lloyd Jones had brought back from Bury full evidence

[1] Reported in *Christian Socialist*, i. pp. 211, 212.
[2] See above pp. 236-238.

of the desire for closer union among co-operative bodies all over the kingdom, and of the need of some central establishment which should link them together. Attempts had already been made, as we have seen, to unite the scattered efforts in a common conference ; but such meetings could only be occasional and by themselves would be impotent to free them from the danger of parochialism. Unity was one great need. And another had been revealed at the same time. The stores had no means of procuring goods wholesale except by purchasing them in the ordinary competitive market, and here they were exposed to the risks of fraud and adulteration which the *Lancet* had recently revealed, and which it was one chief purpose of co-operative supply to eliminate. So long as the movement dealt only with retail trade the difficulty was insuperable.

Neale conceived a plan for meeting these two requirements, the need for a central body to direct the movement and link together its branches, and the need for a market whence stores could rely upon obtaining unadulterated goods wholesale and on co-operative lines. Early in 1851 he drew up and circulated ' Laws for the Government of the Society for the Formation of Co-operative Stores,'[1] a proposal which, if accepted, would constitute for the distributive side of the movement a body analogous to the Society of Promoters. The scheme was not wholly followed up : but he began at once to develop the wholesale side of the business, and to raise some £9000 capital with a view to further extension. After these preliminaries he proceeded to the creation of a Central Co-operative Agency. This, though primarily concerned with wholesale supply, would serve as a point of contact for all the stores, would

[1] A copy is among Furnivall's papers, vol. i. No. 13 ; and in the Ludlow tracts, vol. xx. No. 6.

supply a market for the products of the Associations, and would thus go far towards reconciling the interests of producers and consumers, eliminating middlemen and simplifying the whole process of exchange. Its regulations had been drafted, and were quoted by Lloyd Jones in his speech at Bury, on April 18th; and they met with general approval. On May 30th a meeting of supporters of the Charlotte Street Stores was held to consider the proposal: and at it the decision was reached to wind up the retail Stores; to open their premises as a wholesale depot for the supply of goods in bulk to Branch Stores, and to such existing retail establishments as might wish to have dealings with them; and through the Agency thus constituted to develop a system of Banking and Mutual Insurance.[1] Neale himself supplied the funds for the new undertaking, and Hughes, though he could only contribute as an ordinary subscriber, became his co-trustee, the whole property being vested in the two names. Three managers were appointed as heads of the commercial firm, Le Chevalier, whose business was to supervise the sales and conduct of the depot, Joseph Woodin, an experienced and highly skilled buyer with an expert knowledge of the grocery trade, who was to make the purchases and settle all matters of quality and price, and Lloyd Jones, who was to be responsible for developing the connection of the Agency with co-operative stores throughout the country and for assisting in the formation of fresh branches for retail trade.

---

[1] A *Report* of this meeting was printed—a pamphlet of 24 pages, explaining the principles of the Agency : cf. Furnivall's papers, vol. i. No. 25, and *Five Years*, App. pp. 9-16. Copies of Neale's first sketch of the 'general establishment for the realisation of industrial reform to be called the Co-operative Agency,' and of its first circular, are in the same collection, vol. ii. No. 5 and vol. i. No. 24. An explanatory leaflet of four pages, giving the objects and constitution is in the Ludlow tracts, vol. i. No. 20.

The accounts of the partnership were to be audited half-yearly, and the profits devoted, one quarter to form a reserve fund, one quarter for bonuses to deserving employees, and the remainder to promote co-operative Associations. The trade name of the firm was Woodin, Jones and Co. Woodin, who had had a grocery business in Great Marylebone Street, had already been employed at Charlotte Street, and had represented the stores at Bury. He set himself at once to the production of a catalogue, a substantial little volume of 158 pages. In the introduction to this he commented fully on the various methods of adulteration, and described not only the frauds freely practised in the trade but also the processes employed in the correct manufacture of groceries. It is reviewed with warm praise by Ludlow in the *Journal of Association* [1] for January 10th, 1852.

By the formation of this Agency Neale definitely extended the work of the Christian Socialists to the sphere of consumption and distribution. He had acted throughout largely on his own responsibility, and though the Council of Promoters had discussed his proposals on several occasions, they had exercised no real control over his policy. This inevitably raised the question as to how far the Society, existing as it did for a specifically religious object and being careful to act only after corporate agreement, could hold itself responsible for an enterprise upon which it had hardly been consulted. Ludlow in his criticism of Le Chevalier's original scheme in June 1850 had warned the Society that to give exclusive privileges to the Agency or to adopt it as their sole executive would be ' to stake a great spiritual movement upon the working of a mere piece of

[1] Pp. 11, 12. A copy is in the Furnivall papers vol. ii. No. 20.

intellectual machinery.'[1] And six months later Neale and Ludlow had engaged in debate over the respective merits of productive and distributive co-operation in the pages of the *Christian Socialist*;[2] for Neale had criticised with some warmth an article signed with the familiar ' J.T.' on ' Working Associations and Co-operative Stores,' and Ludlow had defended himself, without bitterness but in such fashion as to reveal the gulf between them.

So when the Agency was founded, although the Council of Promoters and the Central Board passed resolutions [3] expressing formal approbation, it was evident that the relationship between the two bodies would have to be fully discussed.

A further aggravation of the point at issue was created by the address already mentioned,[4] sent out by the Agency to the Trades Societies of the kingdom and inviting them to support it as ' a legal and financial institution for aiding the formation of Stores and Associations, for buying and selling on their behalf, and ultimately for organising credit and exchange between them.' The Promoters had not been consulted about the compilation of this document, and Ludlow, when he returned from his tour in the north in October 1851, criticised it as a barefaced appeal to the commercial instincts and as false to the moral principle of their movement. A complete rupture between the Society and the Agency was even suggested, though this would have meant the retirement of

[1] In *Five Years*, Appendix, p. 8.

[2] Vol. i. pp. 241, 242 ; 261-263 ; 266, 267.

[3] On June 12th and Aug. 18th. The Council added to theirs a recommendation that the Agency should endeavour ' permanently to associate with themselves those whom they may employ in the business ' —a proposal that was never carried out.

[4] See above pp. 238-242.

Neale and Hughes and the abandonment of the Central Office, which ever since the opening of the Charlotte Street premises had been located there.   At the critical meeting of the Council on November 6th Ludlow, who had formally raised the question of the relationship between the two bodies, was not able to be present.   Instead he wrote a letter to Maurice as chairman, urging severance from the Agency and insinuating pretty definitely that Neale's views were such as to make further efforts to work with him difficult and compromising.   Maurice on his own initiative suppressed the letter; but insisted that it must be publicly declared that the Society was distinct from the Agency and was not responsible for any of its acts nor pledged in any way to support it.   Neale and Hughes accepted the position and consented to remain on the Council, Neale even requesting Maurice to take sole control of all the Society's publications so as to ensure their definitely Christian character.[1]   This Maurice refused, and after the meeting sent a full account of his action to Ludlow,[2] pointing out that the decision secured all that his letter had aimed at, namely complete independence for the Society, and had avoided the injury to the cause which any schism would have inflicted.   He concluded by appealing to him to continue his work, ' that the dividing, warring, godless tendencies in each of our hearts which are keeping us apart and making association impossible may be kept down and extirpated.'   ' We cannot,' he adds, ' be Christian Socialists on any other terms.'   Ludlow accepted the rebuke loyally, and the danger of a split was at an end.   Maurice himself developed his own point of view in the last of the *Tracts on Christian Socialism* (Number

[1] So he said.   He recognised that Maurice would favour breadth and inclusiveness more readily than Ludlow.

[2] *Life of Maurice*, ii. pp. 76, 77.

VIII), entitled *A clergyman's answer to the question 'On what grounds can you associate with men generally ?'* published in November, but written before the final meeting to serve as the basis and explanation of his attitude.[1]

This meeting of the Council had left it to Maurice's sole discretion to define the grounds on which the difference between Society and Agency was based. And this he proceeded to do in a leaflet circulated early in December and referred to in the number of the *Christian Socialist* published on the 5th of that month.[2] In it he comments upon the existing confusion as to the relationship of the two bodies and explains it by saying that the Society is definitely concerned with the application of Christianity to trade and industry; that the Agency is in fact doing this very thing in a practical way, its two trustees being ordinary members of the Council of Promoters, and two of its partners, Le Chevalier and Lloyd Jones, extraordinary members of the same body; that nevertheless, since the Agency does not have the same specifically religious purpose of teaching men their relations to each other, which is the main and characteristic work of the Society, the two bodies must each be free to use their own best methods for attaining their objects. As a practical evidence of their distinctness, he suggests that it is necessary to arrange for the removal of the Central Office of the Society, which has hitherto occupied rooms at Charlotte Street, to some independent position.

This suggestion was promptly followed up by the proposal to open a Co-operative Bazaar in some suitable thoroughfare, to which the office could be transferred,

---

[1] Cf. *Life of Maurice*, ii. p. 88. (Letter to Hare enclosing this tract.)

[2] Vol. ii. pp. 362, 363. A copy of the original leaflet is amongst Furnivall's papers (vol. ii. No. 5).

and where the goods manufactured by the Associations could be exhibited and sold. The scheme was never carried out, largely on the ground of its cost, though an elaborate plan for it was drawn up and printed in the *Christian Socialist* :[1] but the question was not allowed to drop. On February 5th, 1852,[2] Penrose, the architect, an original member of the Council, got out plans for the construction of a large hall to seat three hundred, and of offices for the Society, under the workshops of the Tailors' Association at 34 Castle Street. The cost was £229, raised by shares repayable with 5 per cent. interest out of the subscriptions of the Society, and the work was entrusted to the North London Working Builders.[3] This hall was first used by the conference of Co-operative Societies held on July 26th,[4] and afterwards played a very important part in the educational work of the Christian Socialists.

When the project for a bazaar failed, the Central Agency made new and special arrangements for the storing and sale of goods produced by the Associations ; and indeed it was by now in a strong position to do so. During the first year of its existence its success had been remarkable. Two branch Stores in direct connection with it had been founded, and, though one of these, opened at 18 Newnham Street, Edgware Road, in April 1851, was the victim of ' internal quarrels '[5] and had to be wound up after one year,[6] the other, at 13 Swan Street, Manchester, was started as early

[1] Vol. ii. pp. 373-376.

[2] *Journal of Association*, p. 52.   [3] *Journal of Association*, p. 122.

[4] *Journal of Association*, p. 213.

[5] *Christian Socialist*, i. pp. 198, 244.

[6] *Journal of Association*, p. 143. This Marylebone Store had been transferred soon after its formation to 35 Great Marylebone Street, which had been Woodin's private shop. It was closed largely because he was drawn into the work of the Agency and could give it no supervision.

as December 1850 and flourished exceedingly. This latter had as its manager William Stork of Salford, an enthusiast for co-operation: it was for most of the year the head-quarters of Lloyd Jones and served as the northern agent for the wholesale business, and as a rallying point for co-operative stores throughout Lancashire.[1] The reports of the Agency's trade in the *Journal of Association* show that by the spring of 1852 an average of fifteen stores a week were sending orders for goods to Charlotte Street.

In March of this year Le Chevalier, who had admitted that the failure of the London Co-operative Stores had been largely due to his incompetent supervision, resigned his post as a partner, and left the Society.[2] He had written a lengthy letter to the Trustees,[3] criticising the conduct of the Agency, proposing drastic reforms, and suggesting his own resignation if these were not carried out—a suggestion which they accepted with alacrity. His statement of his motives, in this letter and in his book, makes it appear that the Promoters had disapproved of his share in the sending of the address to the Trades' Societies, and that in addition he had been continually thwarted in his work as manager of the Agency by Neale's interference and neglect. But the fact that he had already incurred a debt of £600 to Neale, when added to the ' incompatibilité d'humeur,' as Huber

---

[1] Ludlow, realising the difficulty of the northern stores in procuring their wholesale goods from London, urged that this be made a wholesale depot : cf. *Christian Socialist*, ii. p. 251. A plan for this had already been drawn up by Lloyd Jones, and is printed in Redfern, *Story of the C.W.S.*, pp. 405, 406.

[2] His name still appears in the list of the Council in the *First Report*, and he remained nominally an extraordinary member until November : cf. his final letter to Shorter, *Five Years*, App. pp. 32-34.

[3] Printed in Appendix, pp. 24-29, to his book, *Five Years in the Land of Refuge.*

calls it,[1] between him and the Christian Socialists, warns us to accept his apology with reserve. His subsequent conduct justifies Maurice's description of him as a ' clever sharper.' In June 1852 he issued an address ' to the Clergy and Laity,' full of professions of attachment to the Tractarians. This brought him into touch with the Rev. Charles Marriott, of Oriel, from whom he received support and financial aid. At the same time he put forward schemes for a Board of Supply and Demand and for a Consumers' Protection Society ; and these led to the formation in December of the Universal Supply and Demand Establishment at 159 Fenchurch Street. This rival to the Central Agency did not succeed in obtaining much custom, and seems to have been dissolved after a meeting of its patrons on April 27th 1855.[2]

Meanwhile Lloyd Jones was recalled from Manchester to undertake the selling department of the Agency. His coming was the signal for a notable, though, as events showed, probably a premature, development. In May [3] it was announced that the Charlotte Street premises had become too small for the business, if it was to meet the demands upon it satisfactorily. To secure purity in the pre-paration of many articles, such as coffee, cocoa, and spices, it was essential that they should be ground and mixed on the spot ; and there were other supplies, pickles and sauces for example, which the Agency ought to manufacture itself if it was to guarantee their quality. To do this there was need of space for the installation of steam power and the employment of a large staff. So the Agency proposed to secure a bigger establishment and was already making

---

[1] *Reisebriefe*, ii. p. 169.

[2] *Guardian*, 2nd May, and Holyoake, *History of Co-operation*, ii. pp. 389, 390.

[3] *Journal of Association*, pp. 157, 188, 189.

enquiries with this object. At first their efforts were unsuccessful, but after at least one disappointment a fine block of buildings, comprising showrooms, factory and warehouse, was obtained at 356 Oxford Street. The business was transferred thither in the spring of 1853, figuring in the *London Directory* as ' Woodin and Jones, wholesale and retail grocers.'

The influence of this Central Agency upon the history of the co-operative movement can hardly be overestimated. Not only was it the direct forerunner of the great Wholesale Societies of the present day, but it served to give a sense of unity and solidarity to co-operators everywhere, to co-ordinate the existing efforts by supplying them with a source from which they could receive help and advice, and to stimulate the spread of co-operative ideals and the formation of co-operative societies throughout the country. Neale himself, with his unfailing interest and lavish expenditure of time and money, was able to act as ' friend in need ' on the innumerable occasions in which he was summoned to investigate difficulties, formulate policy, and assist fresh developments. And it was the Agency which gave him his position and opportunities.

Before we consider the legislative changes which made the summer of 1852 an epoch in the history of co-operation and of Christian Socialism, there remain three further developments of some importance to be noted. They are significant of the great strides which the movement was making at this time.

On January 16th, 1852,[1] a meeting had been convened at the chambers of William Coningham to consider the foundation of a Co-operative League. Coningham, who lived in Brighton, where he was afterwards for a time Member of Parliament, had been a good friend of the

[1] *Journal of Association,* p. 46.

Christian Socialists, and had delivered the lecture for them at the monthly meeting of the Society in July 1851, his subject then being ' the Co-operative Associations in Paris.' The objects of the Co-operative League were to promote inter-communication between all those interested in the principles of association, to form a centre for the diffusion of knowledge, to collect all books and documents bearing on the subject, and to get into touch with the co-operative societies throughout the country. Thus it aimed at doing directly what Neale and the Agency had already to some extent done. Several of the Christian Socialists threw themselves heartily into the scheme, and at its first public gathering on March 30th [1] Neale read a paper on the aims and purpose of the League to a large and sympathetic audience. In May the first number of its *Transactions* appeared containing an extended statement of its objects, its constitution and a digest of its doings. Other volumes containing articles, lectures, and reports followed, three of these being preserved in Ludlow's collection of pamphlets.[2] The League served a useful end in arousing public interest and providing a source of expert information.

' In the second place we must refer to the proposal put forward at the end of June 1852 to establish a Co-operative Investment Society. The plan on which this was to be founded was printed in the closing number of the *Journal of Association*,[3] which also contains a long extract from its prospectus. In brief, its aim was to receive deposits from individuals or from Trade and Benefit Societies, and

[1] *Journal of Association*, p. 157.

[2] Vol. i. Nos. 21, 22, 23. In the issue for Oct. 1852 is the report of a lecture given to the League by Robert Owen on ' the Science of Society.' The officers of the League were—President, W. Coningham ; Librarian, Thornton Hunt ; Secretary, E. V. Neale.

[3] Pp. 215, 216. Reference is also made to it at some length in the *Report*.

to make advances after the method of a Building Society to bodies of working men in need of capital for the development of co-operative efforts. It was to be formed under the Joint Stock Companies' Act with a capital of £100,000 invested in the names of trustees, and was to be run in connection with the Central Co-operative Agency. It was further proposed to establish a bank for co-operative societies with which the Investment Society would be in close relationship.

This project seems never to have been carried out, but is interesting as an example of the versatility and anticipation of later progress among the Christian Socialists. We may note that the matter of co-operative banking and investments was taken up at the Congress of 1869, the first of the present series, and has figured largely in discussions of the movement ever since. This proposal in 1852 seems to be the first attempt to deal with the subject.

The third, and in its culminating event the most important, development was directly the work of the Society of Promoters. In the early days of the movement the direction of future progress had been determined and the opportunity for action had arisen out of the holding of open conferences between members of the group and representative working men at the Cranbourne Coffee Tavern and elsewhere. After the foundation of the Society and its Associations, these open meetings had been discontinued ; and in their place had been held conferences and lectures limited to members and their friends, at which subjects definitely connected with their enterprise could be discussed with greater freedom than would have been possible in public. This had led to complaints from persons outside the Society ; and the members soon felt that further discussion, if restricted to those who were actively engaged in co-operation, was becoming unprofitable. For a time no meetings at all were held. Then recognising the need for educative work and the value of external criticism of their methods, they determined to resume the holding of public debates. The Castle Street premises offered a suitable room and the new Hall was already being constructed. So on March 10th, 1852,[1] the first of the new series was held, a programme was discussed, a committee appointed, and Shorter asked to act as secretary. They were continued fortnightly, and were from the first well-attended and full of interest. Several prominent socialists and reformers visited them and spoke, among these being Bronterre O'Brien,[2] the ablest leader of Chartism and for some time editor of the *Poor Man's Guardian*, one of the first unstamped newspapers. These meetings paved the way for a still larger effort in the same direction.

This was nothing less than the gathering together of co-operators from all quarters in a general conference. Local meetings of members of various co-operative societies had been held, as was only natural, for some years. But since the abandonment of the Owenite 'Congresses' no serious attempt had been made to constitute a representative body for the guidance of the whole movement. The first step in this direction was taken in June 1851, when at a conference of Lancashire and Yorkshire societies it was resolved that Lloyd Jones and four others representing the movement in the North should be appointed a committee to draw up rules for the help and unifying of local stores and associations. The Society of Promoters were fully aware of the need for some closer connection and of the dangers of parochialism ; and in the columns

[1] *Journal of Association*, pp. 73, 74.
[2] Cf. Beer, *History of British Socialism*, pp. 285, 304, 336-8.

of the *Christian Socialist* the formation of a Co-operative Union had been definitely suggested. But it was not until the passing of Slaney's Act that an opportunity arose for putting this proposal into effect. Then the matter was raised at a meeting of the Council, and it was recommended that ' a Conference of delegates from all bodies engaged in practical co-operation, whether as respects production or distribution, throughout the kingdom be summoned to determine the best mode of carrying on their work with reference to the Industrial and Provident Societies Act,' and to attend a festival.[1] On June 17th a special committee met to settle the arrangements and draw up the programme, and a series of resolutions was passed by them and submitted to the Council.

The Conference met on July 26th and 27th in the Hall of the Society at Castle Street. Delegates had been invited to attend from all known co-operative bodies, their number being fixed in proportion to the size of the society that they represented, though those unable to send a member were allowed to select a proxy. Twenty-eight different bodies were represented by the twenty-five delegates ; Banbury, Bradford, Halifax, Liverpool, Manchester, Portsea, Southampton and Ullesthorpe sending representatives from their own members, while proxies were chosen by societies in Edinburgh, Galashiels and Norwich. A large number of letters of apology are printed in the *Report* of the Conference [2] ; and in nearly all of these the cost of travel is alleged as the reason for non-attendance : the stronghold of the movement was in the North, most of the societies were young and poor, and several seem to have abstained from dislike of the Promoters. A full account of the proceedings and speeches at the various sessions

[1] *Journal of Association*, p. 204.
[2] Appendix C.

and at the Festival is given in the *First Report*.[1] Henry Smith of Liverpool [2] was voted to the chair ; and the first business, the delivery of reports by the delegates, occupied a large part of the first day. These being finished the question of enrolment under the recent Act was raised by Hughes, who gave an account of its scope and value. After considerable, but rather ill-informed, debate various other important questions were raised and discussed. Among these were the following : the consideration of the steps to be taken for giving unity and power to the movement, and the suggestion that this might be effected by the foundation of a Co-operative Friendly Society ; the desirability of capitalising a portion of the profits of Associations and of applying some of them to the creation of a provident sinking fund ; the adoption of a universal code of rules ; the establishment of a newspaper as the official organ of co-operators—this last being the more urgent in view of the recent disappearance of the *Journal of Association*. An Executive Committee [3] was appointed to deal with these matters and especially to arrange that a similar meeting be held every year, Manchester being chosen as the place for the Conference of 1853.

The Festival, held on the first evening, represented both a welcome to the Conference and the anniversary gathering of the Society. In 1851 this gathering had been held at St. Martin's Hall, and the guests had numbered

[1] The *Proceedings* occupy pp. 37-73, the *Appendices* (names of delegates, reports of societies, etc.) pp. 75-105.

[2] He was secretary of the Liverpool Tailors' Institute (cf. *Christian Socialist*, ii. pp. 109-111), and had been a Chartist (Gammage, *Chartist Movement*, p. 301).

[3] The names were—Lord Goderich, Hansard, Neale, Ludlow, Newton, Pickard, Hughes, Woodin and Cooper, with a number of representatives of provincial bodies as corresponding members. Ludlow withdrew on the ground that neither the committee nor the Conference adequately represented the whole movement. Furnivall was chosen in his place.

three hundred : now their own Hall was used, and the numbers were nearly twice as great. Nor was this the only change. Visitors, who had been present on the previous occasion, could hardly believe that these highly prosperous and well-dressed families were the same Associates that they had met before. The proceedings opened with a ' high tea ' in two relays : then Maurice was presented with a silver inkstand, a gold pen, and a testimonial signed by working-men : after which there were many speeches, concluding with one in English from Louis Blanc.[1] The Tailors' Association finished the evening with a dance.

The warm regard for the Christian Socialists felt by co-operators everywhere was plainly expressed in the Conference's first resolution. By it the Council of the Society for Promoting Working Men's Associations (to give it its original title for the last time) was asked to prepare a statement explaining to all co-operative societies the advantages which they would secure by registering themselves under the new Act. During the vacation this resolution was acted upon, and in September 1852 the required memorandum was duly issued and circulated. With it appeared also a copy of the *Model Rules for Industrial Societies*, as necessitated by the Act ; and these had also been drafted by the Council. They were approved by the Registrar, J. Tidd Pratt, on September 16th. A somewhat similar series for Co-operative Provident Societies was drawn up by them shortly afterwards and was approved on February 1st, 1853.

Under these the various co-operative bodies, which had been hitherto struggling against great legal disadvantages, were enabled to register themselves ; and the

---

[1] *Report*, pp. 63, 64. A delightful account of the Festival, presentation and speeches is given in *Life of Octavia Hill*, pp. 24, 25.

whole movement was at last put upon a secure basis, with the Christian Socialists as its recognised leaders and friends.

The holding of this conference may indeed be reckoned as the culminating event in their efforts on behalf of co-operation. The group, as the list [1] prefixed to the *First Report* proves, had increased in numbers and influence : Henry J. Hose, at this time mathematical master at Westminster School, who was soon afterwards ordained and eventually went out to Australia,[2] and Alfred H. Louis, a law-student at Lincoln's Inn, were enthusiastic in the cause : a number of wealthy supporters had also been attracted to them, including Lord Ashburton, who had joined them since the publication of the *Christian Socialist*, but not avowedly, and whom they therefore called ' Nicodemus,' Charles Buxton, the Hon. William Cowper, afterwards Cowper-Temple, and W. Powell : and they had enlisted the help of sympathisers all over the country, both young men like Charles Kegan Paul, who had been under Kingsley's influence since 1849 and as curate of Bloxham had written lengthy reports on the Banbury Plush-weavers to the *Journal of Association*,[3] and veterans like the Free Church minister Thomas G. Lee of Pendleton, who had welcomed Maurice and the deputation in Manchester in 1851 and had been their champion in the north ever since. And their achievements had been worthy of their growth. It was due to them that the Act, of whose scope and utility we shall speak in the next chapter, and which has not unfairly been called the ' Magna Charta ' of

[1] Reprinted in Appendix B, pp. 378, 379.

[2] He published a volume of sermons at Sydney in 1861.

[3] Pp. 41-3, 216. For his connection with Kingsley and the group, see his *Memories*, pp. 157-165.

organised Labour, had been proposed, drafted and passed
into law : it was due to them that a gathering of those
for whose benefit the Act was designed, could meet
together in council to consider its application to their
various needs. The double event was indeed a
magnificent achievement, a triumph beside which all the
difficulties and disappointments of their task sink into
insignificance. Before we come to consider the dis-
tractions which befell them and the country soon afterwards, and inevitably diverted their attention, before we
treat of what is commonly called their failure, it is well
to emphasise the measure of their success. Five years
before, the Church and respectable people generally had
been indifferent, if not hostile, to social reform : co-
operation had been practised only by a few gallant, but
wholly insignificant, groups of working men, and to champion it was to be regarded as a crank and an outcast :
all the forces of religion and politics were arrayed against
it : and the movement itself seemed condemned to suppression and failure. Three years before, when the first
Association was started, it seemed that one more spasmodic
effort in a hopeless cause was being made : how could
a few young barristers of no special influence, a couple of
unimportant parsons, and a handful of other oddities,
achieve anything but a fiasco ! Co-operation, where it
existed at all, was confined to a few tiny and disconnected
societies hampered by lack of legal status, unrecognised
by the press,[1] unknown to the public, and where known,
suspected. Even during the three years, it had often
seemed as if the cause was inevitably doomed. Working

---

[1] Huber, *Reisebriefe*, ii. pp. 164, 165, admirably summarises it :
' The Conservative press confined itself to reminiscences of the older
socialist systems ; the Liberal remained true to its god, Mammon ;
the Radical took no interest in a movement subversive neither of
religion nor of society nor of the constitution.'

empirically on material collected at random and frequently unsuited to their purpose, working against every kind of opposition so soon as their doings became noised abroad, working with an intensity to which the last four chapters give abundant testimony, and yet without seeming to do more than barely overthrow the obstacles that sprang up hydra-headed in their path, they yet in these three years managed to win the confidence and support of the leaders of Labour, to lay the foundations for the unity of the whole co-operative movement, to extend the knowledge of its principles throughout the industrial world, to promote the foundation of new centres in all quarters of the country, to force the subject upon the attention of the educated classes,[1] to compel the legislature not only to recognise its existence, but to accept and sanction a measure drafted by themselves, and so to establish on an impregnable foundation this great outpost of social progress.

Had they been able to carry on peacefully and without interruption the schemes which they had now set on foot, their history, and with it the relation of Christianity to modern industrialism and democracy, might have been profoundly changed. As it was, their whole effort, so nobly planned and so energetically and successfully carried on, has seemed to the unsympathetic and the unseeing to have ended in collapse and disaster. But if all their labours had been abandoned in 1852, they would still have accomplished a result of larger scope and more abiding fruitfulness than any other group of constructive reformers have effected in a similar time in the history of our country.

[1] The Oxford Union Society had a debate on the principles of Christian Socialism in June 1852 : cf. report in the *Leader*, p. 558 (issue of June 12th).

CHAPTER IX

THE INDUSTRIAL AND PROVIDENT SOCIETIES
ACT, 1852

HITHERTO we have dealt solely with the efforts of the
Christian Socialists to develop their work in face of the
difficulties raised by the attitude of the government
and the state of the law. These difficulties have been
repeatedly indicated, and we have seen in our account of
their constitution [1] the elaborate devices, by which
it was endeavoured to circumvent them. But the legal
members of the Council of Promoters by no means confined
their activities to the attempt to adapt themselves to a
position that was in many respects entirely unsatisfactory ; and it was in their efforts to induce the government to modify its own industrial policy that some of their
most valuable results were accomplished.

The grievances were two-fold. In the first place the
system of contracts adopted in all departments of the
administration was calculated to promote all the worst
evils of competition. In the second the state of the law
with regard to co-operation was such as to deprive the
Associations of all protection against fraud, and indeed
of all legal recognition, except on conditions which were
practically prohibitive.

It has always been complained, and generally with
entire justice, that Government is a bad employer of

[1] See above pp. 193, 194.

labour. Public contracts at this time certainly deserved all the abuse which the fiercest critic of our national methods could direct upon them. As soon as the Christian Socialists got into touch with the journeymen tailors, they discovered that the most iniquitous cases of sweating were those of the workers employed in the making of uniforms for the army, police, postmen, and convicts. Kingsley, in *Cheap Clothes and Nasty*, had reported the substance of the tailors' indictment, of their proof that Government had itself been the originator and was still the chief supporter of the ' slop-system,' and of the evidence of its refusal to interfere even when the terrible consequences of such refusal were demonstrated. Indeed, the method in force in the army was monstrous enough to recall the worst days of Horace Walpole in its bare-faced corruption. Commanding officers were allowed to receive a fixed sum for the clothing of each man in their unit, and then to contract privately, subject to no conditions and no supervision, for its supply, putting into their own pockets whatever they could save over the transaction. No wonder that Ludlow, who had exposed this enormity in his article on ' Labour and the Poor,' wrote of it with righteous indignation. Even the very contractors felt the shame of it ; and the official reply to the petition of William Shaw,[1] one of their number, is among the evidence in Kingsley's pamphlet. As an example of *laissez-faire*, nothing could be more logically correct—and nothing more damning : ' I am commanded by their lordships to inform you that they have no control whatever over the wages paid for making up contract clothing. Their duty is to take care that the articles

[1] A copy of Shaw's heroic protest, a substantial document of 40 pages, is preserved among Ludlow's pamphlets in the Goldsmiths' Library, vol. i. No. 5.

supplied are of good quality, and well made : the cost of the material and the workmanship are matters which rest with the contractor. . . . The men's wages depend upon the amount of competition for employment amongst themselves.'

Against such an attitude deliberately adopted in face of the courageous criticism of one of their own contractors, it might seem hopeless for the Christian Socialists to interfere. Vested interests and long-established customs, ' clothing colonels ' and Chancellors of the Exchequer, were powerful antagonists. Nevertheless, after their first efforts in the winter of 1850, they did not let the matter drop. In the following year the prospect of a surplus revenue gave Ludlow an opportunity, and in two leading articles of the *Christian Socialist*[1] he devoted all the power of his pen, all his gifts of irony and sarcasm, to make the best use of it. He tells once more, and with an eloquence as noble as Kingsley's own, the tale of wanton and senseless cruelty. Government, by taking contracts at the lowest tender, is depressing wages in all the trades concerned below ' living prices ' ; and by doing so it is not even saving money. Men are starved : there is the expense of an inquest and a pauper's burial. Women are driven to harlotry : night police are paid to ' move them on.' Men and women alike are reduced to beggary : charitable institutions, workhouses, poor-relief are more costly than a living wage. They are driven to crime— starvation knows no law : law courts, judges, penitentiaries, hulks, penal colonies, the hangman, are these cheap ? ' Does it need any further proof that a Government Contract System which fosters starvation wages must be the stupidest as well as the wickedest thing ever devised by human knavery ? ' And the remedy is so

[1] Vol. i. pp. 129, 137.

simple. 'Surely it can be ascertained without much trouble what are "living wages" for any particular employment. Let the payment of such living wages, as a minimum to the actual worker, and if thought necessary, the non-employment of middlemen (although this would probably follow of necessity from the other) be made *conditions of the contract*, with a direct appeal to some Government Board or officer in case of its being infringed.' Then he quotes the objections of the advocates of *laissez-faire*, invites them ' to consider a little before braying any louder,' answers their difficulties, and concludes by inviting all who agree with him to ' unite in petitioning Parliament for a thorough reform of the Government Contract System, so as to secure "living wages" to all workpeople employed under it.'

A petition was in consequence drawn up embodying the conclusions of these articles, and signatures were invited in March 1851. The form is printed in the *Christian Socialist*, and readers were asked to copy it, get it signed as widely as possible, and send it to their Members of Parliament. In this, as in so many of their proposals, they seem to have been pioneers : but despite their efforts the days of ' fair wage clauses' were still far off.

In the other and even more important matter of the legal disabilities of Co-operative Societies and Associations they were much more successful, and conferred one of their greatest benefits upon the community.

At the commencement of their work the position of the law in regard to such bodies as they wished to establish was as follows.[1] The Friendly Societies' Act of 1834 had provided that any society established for a purpose not

---

[1] An excellent summary of the legal position is contained in the *Explanatory Statement* on the Act of 1852 drawn up by the Promoters, a copy of which is preserved among Furnivall's papers in the British Museum (vol. ii. No. 1).

otherwise illegal could register and obtain legal sanction in the name of its trustees. Trading societies were thus put on a level with ordinary Friendly Societies, and the position was satisfactory enough. But in the Friendly Societies' Acts of 1846 and 1850 all bodies other than Friendly Societies were excluded from the advantages of the Act unless they came under the Frugal Investment Clause, by which funds could be used for the supply of food and clothing to members, submitted their rules to the Registrar, and had them certified by him as legal. To obtain this certificate and the subsequent registration thus became a serious business for bodies of working men who had small resources and no influence. And even when they were registered the privileges obtained were quite inadequate to their needs : for though they could hold personal property they could only do so through trustees, while real property could not be held legally by them at all. To avoid this *impasse* it was necessary for them to convey real property absolutely to their trustees, upon whose honesty they thus became entirely dependent. Furthermore, a registered society existed in the eye of the law solely for the benefit of its own members, and thus was forbidden to have dealings with the outside public, or at least to secure any protection for such dealings. Indeed, if it were admitted that the society intended to engage in general trading, registration would be refused. Thus, although Co-operative Stores, existing only to supply goods to their own members, could secure a measure of protection, the Associations could only do so if they confined their production to the provision of what their own members could consume ; and for them the Act was useless.

There remained, therefore, no possibility of covering their proceedings under the Friendly Societies' Act, and they had to fall back upon the provisions of the ordinary company law, as it had stood since the passing of the Joint Stock Companies' Act in 1844. And here there were also serious obstacles to contend with. The *First Report* of the Society of Promoters summarises concisely the dilemma in which they found themselves : ' If the number of members were less than twenty-five, they were all partners ; consequently, under the law as it then stood, every individual member had power to pledge the credit of the society, and might have made away with the common stock ; while the only remedy against such dishonesty was a suit in Chancery. If the Association numbered more than twenty-five, it placed itself outside the pale of legal protection, unless it chose to register under the Joint Stock Companies' Act, the provisions of which, being wholly framed for bodies of persons subscribing capital merely and not labour, were totally inapplicable, and too expensive in any case to be of use.' The former alternative obviously raised insuperable difficulties, exposing the whole undertaking to the danger of ruin at the hands of any dishonest member. The latter was open to almost prohibitive objections ; for the regulations which had to be complied with before a joint-stock company could be registered, laid down that there must be three directors, that the exact amount of money to be raised must be specified, and that the capital must be divided into transferable shares. For the Associations this last clause was fatal : for its acceptance would have exposed them to the risk of having their shares bought up by persons who had no interest in the work, and of thus being reduced to the level of an ordinary trading firm. We have seen how real this danger was in the actual history of the Associations [1] : the Pimlico

[1] Cf. above pp. 206, 207.

Builders especially were anxious to bring in as Associates men not actually taking part in the trade ; and Ludlow had been obliged to warn them that this policy, if persisted in, would destroy the whole principle of the self-governing collective mastership.

The first protest against this state of affairs came from Leeds, at the instigation of the Redemption Society. A public meeting was held, and a deputation sent to the Home Secretary to urge the necessity of altering the law. But they were not successful in winning support from other co-operators, and though he received them on May 4th, 1848, and gave them a sympathetic reply, no action was taken.

The Christian Socialists were in a better position to exert pressure. They were in touch not only with leading lawyers, but with Members of Parliament ; Ludlow had already assisted Bellenden Ker in the drafting and revision of the Joint-Stock Companies' Winding-up Acts of 1848 and 1849 ; [1] and as soon as they undertook the promotion of associative production they began to move for a modification of the law, their object being to get the machinery of the Friendly Societies' Act extended to cover Working Men's Associations.

At this stage Hughes got into touch with Robert Aglionby Slaney, a gentleman upon whose name as the promoter of Slaney's Act Christian Socialism has conferred an undeserved immortality. He was an unattached M.P., and already known as having counte- nanced several impracticable schemes.[2] Huber describes him as a man ready to accept any 'parliamentary *cheval de bataille*' that would carry him into public life.[3] So, although he was completely ignorant of the subject, he

---

[1] So he states at the opening of his first book upon them.

[2] Brentano, *Chr.-soz. Bewegung*, p. 50.   [3] *Reisebriefe*, ii. p. 162.

undertook without hesitation to become its champion. The group supplied him with facts and coached him carefully : and in the spring of 1850 he moved for the appointment of a Select Committee of the House to report upon ' Investments for the Savings of the Middle and Working Classes.' A Committee [1] was established with this object and conducted an enquiry into the subject forthwith. The first witness to be examined was Ludlow, and his evidence covered practically the whole ground. At the outset he was met by a cleavage of opinion in the Committee on the subject of limited or unlimited liability, a cleavage which manifested itself throughout their proceedings and involved them in much waste of time. On this his own evidence was clear enough ; ' in any numerous partnership you want absolutely limited liability.' As to the Associations, he pointed out the difficulties arising out of the Joint Stock Companies' Acts, and urged that provisions analogous to those of the Friendly Societies' Act, with powers to associate in unlimited numbers, to trade for the benefit of members, to receive the rights of easy registration, summary jurisdiction, and arbitration, to sue and be sued, to choose a manager who need not be a trustee, to receive loans and to invest their funds in their own trade, should be bestowed upon them. He illustrated his remarks by reference to the Castle Street Tailors and to his experiences in Paris. He emphasised the contentment of the workers with the Friendly Societies' Acts, the machinery of which was smooth, easy and expeditious, and represented that to extend their principles to the Associations would give widespread satisfaction, and would enable the working classes to test for themselves the practicability of the method without feeling that the law was against them.

[1] The names of its members are given in Holyoake, *History of Co-operation*, ii. p. 344.

He was followed by Neale, who dealt with much the same topics, quoting the cost of registration under the Joint Stock Companies' Act as ' coming to £50 or £60,' and declaring that under present conditions men were not being prevented from association, but that if fraud arose there was no means of redressing it.   He also showed how, under existing conditions, although men had been found ready to advance money for the starting of Associations, these men had no power to recover their loans, and if the Associations were disposed to be dishonest there was no remedy available.   Hughes, who also gave evidence, explained very clearly how suitable the methods of the existing Friendly Societies' Act were to the needs of the Associations.   The only two points on which they required special treatment were the power to receive loans and the power to invest their funds in their trade instead of in Government stocks or the other specific objects prescribed for Friendly Societies.   Among working men examined were several connected with the Society ; Millbank, who pointed out the special claim of poor men to limited liability, since they could not hope to obtain an Act of Incorporation, and testified to the desire of the workers for facilities in associating, and who also gave a very striking forecast of the possibility of extending the method until ' all orders of industry are associated and exchange their commodities with each other,' and of the effect of such a change upon social life; Cooper who related the history of the Tailors' Association and explained that at present he was legally the possessor of the funds advanced to him by the Promoters, that this was undesirable and contrary to the whole idea of association, but that in the present state of the law to entrust the money to the body of Associates would be to expose them all to the possible dishonesty of any one of their number ;

Clarkson, who spoke of the value of association for bakers in improving the conditions of their work; Lloyd Jones, who mentioned the Rochdale co-operators and the difficulties which they, in common with other societies registered under the Friendly Societies' Act, had to face; and Le Chevalier, who spoke only about the liabilities of partners. Seven other witnesses were examined; and then at the end of their labours the Committee interviewed two acknowledged experts whom the Promoters had induced to appear.

The first of these was H. Bellenden Ker, Counsel to the Board of Trade, and one of the greatest living authorities on Company Law. He was the barrister in whose chambers Ludlow and Furnivall had read; and it was at the personal request of the former that he consented against his will to give evidence. On the whole his testimony was disappointing; for the Committee, which had been divided from the first on the question of limited liability, now that they had got an acknowledged expert, insisted on spending most of their time on this subject. But what he did say about Associations was favourable; and he recommended that in view of the complexity and expense of procedure under the Joint Stock Companies' Act, they should be given recognition on terms similar to those enjoyed by Friendly Societies.

But the crowning triumph of the Promoters was the evidence of John Stuart Mill, who was at that time in the zenith of his fame and accepted as the leading economist of the day. We have seen in the introductory chapter that from the economists hitherto Christian Socialism could extract but little comfort. They do not seem to have hoped for much praise from Mill: for although in the preface to the third edition [1] of the *Principles of*

[1] In the first edition the tone towards Socialism ' was on the whole

Political Economy he protested that his views on property should ' not be understood as a condemnation of Socialism, regarded as an ultimate result of human progress,' this was not published until 1852, and there was as yet no strong reason to suppose that he would be sympathetic : indeed his reply to their invitation had been decidedly cold.[1]   He was subjected to a lengthy examination by the Committee, much of which is irrelevant to our subject : but Ludlow has given an excellent summary of his views in the *Christian Socialist*, [2] and as these contain his opinion on the general merits and practicability of association, the passage is worth quoting in full.   It will prove, at least, that the one of their contemporaries best qualified to pronounce a verdict did not think their scheme ill-advised or foredoomed to failure.

Ludlow writes : ' The first political economist of the day, not only in this country but in Europe, tells us that " the laws of partnership oppose obstacles of various kinds to the improvement of the working classes," that " perhaps the most important is the obstacle which they throw in the way of combinations among the workmen engaged in any particular branch of industry, for the purpose of carrying on that industry co-operatively, either with their own capital or with capital which they borrow " ; that " hardly anything which the legislature could do in the present state of society and the present state of the feelings of the working classes, would be more useful " than to give facilities to working people associating ; that the want

that of opposition ' : in the second there was little change : in the third his support was ' unequivocally given.' Cf. *Autobiography*, p. 234.

[1] Hughes described the interview in a paper read before the Social Science Association and printed in its *Sessional Proceedings* for 1871-2, p. 2, and in *Co-operative News*, i.

[2] Vol. i. p. 51.   For Mill's own view of Slaney's Act, cf. Elliot, *Letters of J. S. Mill*, i. pp. 171-2.

of such facilities is "a great cause of discontent, and a
very just one." He goes further and states that "he sees
no reason why such associations should not succeed."
He thinks "there is *no way* in which the working classes
can make so beneficial a use of their savings, both to
themselves and to society, as by the formation of associations to carry on the business with which they are acquainted, and in which they are themselves engaged as
work-people." He wishes to see the enterprises in which
the working classes are now engaged carried on, not as
now "by a capitalist hiring labourers as he wants them,
but by the labourers themselves, mental as well as manual,
hiring the capital they require at the market rate." He
points out, we may say repeatedly, how small "a portion
of the price paid at a shop for an article really goes to the
person who made it," and what an "extravagant portion
of the whole produce of the community now goes to mere
distributors"; how "the greater the number of productive
labourers, the greater in general is the produce; but an
increased number of mere distributors has no tendency
to increase the quantity of wealth to be distributed, but
only quarters an additional number of persons upon it."
Co-operative shops or bazaars thus meet with his approval,
as well as associations for co-operative labour; and he
thinks "we can hardly set limits to the consequences
that might arise in the way of improvements from the
feeling that would be diffused, through the whole of the
persons employed in an undertaking, of personal interest
in its success." He considers it advantageous, if it can
be done without restricted laws or privileges, to " limit
the number of distributors,"—and that "on the same
principle on which it is advantageous to suppress any
useless intermediate steps in the process of production."
He answers "decidedly," "certainly," that "it would be

desirable to encourage associations of the co-operative character, to give them all possible facilities, but no premium." Even as respects the security of the 3 per cent. consols, he thinks "the associations by the working classes to carry on, as their own capitalists, their own employment," have "very great advantages over *any other* investments for the working classes"; contrasting them with ordinary joint-stock companies on account of the familiarity of all the associates with the business, their daily attention to it, and the facilities thereby afforded for keeping a proper control over the managers and selecting them properly.'

It is hardly surprising that Mill's evidence, of which the above is a very fair précis, filled the Christian Socialists with delight. Their efforts, heretofore, had been greeted with a chorus of contemptuous censure, and the names of Ricardo and McCulloch, those apostles of unrestricted competition, had been sufficient excuse for the attitude of their critics. And now here was an authority greater than these openly behaving as Balaam did to Balak. ' The question of co-operation '—so Ludlow expressed it—' could no longer be laughed or hooted down.'

Nor is it surprising that the Committee was convinced by his testimony. In their official Report they mention, though not by name, the Associations for production, express the conviction that ' at present the law affords no effectual remedy against the fraud of any one dishonest contributor or partner, and no summary mode of enforcing the rules agreed to for mutual government,' and state that ' any measure for the removal of those difficulties would be peculiarly acceptable to the middle and working classes.' The Report and the proceedings of the Committee were ordered to be printed as a Government Blue-Book on

July 5th, 1850. To Ludlow [1] the contents of the former were somewhat less explicit than he had hoped, as it 'did not distinctly allude to the expediency of applying the machinery of the Friendly Societies' Acts to the Working Men's Associations.' However, soon afterwards he himself was asked by Labouchere to draft a Bill for submission to the Board of Trade; and this was received with apparent friendliness. The Council [2] thereupon prepared a petition to be signed by working men for the legalisation of Industrial Associations, asking specifically 'that the provisions of the Acts relating to Friendly Societies may be extended to all Associations of working men formed for the purpose of carrying on their trade, labour or handicraft for the benefit of themselves and their families.'

On February 4th, 1851,[3] the opening day of the new session, Slaney again asked for the appointment of a Committee for the same purpose as before, but in addition to consider 'the improving the law of partnership.' On February 20th [4] his motion was taken and passed with the further addition of 'the expediency of limited liability.' This Committee reported its results in July 1851, and a Blue-book was issued which did not, however, contain a statement of the evidence taken. As regards the Associations it simply adopted the language of the previous report; and in the further question of partnership did not do more than recommend the appointment of a Commission to enquire into limited liability. Ludlow's [5] only comment upon their work is that 'they do not appear to have gone to the bottom of their subject.

[1] *Christian Socialist*, i. p. 187.   [2] *Christian Socialist*, i. p. 117.
[3] *Christian Socialist*, i. p. 125.   [4] *Christian Socialist*, i. p. 141.
[5] *Christian Socialist*, ii. p. 66, where the Report is fully summarised.

In July 1851,[1] a deputation of the supporters of the Bill, collected by the Promoters and consisting of Lord Ashburton, Slaney, James G. Marshall another M.P., Neale, Hughes, Ludlow, Cooper, Jennings, and a representative of the People's Mill at Leeds, saw Labouchere and obtained from him a promise that the Bill should be introduced ; but he gave no sign of acting up to his words. All through the autumn the Bill was quietly ignored. The Whig party was occupied with internal dissensions, and the disagreement between the 'great little man,'[2] Russell, and the 'little great man,' Palmerston, left them small leisure except for intrigue. Ludlow might write despairing appeals to them to crown their last days with one piece of honest social legislation; but though the fall of the ministry was postponed longer than he expected, no steps were taken to bring in the Bill or to act upon the Committees' reports.

In the new year a fresh attempt was made, and another deputation,[3] Lord Goderich and Hughes from the Promoters, and Cooper, Jennings and Pickard from the Central Board, again saw Labouchere on February 27th. This time he was even definitely unfavourable in his reply, warning them that the Engineers' lock-out complicated the position and that he would have to submit the Bill again to the Law Officers of the Crown. However, a few days later came the defeat of the Government : Lord Derby and the Tories came into power, and a new start had to be made.

---

[1] Cf. *Christian Socialist*, ii. p. 23. It is interesting to notice that the Chartist Convention, meeting on March 31st, with Bezer and Thornton Hunt among its delegates, had inserted in its programme the enrolment and registration of Co-operative Societies (Gammage, *History of the Chartist Movement*, p. 371).

[2] So Edward Ellice to J. T. Delane (*Life of John Delane*, i. p. 327).

[3] *Journal of Association*, p. 44.

This time their success was rapid. The party was less obsessed by the *laissez-faire* doctrine than its rivals, and had a better record in respect of philanthropy. The question of industrial unrest was brought prominently before the legislature. Slaney's Committee had laid special stress on the importance of their recommendations as a sedative for labour discontent ; the Bill might help to pacify the workers and was not likely to arouse any violent opposition ; let it therefore be introduced. Such was the line which the former critic of Christian Socialism, W. R. Greg, followed in a long and weighty article in the April number of the *Edinburgh Review* [1]: it fairly represents opinion at the time, even among those who like the reviewer disliked the method of association and only wished to give it a fair trial, in order the more clearly to demonstrate its futility. And so, on Friday, March 19th, 1852, ' the Bill to legalise the formation of Industrial and Provident Partnership was brought in and read a first time, on the motion of Mr. Slaney, and ordered to be read a second time on Tuesday week [2] ' : and Ludlow was at last able to send out a whip to co-operators to send in their petition.[3]

There was, however, one ' fly in the ointment.' When the Promoters studied the Bill they found that a new clause, number VIII., had been introduced since its preparation by Ludlow, making all members of an Association liable without limit for the ' lawful debts ' of the Association. ' Every such member shall, in respect of such debts and engagements, be subject to all the liabilities imposed by law upon the partnership ' : as by Clause VI. the interest of all members was restricted to £100 each, this provision was ' obviously unjust.' The Promoters

---

[1] Vol. xcv. pp. 405-453 ; Greg, *Essays*, i. pp. 389-457.
[2] *Times*, March 20th, 1852.   [3] *Journal of Association*, p. 104.

deputed Hughes and Neale to wait upon Slaney and
Sotheron, the Members backing the Bill, and press for
its alteration.

On April 21st the Second Reading was moved by Slaney
in a short speech, seconded and carried without opposition,
and the Bill was referred to a select Committee. ' The
House of Commons has therefore solemnly admitted
that Industrial Associations ought to be legalised and
assimilated in their machinery to Friendly Societies ' :
so the *Journal of Association* [1] comments. But the offensive
clause was still in the Bill ; and under the threat of
opposition from the representatives of certain manufacturing districts, it appeared doubtful whether it would
be possible to remove it : for to do so, however just
the concession, would be to give Associations preferential
treatment over other partnerships.

On May 27th the Bill passed through Committee,
Ludlow, Hughes and Neale being present by invitation
at its sittings. Four new clauses were inserted, three of
them to define the legal procedure in case of refusal to
accept the award of the arbitrators, and the fourth to
cover the bankruptcy of a member. Various other
amendments were introduced, but these were not of a kind
to alter the scope of the measure. The most important
clauses, those legalising association for production and
trade, making the interest of members non-transferable,
exempting them from the Joint Stock Companies' Act,
and extending to them all the provisions of the Friendly
Societies' Acts, except the restrictions as to the investment of funds, were accepted without any modification :
and that defining the scope of the rules of Associations,
though slightly altered, was not injured. Clause VIII.,
now become XI., was only so revised as to allow that

[1] P. 137.

' no person shall be liable . . . after the expiration of
two years from his ceasing to be a member.'

On June 3rd the Bill was read a third time, an amendment to limit the liability of partners to the extent of
their shares being moved but negatived without a
division.

In the House of Lords it was taken in charge by the
Earl of Harrowby, was read a second time on June 8th,
passed through Committee on June 10th, and was read
a third time next day, with only one trivial amendment.
Thus amended, it was finally passed by the Commons
on June 15th, and received the royal assent on June 30th.
The Industrial and Provident Societies' Act, 1852 (15 and
16 Vict. c. 31), which gave the whole co-operative movement
its status and was in some respects the most important
piece of social legislation of the century, had been passed
almost without notice from the outside world. Even
up till the last Ludlow had feared that it would fail to
obtain the force of law, since the session was nearly over,
and it was the close of that Parliament's life, when any
opposition would inevitably have been fatal, and postponement would have meant that all their labours must begin
again. It was this pressure of time that compelled him
to accept the refusal of limited liability : it was wiser
to get the Act passed, even in a somewhat disappointing
shape. He could claim [1] that ' although not a full measure
of justice, the instalment given is certainly a much
larger one than is usually obtained ' : if there was no
limited liability, at least the Associations were even in
this respect no worse off than before, or than all other
registered companies, unless they could afford £1000 or
more for the privilege of incorporation. ' Fifty workmen
in a shop can be as true to one another as fifty subscribers

[1] Cf. *Journal of Association*, pp. 201-203.

in a Joint-Stock Company ' ; besides which their liability is restricted to two years instead of the three of Joint Stock Companies, and to ' lawful debts and engagements,' so that ' an officer exceeding his powers will not bind the members.'

CHAPTER X

THE ' FAILURE ' OF CHRISTIAN SOCIALISM

THE passing into law of ' Slaney's Act ' not only altered the whole legal situation in the co-operative movement, but also made necessary certain changes in the constitution of the Society of Promoters. These they proceeded to consider during the winter and spring of 1853.

It was obvious that the function of the Christian Socialists had been modified by the Act. Hitherto they had been serving as champions of a cause which had not yet won recognition. So long as co-operative efforts were unprotected by law, there was no likelihood of their being undertaken by the workers, unless a body of persons, prepared to supply not only advice and guidance, but also financial support, was behind them. The Society had provided a guarantee and to some extent a safeguard against embezzlements within and legal interference from outside. They had given a sense of security to all those engaged in co-operative work.

Now the position was altered. Associations and Stores could stand upon their own feet. The law might not give them limited liability ; at least it enabled them to be protected, in the carrying on of their business, from the risks which had before frightened many of the best and most cautious workers. Under the Act the existence of a Society of Promoters was not recognised, and many of their previous tasks, such, for example, as the drafting and considering of constitutions and rules for co-operative bodies, were now provided for by other means. They had, therefore, to decide to what extent their continuance was valuable, and by what methods they could best make it so. And when once reconstruction was undertaken, the way was opened to the raising of those fundamental issues which had already threatened to divide them.

Neale, as we have seen, had never liked the name 'Christian Socialism,' or the definitely Christian basis upon which the Society had rested. Such a basis does not seem, in fact, to have prevented any honest sympathiser from joining them ; at any rate Lloyd Jones, who was not a professing Christian and was certainly as honest as the day, had found it no barrier. But Neale did not like it. His ideal for the Society was that it should be professedly as wide as the co-operative movement, that it should welcome all 'men of goodwill' (as we call them nowadays), and by uniting them with the strong Christian element in the body should leaven them, and from them the whole movement, with Christian principles. To insist upon the express statement of Christianity as the mainspring of their action seemed to him like the imposition of a test creed, and therefore certain to frighten away the very people who would be most valuable as allies : it was to give needless offence over a matter of words, since, so long as Maurice remained its leader and Ludlow its chief member, the new Society would be, in fact, if not in name, as Christian as the old one. On the other hand to refuse any change, especially now that the question had been raised, would be to limit the Society's membership and usefulness to those who were prepared to accept and endorse an explicit confession of faith ; and this would be to start a work of co-operation by deliberately encouraging a schism. Christians ought to

set a better example of brotherhood, and ought to remember that the spirit was more important than the
letter.

Ludlow, now as heretofore, took the opposite view.
Much as he valued co-operation he valued Christianity
more. He deplored the tendency which would maintain
that, so long as a man showed goodwill, it was a matter of
comparative indifference whether he had any or no religious belief. He wished to socialise Christianity in order
the more effectively to make society Christian; and
co-operation only mattered because it promoted this
object. If, after the struggles and hostility of the previous
years, they were now to abjure the basis from which
their whole work had drawn its power, they would seem
to be pandering to the commercial side of the movement,
to be encouraging the idea that co-operation was an end
in itself, and to be denying all that was really vital in
their undertaking. For morals without religion, for a
spirit which shrank from the effort of confession, he had
not that admiration which possessed some of his colleagues.
If they really believed that Christianity was the sole
power capable of redeeming the world from materialism
and selfishness, capable of inspiring and uplifting the
co-operative movement and saving it from becoming a
mere money-making concern, then surely they could
not leave that belief unexpressed, or treat it as a matter
of indifference. Now, when the movement over whose
travail they had spent so much effort, had come successfully to its birth, now, if ever, was the time to christen it.
They had won the affection and trust of its members
everywhere; if they took up a strong and definite attitude,
and were not ashamed to proclaim that what they had
done had been done in the name of Christ, and that in
His name they would carry on their work, would not their

lead be followed ?   If they were to refuse, the men for
whom they had toiled would be left to fall into the hands
of those like Holyoake, who were not ashamed to profess
hostility to Christ, and who would not be slow to take
advantage of their silence and to put upon it the interpretation which best suited their own anti-religious
propaganda. To omit or to water down the confession
of the faith of their Society would be an act of apostasy.

   The discussion and settlement of this question took a
considerable time. The details need not be treated with
much fulness, although certain speeches of Maurice—
which have been recently printed for the Working Men's
College with an introductory notice by his son—give us
a complete account of his attitude and incidentally of the
difficulties which he had to face. The procedure was as
follows. The Council drew up a series of resolutions
indicating the main lines on which they wished the
constitution to be framed. Details were then left to a
committee. At this committee the question was thrashed
out. Maurice, whose conception of Christ as the Head
of every man, acknowledged or not, had been not only
expressed in his whole theology, but developed in reference to this special point in the eighth and last of the
Tracts on Christian Socialism at the time when this
matter had previously arisen, was unwilling to make
the Christianity of a man, or the Christian quality of his
actions, appear to depend only upon his acceptance or
refusal of a credal test. To him, Neale, and even Lloyd
Jones, were Christians, in so far as they were doing the
works of Christ and showing the fruits of His Spirit.
The ' Light that lighteneth every man ' was theirs,
although they might refuse to believe it. As a student
of the Fathers he knew the futility and the peril of
dogmatic assertions of orthodoxy, he knew the schisms

and scandals to which they had given rise, he knew how easily religion was debased into a repetition of shibboleths. So he set his face against any policy which would exclude those who otherwise would be his fellow-workers ; and with this purpose endeavoured to formulate a statement of the basis of the Society, that should secure for it its definitely Christian character, without employing language which might strain the consciences of those out of sympathy with Christian doctrine.

In doing so he laid hold upon the Pauline teaching of membership which has since figured so prominently in social ethics. That the body was one, having many members differing in function, but none the less all truly united, this was a conception which all his colleagues in the co-operative movement would accept. To the Christians, and, so long as he, a priest of the Church, remained its president, to the Society, such a conception would inevitably involve belief in Him who alone supplied the unity of the body, and from whose religion the whole idea was derived. But as a definition such language would be less liable to divide, less difficult to accept, than the clause which had stood in the previous constitution. So, in the two speeches preserved for us, he strove to maintain.[1]

Ludlow was naturally distressed. Maurice's long letter to him on the morning of the final meeting, March 9th, 1853,[2] sent to explain the course which he proposes to take, is a fine example of the candour upon which their friendship was founded. In it he urges that to insert a clause insisting upon the Christian character of the Society in so many words would be to go beyond, and be false to, the terms on which the committee had been

---

[1] Printed in 1906 for the Working Men's College.
[2] Life of Maurice, ii. pp. 159-161.

appointed; but he admits that if Ludlow's amendment is brought forward and approved, he will himself be delighted. In any case he will not regard the Council's action as a test of their belief, nor will he refuse in either event to carry on the work.

Finally, at this meeting, the name of the Society was changed into the Association for Promoting Industrial and Provident Societies, and the preamble of its constitution consisted of the following statement :

' The Promoters of Working Men's Associations, having united together for the purpose of applying the principles of Christianity to trade and industry, and desiring to state more definitely what those principles are, as they find them set forth in Christ's gospel, that they may serve as the basis of a society to be formed for the objects after mentioned, declare :—

1. That human society is a body consisting of many members, not a collection of warring atoms.
2. That true workmen must be fellow-workmen, not rivals.
3. That a principle of justice, not of selfishness, must regulate exchanges. [1]

And on this basis the newly-constituted Association set out to contribute whatever it could to the life of the co-operative movement.

And its career was now more difficult than ever. In a sense, as we have seen, the work of the Christian Socialists was accomplished. Some of their previous tasks could now be taken over by the Associations themselves : others naturally devolved upon the executive committee of the new Annual Conference : others, and particularly all those connected with the passing of the Act, were now at an

[1] The full constitution is printed in St. André, *Five Years*, App. pp. 67-74.

end. Further, even the continuance of such work as remained was rendered difficult on financial grounds. Although their numbers had increased,[1] they had all lost money over the Associations : they were all committed to an expenditure as heavy as they could afford : Neale, their man of means, was deeply involved in the Agency and the Atlas works. Under such circumstances fresh ventures were quite out of the question. Indeed, it became doubtful how long they could carry on the old ones.

And at this stage these began to fail. Vansittart's ironworks in Mile End were particularly unfortunate. Under John Musto they had made an excellent start : he was vigorous and sensible, very keen on his business, and with a firm hold over his fellow-workmen. The *coup d'état* by which he had become manager had been so amply justified by results that at Manchester he did not hesitate to ascribe their success to the concentration of control into the hands of a few.[2] Though he had only eight Associates, there were twenty-two Probationers awaiting admission and employed on whole-time work. Their capital was now £2804, and they had done business to the value of £4280. In August 1854 Huber visited them, and has given a lively and very encouraging account of their doings.[3] Musto had persuaded two of his brothers to join him, was employing twenty workmen and several boys in the shops as well as others in the office, and had fitted up a room with a blackboard and drawing materials in which he trained the apprentices after hours. Thanks to the war business was very brisk : interest was being paid regularly upon the loan, and all profits were being

[1] Huber says that at this time there were seventy members of the group, of whom were nine ministers of religion, nine lawyers, two M.P.'s, two peers and ten more of the upper classes (*Reisebriefe*, ii. p. 171).

[2] *Report of M. Conference*, p. 33.   [3] *Reisebriefe*, ii. pp. 484-492.

devoted to increasing the plant : expansion of output
was only limited by shortage of capital and by the size of
the premises. Shortly afterwards the crash came. 'The
men worked hard, and everything seemed going on successfully, until the Association had to tender for a large job.
. . . They made a large contract at a price which involved
a considerable loss, and the result was that they had
to be wound up!' Such is Hughes' account.[1] Vansittart
could spend no more, and decided to cut his losses and
to close the works. This was late in 1853. Neither the
members of the Association nor the A.S.E. made the
slightest effort to share in the repaying of the sum
advanced to them for their start.

Nor were the Atlas Works more satisfactory. Their
commencement, though it had not been so brilliant as
that of their friends at Mile End, had been extremely
promising. Their business was on a larger scale, and
Neale had taken pains to give them every chance of
success. In the summer of 1853, though they had only
ten full Associates, they were employing some sixty
hands, and regarded their method as satisfactory.[2]
But here, too, there was almost from the first disappointment. The executive of the A.S.E., who had unanimously
resolved during the strike to devote themselves seriously
to association, now refused to support the venture.
Neale and the original Associates were left to carry on.[3]
One crisis followed another. Self-government, which had
admittedly been a risk for members of unorganised
trades, proved to be too much even for these élite of the
working-classes. The manager and foremen could not
secure regularity. Orders and contracts could not be

---

[1] Co-operative News, i. p. 158.   [2] Report of M. Conference, p. 33.
[3] Cf. Neale's own narrative in B. Jones, Co-operative Production, i.
p. 134.

finished up to time. The quality and quantity of the output was constantly diminishing. Again and again affairs seemed desperate. And still Neale persisted, and would not admit himself beaten. Deeply involved as he was, he seemed ready to make any sacrifice in this final test, hoping against hope that the men would eventually respond to his efforts, or that the A.S.E. would decide to assist him. With ' a patience verging upon obstinacy,' as Hughes calls it,[1] he held on for several years, and when at last the end came his losses over it contributed largely to make him a poor man. He sacrificed not only the money originally spent for the purchase of the site and buildings, but also the sum paid by him to discharge the debts of the Association, which were not covered by the sale of the tools and plant. Here again the A.S.E., by whose resolutions he had been led to the enterprise, made no suggestion of help, but left him to bear the whole burden unaided.[2]

And if the skilled workers could not rise to the demands made upon them, it was hardly to be expected that the struggling groups in other trades, whose difficulties we have already described at length, would fare better. In the *First Report*[3] the document issued after the Conference in 1852, it had been admitted that the Amalgamated Shoemakers' Association had been deprived of self-government, and was still in serious difficulties.

[1] *Economic Review*, iii. p. 48.

[2] The National Association of United Trades which had also endorsed the policy of co-operative production sank into insignificance about this time : cf. Webb, *History of Trade Unionism*, p. 206. Of the A.S.E. Newton and Allan remained loyal to association, and nearly succeeded in carrying the Society with them : but Joseph Musto, their president, was discouraged by the experience of the East London Ironworks of which John Musto was manager ; several of the executive were hostile ; and to press the matter might have meant a split, just when they were recovering from the lock-out. So it was shelved.

[3] P. 47, cī. above p. 183.

In the *Report of the Conference at Manchester* [1] in 1853 there is mention of yet another reconstruction of the Association in March of that year : the number of members had fallen to fifteen, and it is complained that they cannot secure custom. Yet in spite of all their mishaps they rallied, and for some years worked well. Indeed, they are mentioned as still surviving and paying a fair interest on their loan and a dividend to their members as late as 1863. But they never recovered self-government, and finally Thomas Christmas, then their manager, took over the business and conducted it as a private firm. [2] The Printers, loyal and courageous as they were, resolved when the *Journal* was discontinued to produce a new halfpenny weekly paper, to be called the *Bee-Hive*, and to include in it the ' Association News ' which had been so valuable a feature of its predecessor. [3] But it does not appear that this project was ever carried out, and the Association, which had always been kept going only by the work put into its hands by the Promoters, struggled on with great difficulty. In August 1852, when the cessation of the *Journal of Association* had deprived them of their regular work, Isham, the manager, insisted on taking full control into his own hands, and refused to furnish accounts or divide profits : Leno and Dodd, two of the original Associates, left : and the business became a private concern, Isham carrying it on till about 1858. [4] In 1853 he was present at the Manchester Conference though admitting that his workmen were no longer *bona fide* Associates, and claimed that the improvement in

[1] P. 31.

[2] Cf. B. Jones, *Co-operative Production* quoting the *Quarterly Review* and Leno, the printer, i. pp. 117, 122.

[3] Cf. their manager's letter in *Journal of Association*, p. 117.

[4] *Report of Manchester Conference*, p. 37, and B. Jones, *Co-operative Production*, i. p. 122.

the standard of his printing had enabled him to replace the Promoters' custom by securing outside orders : Allan complimented him on the quality of the A.S.E. Reports. Next year all pretence that his firm was an Association was dropped.[1] The Pianoforte-makers who had always had a hard struggle had by July 1853 lost nine of their fourteen Associates, two having been expelled for misconduct and seven having left in disgust.[2] But the greatest disappointment was with the Association which had seemed the most successful and energetic. In the *Report of the Manchester Conference*,[3] though the North London Builders made a very cheerful statement of their success, there is a sad story from Pimlico. In the early spring of 1853 the creditors had pressed for payment, the manager was unequal to the situation ; and the business was wound up. When the assets were realised, it was found that the position was not really unsatisfactory : after settling all claims, there remained between £500 and £600, and this was divided up. Failure seems to have been due more to the want of authority on the part of Jennings than to financial difficulties : but the Association was not reconstituted, though seven of its members set up the ' Pimlico Industrial Building Society ' at 8 Ponsonby Place. Stevens, the manager of their Co-operative Store, had already in August 1852 transferred his energies to the ' Metropolitan and Provincial Joint-Stock Brewery Co.,' a business run on associative lines in New Brentford with an office at 18 Upper Wellington Street, and had thereby brought grave searchings of heart to the teetotalers among the

---

[1] The printers' name on the A.S.E. Reports is significant : it is in 1852 The Working Printers' Association ; in 1853, R. Isham, manager of the Working Printers' Association ; in 1854, R. Isham & Co. Then he lost the contract.

[2] *Report of M. C.*, p. 36.   [3] Pp. 30, 31.

Promoters. The North London Builders seem to have carried on their Association till 1860, after which Pickard took it over as his own business. Even the Castle Street Tailors, the pioneer and model of them all, though it survived until long after the Association of Promoters had been disbanded, came at last to grief, though through no fault of its own. Walter Cooper, who had worked so well during the years of effort, had then become respectable ; he was a pillar of the Church, vicar's warden at All Saints', Margaret Street, and apparently unimpeachable. And then late in 1860 the crash came. He was found to have been misapplying the profits of the Association and falsifying the books. He was convicted and sentenced. And the Associates broke up the business. Hitherto they had done well and seemed settled and successful; but his failure, with the scandal and suspicion to which it gave rise, was too much for them.[1]

Nor was the Central Co-operative Agency more successful than the Associations. Although in Woodin and Lloyd Jones it had two business men of exceptional capacity, and although its sales expanded well[2] and the northern stores were coming more and more to obtain their goods through it, the cost of upkeep, and especially the rent of the very expensive premises which Neale had so recklessly taken in Oxford Street, was too heavy, and in 1857 he was obliged to wind up the whole concern. Probably, had it not been for his losses over the Atlas Works, he would have been able to finance the Agency until the growth of its trade made it self-supporting: but the Rochdale Pioneers, who about this time also launched a wholesale society.

---

[1] Holyoake, *History of Co-operation*, ii. p. 339, says of it,' A manager of energy, good faith, and good capacity might have made an industrial mark under these well-devised conditions.'

[2] Huber, *Reisebriefe*, ii. p. 296, states the value of its yearly business as from £50,000 to £60,000.

were equally unsuccessful : and it may be that Abraham
Greenwood was right when, in submitting his proposals
for the North of England Co-operative Wholesale Society
to the conference at Oldham in 1862, he declared[1] that
these two forerunners of his scheme had failed ' from their
efforts being too soon in the order of co-operative developments.'　In this, as in other branches of their work, the
Christian Socialists paid the penalty that befalls the
prophet, the man in advance of his time.

Of the Association of Promoters itself there is not much
more to relate.　On August 15th and 16th, 1853, was
held the second Annual Conference of the co-operative
movement at the Cooper Street Institute in Manchester.
Neale as senior member of the Executive Committee
appointed at the previous Conference, took the chair :
twenty-six delegates, among them Newton, representing
the Atlas Works, Allan, Cooper, Lloyd Jones, John Musto,
Shorter, Furnivall, and Maurice as delegate from the
Association of Promoters, and three visitors, were present.
Ludlow, who had declined to join the Executive, did not
attend.　The *Report* which has already been so freely
quoted, though it lays much less stress upon their difficulties and failures, is rather a disheartening document :
it lacks that note of achievement and confidence which
sounded so clearly in its predecessor.　The discussions,
briefly summarised in it, are concerned mainly with the
problem of unity both in the movement, and in individual
Associations.　Great emphasis is laid upon the need of
securing the authority and permanence of the managers ;
and several resolutions with this object were passed.
In accordance with the resolutions of the previous Conference, a scheme was also submitted for the formation of

---

[1] *Co-operator*, March 1863, vol. iii. p. 161.　His speech contained a
glowing tribute to the Christian Socialists.

an Industrial and Provident Societies' Union,[1] and the
Executive was asked to circulate this to the Stores and
Associations and discover their opinions upon it: and
arrangements were made for the issue of a paper,
which appeared in the autumn with the title, the *Co-
operative Circular*.[2] On the second day, on the proposition of Newton, seconded by J. J. Merriman
of Portsea, the Conference adopted the three clauses
which formed the Association's basis as 'the true
foundation of social reform,'[3] and they were afterwards inserted in the constitution of the Co-operative
Union. Maurice himself presided at the festival held
at the close of the proceedings; and as Hughes tells us,[4]
this was his last piece of active public work in connection
with co-operation. He was already turning to the educational side of the movement, and devoted himself increas-
ingly to those lectures and classes in the Hall of Association
at Castle Street, which were the predecessors of his final
venture in social service. The trouble at King's College
was making him unpleasantly notorious; the co-operative
movement could find many more reputable leaders, now
that it had itself become respectable; and he shrank
from any possible injury to the cause that might arise
from his connection with it.

It is plain that by this time a divergence of opinion was
appearing among the Promoters. The founders of
Christian Socialism, Ludlow, Maurice, Kingsley and Mansfield, had now learnt that the time was not ripe for the
fulfilment of their schemes. They thought it wiser to

[1] Printed in *Report*, Appendix B, pp. 52-62, and St. André, *Five Years*, App. 74-82.

[2] So Huber, *Reisebriefe*, ii. p. 167. This paper abandoned the religious aspect of the movement, and maintained neutrality on political
and social topics, confining itself solely to co-operative topics.

[3] P. 16.   [4] *Economic Review*, i. p. 219.

turn to education, foreseeing that without this the distributive side of co-operation, just because from the business standpoint it was practicable and lucrative, would fail to teach fellowship and might easily degenerate into mere dividend-hunting. The others, who had been more closely connected with this side of the movement, had naturally joined the Executive Council appointed by the first Conference, and were prepared to continue their work even if co-operative production had to be dropped : in doing so, it was their lifelong endeavour to denounce profit-making and selfishness, and to insist that ultimately associative principles must be applied to the whole industrial life of the country.

Nevertheless, during the larger part of 1854 the Association continued to exist, to arrange meetings, and to supervise the remaining groups of workers. The third Annual Conference was held in the Philosophical Hall at Leeds in the third week in August. Huber [1] has described his disappointment at finding only some fifty persons present of whom about twenty were delegates. Maurice who was very unwell refused to preside, and the chair was taken by Neale. Lloyd Jones and Henry Smith were the most prominent speakers, and their eloquence and capacity made a great impression on their German visitor. At this Conference the Promoters decided that their work in this direction could be better done if expressly linked up with the movement ; and so asked that the Executive Committee of the Conference, on which were Neale, Hughes, and several other Christian Socialists, should take over the Association's duties. This was agreed upon, and on November 25th the Promoters met for the last time, and resolved that all future meetings for

[1] *Reisebriefe*, ii. pp. 292-297.

business be suspended. As we shall see, their energies had already been devoted to a new but cognate field of endeavour.

Having thus briefly recounted the failure of the Associations, we have now to consider the vexed question of its causes. Let us take first those usually assigned by the critics, and most fully stated by Mrs. Sidney Webb, then Miss Beatrice Potter, in her book, *The Co-operative Movement in Great Britain.*

We may dismiss in a few words her theoretical objection, although this has been accepted and repeated by several writers whose outlook by no means coincides with hers. Starting from the curious fallacy common to the State Socialists that democracy means bureaucracy, and from the consequent belief that true progress aims at reducing a human being to the level of a reliable machine, she proceeds to contrast co-operative production with co-operative distribution, to label the former individualist and the latter democratic, to apply to their achievements the test of material success, and so to demonstrate to her own satisfaction that this and all other schemes for self-government in industry are futile as well as reactionary. Ludlow's own criticism,[1] whose generosity and kindliness are in striking contrast to her patronising scorn, insists that true reform must start from the sphere of production, and brings out with admirable clarity the distinction between her worship of mechanical efficiency and the Christian Socialist insistence upon the principles of liberty and righteousness : it is moreover, as we have already shown, a remarkable anticipation of recent developments. Suffice it to say that all her arguments against Associations for production apply equally to the

[1] *Atlantic Monthly*, lxxv. pp. 383-388 and *Economic Review*, ii. pp. 214-230. See above p. 249.

proposals of the Guild Socialists. Mr. Cole and his friends are dealing faithfully, if none too gently, with their victim : we need not waste time flogging its corpse. That the methods of the Christian Socialists displeased the advocates of Fabian Collectivism is not to their discredit, nor is it of itself any sufficient reason to account for their failure.

But if Mrs. Webb need not detain us while she is arguing that the scheme conflicts with the ideals of State Socialism and therefore with true progress, we shall not find much more value in her other criticisms. When she is attacking the theory of co-operative production, we can only wonder at her callousness to the interests of the producer as compared with the consumer and agree with Ludlow that she is starting at the wrong end. And when she comes to more practical matters we discover that she has not really grasped what the Christian Socialists purposed to do, or even made herself acquainted with their actual achievements. This is the more regrettable because her mistakes have been either copied, or at least shared, by several subsequent writers on the subject.

The chief count in her indictment is that the Associations tend to ' break a community into tiny self-governing circles of producers which must fight each other to the death or combine to impose price and quality on the public,' [1] that they stand, therefore, between competition and monopoly, and must fall into one or the other. It is interesting to notice that this objection was raised first by W. R. Greg in his article on ' English Socialism and Communistic Associations,' in the *Edinburgh Review*.[2] He had summed up his case by saying : ' The advocates of association, as a cure for competition, are caught between two horns of a dilemma: in case you have

---

[1] *The Co-operative Movement*, p. 156.

[2] Vol. xciii. p. 22 : see above p. 168.

many Associations, you retain all the evils of competition ; in case you merge them all into one, you encounter all the evils of monopoly. We defy the Socialists to escape from this dilemma, except by assuming a remodelling of human nature by Divine or Christian influences.' His contention was answered without delay by Furnivall in the *Christian Socialist*,[1] and by Ludlow in a lecture given on February 12th of the same year and afterwards published as *Christian Socialism and its Opponents*. As the criticism is a very obvious and oft-repeated one and not without present interest, it may be worth while to summarise their replies to it.

Furnivall is brief and drastic. He appeals at once to the Constitution of the Society and quotes from it the rule regarding prices: ' The price of the articles sold by the different Associations of the same trade and place shall be regulated by those Associations, subject to the control of the Central Board, in such a manner as to prevent either monopoly or unfair competition.' He then explains the composition of the Central Board, and demonstrates that even if the Associations are all purely selfish they will find it difficult to indulge their selfishness under the control of such a body. Naturally he concludes by insisting that men who accept co-operation as ' the practical application of Christianity to the purposes of trade and industry ' are not always or only actuated by self-interest. In passing we may note that the system of control here instituted is closely analogous to the similar method now proposed by the Guild Socialists.

Ludlow, who had constantly foreseen and warned the Associates of the danger of competition between their Associations,[2] admits the risk, mentions the safeguards,

[1] Vol. i. p. 122.

[2] Cf. his repeated denunciation of exclusiveness as degrading the

and surmises that in any case it is easier to control fifty Associations than twenty-three thousand journeymen. As to monopoly he insists that they were seeking ' one which instead of narrowing sought only to extend its circle, and would not cease widening till it had taken in the whole world,'—a proof that already he contemplated nothing less than a world-wide revolution in the methods' of industry.

Mrs. Webb's argument is therefore fairly met by replying that the Christian Socialists were fully aware of the danger, that they had set up a central authority which should prevent it from arising, and that in addition to this precaution they had planned both the scope and the moral background of their movement on such lines as to eliminate it altogether.

Her second count, an attack upon profit-sharing from the stand-point of Trades Unionism, is hardly meant to apply, as she states it, to the Christian Socialists. But although she refers this charge rather to their successors than to themselves, it is worth mention because mis-understanding of this point created suspicion of their work among the Trades Societies of their time. The Christian Socialists never contemplated profit-sharing at all. Capitalists did not enter into their scheme except as providing the initial outlay, and this was simply a loan repayable with interest but giving no title to a share in profits. They aimed at what Ludlow calls ' Collective Mastership,'[1] and at the total elimination of the capitalist. And with regard to Trades Unions, Mr. and Mrs. Webb

Associations to the level of a Joint Stock Company, *e.g. Christian Socialist*, i. p. 242. It may be noted that Mr. G. D. H. Cole's answer to this criticism of Guild Socialism displays more heat than light (cf. *Self-government in Industry*, pp. 281-285).

[1] Cf. *Letters to the Working Men's Associations*, iii. and iv. in *Christian Socialist*, i. pp. 44, 60.

are hardly correct when they state [1] that ' this new form of co-operation was intended not as an adjunct or a development of the Trade Union, but as an alternative form of industrial organisation ' : for the antithesis is misleading. Their purpose was not to group the workers defensively for the raising of wages, but to develop the Unions into self-governing Associations, or, as we should now call them, Guilds, which should take over the whole business of production and with it of exchange. Trades Unions, as we now know them, and wages in the strict sense would disappear. That some of the Christian Socialists, later in life, and in face of the change in the temper and scope of the Unions, should have turned to profit-sharing as a means of alleviating industrial strife and as a step towards their ideal, need not concern us here. Such schemes had no place in the original programme of the movement.

Finally she brings a further charge against them, and one which has been freely repeated that ' they overlooked the fundamental changes brought about by the industrial revolution, increasing returns from the use of large capitals, the elaborate discipline of the factory system, the skilled intelligence needful for securing a market under stress of competition.' [2] Before we go further into the matter, Ludlow's comment on this is worth quoting : [3] ' As for saying we overlooked . . . the simple fact is we had not these things at our disposal. . . . We tried to do the best we knew how with our materials.' And his words only restate those of the First Report [4] : ' That our efforts have as yet been confined to hand-workers is an accident. We believe and teach that association,

[1] History of Trade Unionism (edition of 1911), p. 207.
[2] The Co-operative Movement, p. 167.
[3] Economic Review, ii. p. 215.   [4] P. 5.

fellow-labour, is the true law of all work, from ruling a nation to sweeping a street.'

But the argument as developed for example by A. V. Woodworth[1] is so familiar that we must not brush it aside. It is maintained that the scheme of Associations was only applicable to the petty trades in which it was most freely tried, that modern industry is too vast and complicated to be conducted on associative lines, that the attempt to introduce self-government would involve the return to conditions which have passed away for ever in all but a few trifling businesses, that for the larger operations of commerce and manufacture the individual must be rigidly subordinated to autocratic control.

Now it must first be noted that those who glibly produce this argument, seem quite unaware of the efforts made by the Christian Socialists to extend their principles to the great industries. We have seen how conscious they were of the need of a test on a larger scale than at first they were able to employ, and how eagerly they seized the opportunities which came through the lockout. In the Constitution prepared for the Windsor Ironworks, which Woodworth, whose book is very superficial,[2] seems not to have studied, we can judge of their readiness and ability to conduct a large undertaking. Admittedly the plan, on which the small Associations were founded, could not be applied unmodified to a complicated and highly organised industry. But in the records of the Mile End and Atlas Works there is no sign that such modification was impracticable. If we omit for a moment the moral difficulty, there seems no

---

[1] Cf. *Christian Socialism in England*, pp. 31, 40.

[2] Ludlow writes to the Rev. J. Carter, ' Yes, I have read Woodworth's book, which is a fairly good one, allowing for some inaccuracies ' (March 8th, 1904).

other reason why the workers should not combine to run a factory, any more than to run a builder's yard ; the principle of differentiation of function must be introduced in one just as in the other : the arrangements for control will be more complex, they need not be less attainable—unless of course we are to surrender our whole faith in democracy, as Mrs. Webb apparently does, when she insists upon ' the subordination of the individual worker to masses of capital ' as a fact that ' has come to stay.' [1]

The difficulty is indeed rather moral than economic, as the Christian Socialists realised more plainly than their critics. If we rely upon the capacity of a ' free and independent electorate ' to control the destinies of a nation, surely there can be nothing inherently impossible in the government of industry by the workers. At any rate the Christian Socialists thought it practicable, and their plans failed not through anything inevitable in the circumstances of the case, but because, in their large as in their small undertakings, the human material at their disposal could not stand the moral test.

Before we examine their own account of the failure we must not omit Mrs. Webb's culminating charge against the ethics of the movement. And in this she falsifies the evidence both by suppression and misrepresentation. In endeavouring to prove that they based their inducement to members not on altruism but on selfishness she writes: [2] 'The leaders of this school, in their schemes for self-governing workshops, appeal to the desire for personal independence and personal gain among the workers. A group of workers are to be stimulated to increased effort and more sustained diligence

---

[1] *The Co-operative Movement*, p. 168.

[2] *The Co-operative Movement*, p. 154.

because they, and not the capitalist *entrepreneur*, are to be benefited by this change in their conduct. The idea of the service of one man by another is to be repudiated.' And in the joint *History of Trade Unionism* [1] the same charge is brought even more boldly : ' Unlike the Owenites of 1834, the Christian Socialists had no conception of the substitution of profit-making enterprise by the whole body of wage-earners, organised either in a self-contained community or in a complete Trades Union. They sought only to replace the individual capitalist by self-governing bodies of profit-making workmen.' These statements contain a bare half-truth and even that misstated.

It is true that, in appealing to the starving victims of sweated labour, the Christian Socialists did complain that these men were slaves, and that they were being deprived of the reasonable reward of their toils : for all her belief in strict subordination, Mrs. Webb would agree. But they never at any time represented Association as concerned only or chiefly with financial advantages ; neither its motive nor its goal was selfish : the motive was brotherhood and the goal was the emancipation of industry from competition and wage-slavery. Almost any page of their records will bear out this description of their attitude, and the Constitutions of the original Associations and of the Windsor Ironworks prove it beyond cavil. In the former, though the communist principle of equal wages is rejected as unpractical in the present state of society, it is clearly intimated that this is only a step necessitated by circumstances and not to be regarded as final or permanent, and moreover it is provided that a third of the profits be devoted to the development of the Association—a rule which led the

[1] P. 207.

Tailors to establish baths and a library. In the latter, which more truly represents the fruits of their experience, no profits are to be divided at all ; the whole sum remaining when the standard wage has been paid is to be devoted to the provision of benefits in the shape of insurance and educational facilities, or to be employed in the extension of the principles of association by setting up similar bodies of workers elsewhere. Over and over again in their speeches, discussions, and writings it is insisted that selfishness and lack of discipline will be fatal to the whole movement, and that Associates must never be content until the redemption of their fellow-workers, the slaves of the competitive system, has been accomplished, and the principle of voluntary and self-governing association introduced into every branch of industry. ' At present the payment of wages is nothing but a deception,' said Maurice : [1] ' Pure communism, the having all things common, must always be the ideal of Socialism,' said Ludlow : [2] and continuously the same message is proclaimed. Their fundamental ambition was the destruction of competition, of that craving for personal advantage which Mrs. Webb accuses them of advocating ; and they regarded the division of profits among the workers only as a necessary but temporary makeshift, until a closer approach to their objective could be reached. What else could they have done than promote with every ounce of their strength the extension of the Associations, and of those moral principles of which the Associations were the embodiment ? They might have imitated Owen's disastrous experiment and founded monastic and isolated communities ; utopian dreams of that kind had been singularly fruitless. Or they might set to work with the means ready to their hands, striving

---

[1] *Life of Maurice*, ii. p. 32.   [2] *Christian Socialist*, i. p. 234.

to give expression to their ideals in the world around them, to demonstrate by tangible evidence that man was made for fellowship and co-operation, and so to leaven industry with this conviction that in time a radical and universal change might come.

In concluding this examination of Mrs. Webb's book we ought to explain that her injustice to the Christian Socialists is obviously due to the fact that she has not studied their own works at all, but has relied wholly, and with very inadequate acknowledgment, upon the citations given by Benjamin Jones in the *Co-operative News* and published in his book *Co-operative Production*. Valuable as this is as a painstaking compilation of extracts from rare and little-known documents, the chapter on Christian Socialism is totally inadequate,[1] is indeed a grotesque caricature ; and the selection from their writings appears to have been chosen, not to illustrate their history, but to gather together every scrap that can be turned to their discredit.[2] No wonder that Mrs. Webb and her copyists, drawing their facts from such a source, arrive at opinions which a little independent study would have enabled them to avoid.[3]

But if the details of the scheme itself were not responsible for its failure, if there was nothing inherently wrong either with their ideal or with their efforts to put it into practice, there remains the fact that they did not succeed in accomplishing their purpose. To explain this,

[1] Ludlow while recognising Jones' desire for impartiality protests that his book cannot be safely used without making allowance for his bias. (*Atlantic Monthly*, lxxv. p. 96.)

[2] For example, his summary of the *First Report*—a document which Maurice criticised for its emphasis upon their difficulties—consists solely of quotations descriptive of their failures : Mrs Webb goes one better, and copies only the most one-sided of these.

[3] A notable instance is the summary of Christian Socialism given in Kirkup, *History of Socialism* (5th edition), pp. 365, 366, every sentence of which contains an explicit untruth.

we must first remind ourselves of the peculiar difficulties of a temporary and local character against which they had in the later years of their work to contend. Both in the religious and in the political world there were events occurring that raised obstacles in their way.

The Church of England was already distracted by the threat of 'Roman aggression' from without, and by the suspicion of Roman tendencies within. The papacy, by its action in partitioning the country into dioceses and bestowing territorial titles on their bishops, had aroused a fury of opposition which we to-day can hardly conceive. If the motive of the action had been solely to create embarrassment for English Churchmen, it would have been a master-stroke : for the Tractarian movement had already revived the fear of 'Popery'; and this new move seemed like a deliberate challenge and an anticipation of triumph. Even the pages of the *Christian Socialist* reflect the excitement of the public mind; and Lloyd Jones, who had been brought up a Roman Catholic, has a sad story [1] of how he went to Manchester to attend a Co-operative Congress on December 1st, 1850, and after having been kept warm on the journey by a debate on the doings of Pio Nono, was flung violently out of a meeting for venturing to suggest that the best answer to papal aggression would be protestant progression. And the 'No Popery' campaign did much more than distract attention from more vital matters : it put the Tractarians and their followers in a position of unenviable difficulty, forcing upon them the most disagreable aspect of the Church to which they still belonged, compelling them to recognise the futility of their hopes that the separation might be bridged by their mediation, and exposing them to suspicion and persecution. It was

[1] *Christian Socialist*, i. pp. 58, 59.

openly believed that they were secret agents in the papal campaign, traitors within the city acting in concert with the enemy and pledged to its betrayal. The 'Gorham controversy' and the anti-ritualist riots were symptomatic of the public temper; and in the religious world the topic became universally dominant. All other questions were forgotten; the Church became involved in an orgy of unedifying strife; and however earnestly the Christian Socialists might endeavour to recall their fellow-countrymen to a sense of proportion, to plead for charity, and to urge that Christians had a call to something higher than party-bitterness, their efforts were not likely to prevail, nor their work to receive the support which otherwise might have been given to it. Ludlow may well be forgiven a certain irony of speech when he contrasts the fury of the rioters at St. Barnabas' with the passive acceptance of the aggression of the 'King of Slop-sellers.'[1]

If the interest of Churchmen was diverted from social problems to the familiar but sterile debate upon the claims of Rome, the State was becoming absorbed in an almost equally unsatisfactory digression. When the Duke of Wellington died in 1852, there were already signs that the long epoch of international peace was coming to an end. And with the increase of anxiety and the debates over the Militia Bill it became apparent how unfitted the country was for war. In every department of public service there was confusion. Incompetent methods and careless or corrupt administration had been suffered to go on unchecked. The scandal of the government contracts had long ago drawn indignant protests from the Christian Socialists; but their words had been wasted, and the departments

[1] *Christian Socialist*, i. p. 33.

had taken no steps towards reform.   So when the storm
broke and the expedition to the Crimea was undertaken,
the whole energies of the nation had perforce to be directed
to the remedying of evils that had grown almost incurable
by neglect.   The condition of the medical services, upon
which the labours of Florence Nightingale threw so lurid a
light, was only typical of the general inefficiency.   War at
any time absorbs the vitality and concentrates upon itself
the activities of a people.   Domestic problems must be
postponed, domestic interests must be sacrificed, domestic
reforms must wait for the return of peace.   All that is
best in the nation's manhood must be put at the disposal
of the country, and used directly or indirectly for the
prosecution of the campaign.   And in the fifties, when once
it was seen that war was certain, all hope of social or
industrial reconstruction disappeared.   The government
of the day was far too busy with efforts to conceal or
repair its shortcomings to have leisure : the press found
room for nothing but war news (' the *Times* seems to me
horribly wicked ' wrote Maurice [1] in January 1855) :
the public alternated between bursts of enthusiasm over
the gallantry of the troops and of despondency at the
manifest incompetence of civil and military authorities.
What chance had the enterprises of the Christian Socialists
at such a time ?   They themselves, like all patriotic
citizens, were drawn into the atmosphere of the war.
The Associations could no longer receive their undivided
attention, that hourly supervision which alone had
enabled them to overcome their difficulties.   Maurice
was, as we shall see, already sufficiently involved in other
matters ; Kingsley gave voice to his martial ardour in the
epic pages of *Westward Ho!* ; Ludlow struggled on for a
time, but when the Crimean war was followed by the Indian

[1] *Life of Maurice*, ii. p. 250.

Mutiny his interest in the land of his birth led him to devote himself to its history; Hughes threw himself into war work and before the end of the decade became an officer in the newly-formed volunteers, activities which left him little time except for his professional and literary work ; Neale, though as keen as ever, was seriously embarrassed by his losses and the consequent changes in his way of life ; the rest were scattered in various duties. The Association of Promoters could hardly have carried on its work when once war had been declared.

But while the attention of the Promoters was distracted by national affairs, there was also a matter involving their leader which was even more fatal to their success. It is not necessary in this place to recall the shameful history of the persecution of Maurice by the religious press, or of his expulsion on October 27th, 1853, from King's College. Suffice it to say that it reflects grave discredit upon Dr. Jelf, the Principal, a man too weak to accept Maurice's suggestion and to say frankly that he regarded his further connection with the College as undesirable, and who therefore sheltered himself behind a pretext provided by a newspaper notorious for its tyranny ; upon Bishop Blomfield, who had already made himself sufficiently ridiculous over the inhibition of Kingsley [1] and whose action at the decisive meeting was certainly biassed and probably dishonest ; upon the College which allowed one of its body to be made the victim of a heresy-hunt ; and upon the *Record* whose vindictive partisanship, though only too typical, would have disgraced any secular periodical. Maurice himself

---

[1] The story of his sermon and the incumbent's protest is one of the most familiar episodes in the history of Christian Socialism : cf. *Life of Kingsley*, i. pp. 288-291.   His address on ' The Message of the Church to Labouring Men ' was the third in a course, to which Maurice, Hansard and F. W. Robertson also contributed, during June and July 1851.

came through the ordeal unscathed; but for a man of
his temperament the agony of it was intense, and its
consequences upon Christian Socialism were far-reaching.

In the first place its direct result was to engage
the energies of his friends and particularly of Ludlow in
his defence. If his colleagues and pupils at the College
were with few and honourable exceptions prepared to
allow him to be cast out without protest, if the press
was either hostile or indifferent, the Christian Socialists
at least could not remain dumb.   With a man of his
diffidence, who shrank from anything in the shape of
public demonstration, it was not easy for them to know
how best to proceed: but eventually it was decided to
produce a series of papers on the man and his work, which
might at any rate speak of him as his friends knew him,
and prevent the spread of the libellous caricatures which
the *Record* was sending out to its readers. To this undertaking, in which Ludlow was the moving spirit, we owe
some of the most intimate of our pictures of him. The
material was never published in its intended form [1]:
but much of it is incorporated in his *Life*. Besides this
larger undertaking Ludlow drew up and published a full
and careful statement of the facts of his dismissal; [2] and
this was widely circulated and helped to explain the
revulsion of feeling that followed the verdict.

But the rallying of his friends for this task was the
least serious of the losses involved. Far more disastrous
was the ' cholera of resignations ' [3] with which Maurice
himself became infected. Always shy of the position

[1] A volume of similar intention was printed privately by ' a Cambridge M.A.' but I do not know his identity ; nor does his work reveal
much personal knowledge of Maurice.

[2] *King's College and Mr. Maurice. No. I. The Facts.* By ' a Barrister
of Lincoln's Inn,' published in March 1854—a pamphlet of sixty pages.

[3] Cf. *Life of Maurice*, ii. 172-174.

which he had held in the group, he now became convinced that his continuance in it was unjustifiable, that
he could only injure the cause by being publicly connected
with it, and that his followers realised this but from
motives of loyalty would not admit it. As early as
August 1853, in consequence of a small difficulty about
the appointment of two assessors for the Association
and the refusal of Ludlow to be one of them, he had
insisted that he had lost the confidence of his fellow-
members and must resign the presidency : and this was
the first of a succession of attempts. ' It was awful
work,' says Hughes,[1] ' having to fix him up again against
his will every three or four months in one post or another
which he thought he might slip out of.' The resultant
uncertainty could not but have an unsettling effect
upon them all, especially at the time when the new constitution, which Ludlow at least never liked, had to be
put into working order.   Just when they needed a firm
guidance to steer the movement into its fresh course,
his hand upon the tiller slackened its grasp, and at the
slightest sign of dissension he proposed to surrender
control altogether.   Indeed when once the decision at
King's College was made public, although his friends
would not let him resign, he became so terrified of doing
harm by allowing himself to be associated with them,
that he virtually gave up the public part of his work in
the field of co-operation.

It would be certainly untrue to suggest that the attack
upon their president was directly responsible for the
failure of Christian Socialism ; it seems evident that it
was a contributory cause of considerable importance.

One final difficulty of a general kind may be noticed,
arising out of the local peculiarities of London.   As

---

[1] *Life of Maurice,* ii. p. 172.

subsequent experiment has repeatedly proved, London is the most difficult city in the country for such an enterprise. It still remains the one centre almost untouched by the co-operative movement : indeed, apart from Woolwich, where the conditions are more like those of a north-country industrial town, no really successful attempt to plant either Stores or Associations there has been recorded. And the obstacles which still prove unsurmountable were even stronger half a century ago. Briefly speaking, the Londoner is the only townsman in Europe who prides himself on not knowing his next-door neighbour. Local patriotism, so strong in Lancashire, is completely absent. Diversity of employment fosters secrecy and suspicion. Size forbids corporate action and prevents the discovery of natural leaders. The 'cockney' is a thorough-going individualist, proud of ' minding his own business ' and delighting in an excuse to consider himself ill-used. He will take up a novelty with enthusiasm, but, unless he comes under the personal influence of one to whom he can be utterly loyal, he will tire of it in a month. The war may have shown that the popular conception of him has been unjust ; those who know and love him best, must admit that it was not pure fiction.

The characteristics of the Londoner go far to explain the special difficulties which the Christian Socialists had to overcome. In the North they would have had no trouble in finding managers for their Associations ; for the qualities of each man are intimately known to his comrades and fellow-workmen, and the ' windbag ' is not mistaken for the leader. Nor would a good man once chosen have had the same risk of disloyalty ; he would have commanded respect from the first, and the recognition of his reliability would have been a guarantee of the security of the undertaking. Moreover the Associates would have been better material, more accustomed to act together, and more sure of one another : they might at first have been fewer in number—the task of selection would have been the simpler for that—but those who joined could have been trusted to have counted the cost beforehand and to have been influenced by other motives than curiosity ; and when once they had started, they would have been slow to stop or confess themselves mistaken. The saddening record of petty jealousies and quarrels, of disloyalty and dishonesty, which marks the history of the London Associations, is in striking contrast with the stories of patient sacrifice and silent effort which brought success to the much less favoured attempts of northern co-operators. It is no mere accident that the Promoters' most enduring venture was that of the Manchester Hatters. The locality of the Christian Socialist movement was alone sufficient to explain its lack of success.

A further point of a more individual kind is one upon which Ludlow himself was not afraid to speak freely. Great as was his admiration for the generosity and self-sacrifice of Neale, he felt constrained to recognise that this lavish expenditure was not wholly advantageous. Very early in their work he had seen the danger of attracting to them the wrong type of Associate, men who had no motive other than the prospect of larger profits and easier conditions. After the start he had set himself to make it hard for the workers to get assistance or recognition, until they had shown by real self-denial that their aim was brotherhood, rather than financial benefit. Neale, with his impetuous willingness to supply money, did much to undermine the morale of the men. They became pauperised, lost their self-reliance, and

then when difficulties arose had not the courage or conviction to meet them.   Neale himself in later life recognised and deplored the ill-effects of his enthusiastic
liberality.[1] Greening in his account of Ludlow[2] lays much
stress on this, and considers that it goes far towards
explaining the failure of the Associations, as compared
with the co-operative experiments in the North.   Fay
is probably right in reckoning ' over-assistance from
above and consequently lack of initiative ' as the primary
cause of the failure.[3]   If it be true that Neale lost
£60,000 over the movement, it may well be that his
sacrifice was not an unmixed blessing.

But when we have made all allowances for these special
difficulties of time and place and circumstances, there
remains the conviction that in London at any rate, and
probably elsewhere, the scheme made too great a demand
on the moral qualities of the human material, upon whose
efforts and power of corporate life its success depended.
In the *First Report of the Society*[4] it is admitted that
' working men in general are not fit for association.
' They come into it with the idea that it is to fill their
pockets and lighten their work at once, and that every
man in an Association is to be his own master.   They find
their mistake in the first month or two, and then set to
quarrelling with everybody connected with the Association,
but more especially with their manager, and after much
bad blood has been roused, the Association breaks up insol-
vent, has to be reformed under stringent rules, and after the

---

[1] In a letter to Seligman quoted in *Owen and the Christian Socialists*
(*Pol. Sc. Quarterly*, i. p. 241).

[2] *Working Men's College Journal*, vol. xii.

[3] *Co-operation at home and abroad*, p. 222.   The other two causes
were in his opinion indiscipline among the workers and want of organisation among themselves and with the consumers' stores.

[4] P. 32.

expulsion of the refractory members.' The document goes on to illustrate this from the history of the shoe-makers; but, as we have seen, it is true in practically every case. No doubt such a disastrous state of affairs was more frequent in the early days, when no special pains were taken to select the Associates, or to test their fitness and keenness by a period of probation or by expecting them to do anything towards the raising of funds. The first few months ·were sufficient to demon-strate to the Promoters, that their belief that any group of workers would recognise the benefits and respond to the duties of the new method was too optimistic. But even later, when much greater precautions were devised, the same faults appeared sooner or later. Finally, when the Engineers' Associations exhibited exactly the same defects and it was proved that they could no longer excuse the failure of their members on the ground that they were all taken from the *déclassés* of the labour world, the Promoters were forced to confess that their enterprise had been premature, that though the ideal was, as they still unanimously maintained, right and worthy, it was not yet capable of being put into practice, and that education must be extended and developed before a successful result could be obtained. The *Report of the Manchester Conference* is equally clear, though its admissions are less outspoken. In its Appendix is printed a list of replies to a *questionnaire* submitted to the various bodies. One set of these deals with ' the methods most conducive to success' ; and though they are often simply the reflection of the mood of the moment, and sometimes directly contradict one another,[1] there is

---

[1] Atlas reports that success is due to ' equal advantages among the Associates, and the supervision of the management being vested in the members at a general meeting ' : the East End Ironworks ascribes it to ' management being invested in the hands of a few' (*Report*, p. 33).

a measure of unanimity which fully bears out the previous conclusion. Isham's report is characteristic of the majority. ' The great evil,' he writes, ' is too many disputes, too many discussions, too many meetings, too much interference.' [1] A strong manager rendered himself liable to the charge of being false to the spirit of association : a weak one could not secure adequate performance of the work. In the latter case, the complaints of lack of custom or capital are the natural consequence of slackness or indiscipline. In the former we can trace just grounds for apprehension in the repeated insistence that managers must deal frankly with their Associates, and must submit regular statements of the accounts for their inspection. Dishonesty on the one side and insubordination on the other were the real causes of the failure. Kingsley's verdict in 1856, ' it will require two generations of training both in morality and in drill,'[2] must have been by that time the opinion of all his colleagues. They had made their experiments ; they were not in the least ashamed of having done so; they believed that their scheme was adequate, and would have attained its end if the men had been ready for it : but they had discovered beyond dispute that at present it was impracticable ; and so, with a courage and faith beyond all praise, they set themselves to prepare for the day when it should be possible to try again and succeed. So long as the Christian ethic is accepted and men confess that love is more righteous than hate, co-operation than competition, association than selfishness, the experiment will have to be repeated. Many times it may be tried and seem to fail : progress is slow and men are weak. Some day it will succeed. Kingsley's two generations have passed away : the

---

[1] *Report*, p. 37.   [2] *Life of Kingsley*, i. p. 474.

Guild Socialists are attempting a similar reform : will they be better supported ?   Will they find humanity able to rise to the level required of it ? And will the Church of the Christian Socialists give them, for what it is worth, its assistance ?

But we cannot close our history of the Associations on a note of failure.   To do so would be false to them and to the great men from whom they drew their life.   Ludlow, reviewing the history of co-operative production in his book on the *Progress of the Working Classes 1832-1867* (the joint work of himself and Lloyd Jones), has thus summarised his verdict upon association : [1] ' It has a moral value which is not indicated by the number of the men whom it sets at work, or the figure of its business. . . . Co-operation first expels from the shop drunkenness and all open disorder, introducing in their place a number of small adjustments and contrivances of a nature to facilitate work or promote the comfort of the worker.   By degrees it exterminates the small tricks and dishonesties which the opposition of interests between employer and employed too often excuses ; it is felt to be to the interest of all that all work should be good, that no time should be lost.   Fixity of employment coupled with a common interest creates new ties between man and man, till there grows up a sort of family feeling, the only danger of which is that of its becoming jealous and exclusive towards the outsider.   Let this state of things last awhile and there is evolved a new type of working man, endued not only with honesty and frankness, but with a dignity, a self-respect, a sense of conscious freedom which are peculiar to the co-operator. . . . This development may be confidently looked forward to as a normal result of co-operative production.'

[1] Pp. 143, 144.

Such testimony can be paralleled from very many speeches both of the Promoters and of the Associates : similar passages occur constantly in the columns of the *Christian Socialist*. We have quoted this alone, because it represents the considered judgment of one who may be supposed by the time of writing to have been thoroughly disillusioned, and whom we should pardon if he had written with a touch of bitterness. That after his devoted labours and many disappointments, he can still speak so highly of the moral effects of association upon the men who had failed him, is proof not only of the reality of its influence, but of the large-hearted generosity of the writer.[1]

---

[1] Dr. Alfred Marshall's comment is worth quoting : ' Experience has partly moderated and partly confirmed the bright hopes entertained about half a century ago, to the effect that co-operative production and copartnership together would gradually develop a set of working class leaders with wide business experience . . . In the last two generations much has been learnt as to what can be done even under present conditions, and what could be done under a nearer approach to ideal perfection of human nature.' (*Industry and Trade*, p. 838.) The subsequent pages deserve careful study.

CHAPTER XI

THE FOUNDATION OF THE WORKING MEN'S COLLEGE

WE have spoken of the ' failure ' of the Associations at some length, because it has been so emphasised by superficial students of their work as to create the impression that the Christian Socialists were a band of well-meaning amateurs, who made an interesting entry into social history, aroused an amount of attention quite disproportionate to their achievements, conferred a certain indirect benefit upon the workers, but in their real enterprise accomplished nothing but disaster. This notion of them has been sedulously fostered by writers whose motives in desiring to minimise the value of Christian Socialism, though not in all cases identical, are sufficiently obvious. But it has done grave injustice to their memory ; and its advocates show a complete misunderstanding of the position. A brief summary of their history will make this clear, and at this point will not be' out of place.

The Christian Socialists were Christian in no merely conventional sense. One of them has strong claim to be considered a saint as well as a prophet ; and all the leaders were men to whom their faith was the most vital part of their lives. They saw—how could they help seeing—the disease of the body politic. Being Christians, they believed themselves to possess knowledge of a principle which, if it could be expressed in appropriate action, would effect a cure. They diagnosed the malady, discovered as they thought the seat of the evil, and set themselves to find a method of applying Christianity. This they found already employed in the Associations in Paris and somewhat similarly in the Co-operative Stores in the North of England. The former of these seemed to them specially adapted to embody the spirit of brotherhood, of Christianity in action : it covered the sphere of production; and if industry was to be transformed, it was with production that a start must be made. At the same time they recognised that it would not be an easy task to introduce it, since it was at present unfamiliar and would make large demands on the moral qualities of the workers. So they decided to test their method in practice, to experiment upon a few groups or model Associations, and so to learn whether they were right in their estimate of the value of the scheme. They founded their Associations, watched them as the scientist watches his apparatus or the doctor his patient, noted the results week by week for two years, and at last arrived at a twofold conviction. They learnt in the first place a confidence in the value of association as a means of reforming industry, and in the possibility of its ultimate success, which no disappointments could shake; they were prepared to give their lives to the cause on the strength of those two years of trial. But they learnt also that the task was harder than they had hoped to find it, that it would take years of progress before it could be universally accepted, and that the principal difficulty arose from the lack of education and moral training in the workers themselves. Their experiment had thus served its purpose : it had supplied them with an answer as to the worth and the practicability of association, and had suggested to them the next step which they must take for the furtherance of their object.

Meanwhile, though their energies had largely been devoted to associative production, they had not neglected the attempts being made to apply the principle of co-operation to the easier field of distribution. When they began their work, they found a few scattered groups of working men struggling heroically but without influence or unity. To the world at large co-operation (thanks to Robert Owen) seemed essentially godless and revolutionary; the groups engaged upon it were, with the exception of the Rochdale Pioneers, small and weak. The Christian Socialists were content to share the obloquy : they wished neither to flatter nor to patronise, but to stand alongside their fellow-workers as friends in the same cause. At first they were very naturally suspected of ulterior designs. Soon their critics, except the professional agitators like Ernest Jones [1] whose influence depended upon the iniquities of the upper classes, were convinced of their sincerity. And when mutual trust was established, the newcomers were able to do a vast work. They rallied and united co-operators all over the kingdom : they gave them a platform and secured for them the attention of the public and of the legislature : they provided the movement with a legal status and an organic corporate life : they supplied out of their own number men who were prepared to spend and be spent as ' the trusted legal experts and political advisers ' of the leaders of labour for the next forty years : more than any other men, they made the co-operative movement.   Nor was this alone the sum of their achieve-

[1] Cf. debate between him and Lloyd Jones at Padiham (*Christian Socialist*, ii. pp. 369-393, and Gammage, *History of the Chartist Movement*, p. 382).

ment. In every field of social service the influence of their adventure was felt. Ludlow's unobtrusive labours for the Friendly Societies, Maurice's devotion to the education of the workers, Kingsley's enthusiasm for sanitary reform, Octavia Hill's crusade for the better housing of the poor—each of these, and many another half-forgotten heroism, owed its inspiration to Christian Socialism. And all this has been neglected or mentioned with sneers, because ' the Associations failed.'

That was the position when Slaney's Act was passed at the end of their two years' work. With the passing of the Act there was an opportunity for them to pause and take stock of the situation. For the movement had entered on a new phase ; and their connection with it must be revised and readjusted. Hitherto they had been indispensable as leaders and spokesmen of a cause that was striving for recognition and the right to exist. Now they had made it legal and easy for others to carry on, and had created a body, the Annual Conference, which would naturally take their place. What was the sphere in which they could henceforth best serve the ideal with which they had started—the ideal of a Christian industrial system ?

With co-operation as a business method they were obviously not specially concerned. They neither were, nor had ever pretended to be, interested in it except as embodying the principle of their faith. They had always been afraid of developing its outward commercial aspect and thereby obscuring its inward moral meaning : Maurice especially had held back from some of their undertakings on this account ; and we have seen that differences had arisen continually between Ludlow and Neale over it. They were not qualified to take the lead in developing the business and trade of the movement.

Clearly their duty did not lie there. Some of them might and certainly would do much good work in that field; but for the group as a whole it was unsuitable alike to their motive and to their capacities.

Setting this aside there remained a choice between two alternative tasks, a choice suggested by the lessons of the Associations. Either they could continue to study the problems of co-operative production, to demonstrate its value, and to extend the practice of it—which would mean the continuance of work similar to that which had occupied most of their time during the two years; or they could try to hasten the coming of the new age of industry by supplying educational facilities which should remedy the defects in character revealed by their experiment. The former of these had its attractions, although they had all now given up the dream that they had only to found a few Associations in order to 'convert all England and usher in the millennium at once' [1]—a dream which Hughes was perhaps the only one to take seriously. Personal ties with the existing groups of workers were strong : there was a moral obligation upon them to support those whose struggles they had watched so long. And actual experience was the best form of education : they had seen men developing into fine characters, growing in brotherhood, in self-control and self-sacrifice. As propaganda, an ounce of demonstration was worth a ton of theory. And yet after all was it any longer their best work ? Would not the Associations be all the better for more independence ? Had they not shepherded them long enough ? Now that the first trials were safely passed, it might be wise to retire and leave the workers to their own efforts. The Rochdale men had stood alone, and learned more by doing

[1] Cf. Hughes, *Memoir of a Brother*, p. 111.

so than they could have done on easier terms. The managers had gained their experience now, and ought to be trustworthy. Besides, education was plainly needed, perhaps more needed than anything. And they were in a position to supply it : the workers trusted them ; two years' experience had shown them how to set about the task ; some of them were teachers by profession already, and most of them could take a hand somewhere in the curriculum. Surely this was their duty ; they must be content to prepare the way for association by training the workers and impressing on them those moral qualities without which association would never be practicable.

Such was their state of mind during the months after the passing of the Act, while they were considering the reconstruction of the Society, and developing plans for their next year's work. Maurice writing a retrospect long afterwards to Ludlow expresses the situation as he saw it. ' I have never repented, and hope that I never shall repent, of having been united with you in maintaining that co-operation as applied to trade has a Christian foundation. . . . But the more I compared our proceedings in London with those of the men who were working unhelped at Rochdale and elsewhere in the North, the more I was convinced that we should mar the cause grievously and weaken any moral influence that we might possess, by continuing to meddle with the commercial part of the business ; that doing little, and that little badly, we should become the victims of clever sharpers like Le Chevalier, and should bring disgrace upon a principle which we felt to be sound. . . . I was free to consider whether there was not another opening for the assertion of the principle of co-operation, and whether it was not our special calling to avail ourselves of that opening. A college expressed to my mind precisely the work that we could undertake, and ought to undertake, as professional men ; we might bungle in this also ; but there seemed to me a manifestly Divine direction towards it in all our previous studies and pursuits. And so far as we could give a hint of the way in which the professional and working classes might co-operate, so far I believed we should help to heal one of the great sores of the commonwealth, counteract the exclusiveness of literary men, undermine the notion that the patronage of rank or wealth is that which is wanted to elevate the labourer.' [1]

This letter anticipates a later position. In 1852 there was no definite need for a decision between the alternatives which lay before the Christian Socialists. The Society was being reorganised, and much of its work was done ; but much still remained to do, both in relation to its own Associations and to the movement in the country which looked to its members for help in the legal business necessitated by the new law. They need not retire, or even think of retiring, yet. Only in drafting their programme they would give scope for more definitely educational work than had hitherto been possible. Now that they had the Hall of Association in Castle Street and in all probability fewer claims upon their time, they could develop the holding of lectures and classes for the members of their Associations and for working men generally. Maurice had always favoured this side of their enterprise: Ludlow, ever since the old days of the Cranbourne Tavern, had recognised its value to the movement : Kingsley, who had been complaining that they gave him no share in their doings, could help them here : Mansfield, though at the time he was in Paraguay, was

[1] *Life of Maurice*, ii. p. 550.

particularly set upon it, and even before his departure, in May 1852, had mooted the possibility of a Working Men's College: Brewer and Hullah and one or two others of Maurice's King's College colleagues would lend a hand: almost everybody could be used.

For indeed, as Ludlow pointed out in what must be one of the last of his published papers, that on 'The Origin of the College' in the jubilee volume of the Working Men's College, education had never been forgotten in their work. Conferences and lectures in one form or another had played a part in it throughout; and the holding of meetings open to all working men had recently been resumed. In the Laws for an Association in *Tract V.* special mention had been made of schools, of a library, museum and reading-room, as objects which the movement ought to aim at. Nor had this been merely the expression of a pious hope. By the autumn of 1851 the Central Board had taken the matter up; rules for a library were printed in the *Christian Socialist*; and contributions of books began to come in. Special emphasis is laid upon this aspect of their enterprise in the pages of the *First Report.*[1] More definite work would no doubt have been undertaken, but for the lack of a suitable room and the pressure of existing business upon the Promoters. So it was no great innovation to develop alongside of the fortnightly conferences a programme of lectures and classes definitely educational in purpose: the opportunity was favourable: the experiment could do no harm and might lead to more ambitious efforts, such as Mansfield had in mind. There already existed a committee of the Promoters to supervise their publishing, and containing Maurice, Ludlow and Hughes among its members; and the functions of this body were

[1] Pp. 18, 19.

extended by the new Constitution; it became the 'Committee for Teaching and Publication' and was instructed to undertake arrangements.

The first course was therefore fixed for the month of December 1852, and a handbill announcing the titles of lectures and names of the lecturers was printed. The subjects covered a very wide range, no doubt with the idea of testing the feelings of the workers. Maurice spoke on the historical plays of Shakespeare, Cooper on his favourite Burns; of the other Promoters, Penrose dealt with architecture, Goderich with entomology, Johnson with geography, and Hansard with astronomy —in two lectures specially intended for children. There were several lecturers not belonging to the group, Trench, Maskelyne, Deputy Reader in mineralogy at Oxford and afterwards for some time a teacher at the Working Men's College, and Hullah whose subject, 'Vocal Music,' was intended to prepare the way for the starting of a singing class. Lectures were to begin at 8.30. Admission was to cost twopence, or to reserved seats sixpence.

No details of the success of the course have been preserved, but its result must have been encouraging, since a similar programme was arranged for the next year, several new lecturers, including Kingsley, Grove, and Lloyd Jones, being obtained.

In addition to these popular lectures, a more serious effort to provide educational opportunities was made by the holding of weekly classes. These were quite a new undertaking; and their syllabus is of special interest. Being a weekly engagement it was less easy to get outside help for them than for single lectures; and the bulk of the work fell upon members of the group. The proposed classes and their directors were: Grammar—T. Hughes and A. A. Vansittart; English History—Maurice assisted by E. V. Neale and A. H. Louis ; French—J. M. Ludlow ; Book-keeping—Newling ; Singing—J. Hullah. Classes were also to be formed in Drawing and Political Economy. In addition and most important of all Maurice's own Bible-readings, which had been held at his house in Queen Square on Monday or latterly Tuesday evenings, were now transferred to the Hall and held on Sundays. A Bible, presented to Maurice by the members of this ' Hall of Association ' class and containing the signatures of its donors, is still preserved in the library of the Working Men's College ; and the list is an interesting one. No attempt was made to restrict any of these lectures or classes to members of the Associations, and all of them were thrown open to women as well as men.[1]

Such was the position until after the expulsion of Maurice from King's College. Educational work had been started alongside of the Associations and the experiment had proved abundantly successful. The question of extending it by the foundation of a definite College had been raised on sundry occasions by the more enterprising and far-sighted members of the group: to Ludlow and Maurice the ideal had perhaps been present from the very first ; at any rate their earliest contributions to the *Christian Socialist* show that it was already in their minds then. Hitherto it had inevitably remained a distant possibility : they had no leisure for such a project, nor any means of putting it into effect. Now suddenly all this was changed ; and a distinct call came almost at once.

On December 27th an address was presented to Maurice, signed by 967 working men of London and expressing to him their sympathy, gratitude, and affection ; among

---

[1] The fullest account of these lectures and classes is that given by Ludlow in *The Working Men's College, 1854-1904*, pp. 15-17.

the signatories were Allan and Newton of the A.S.E. as well as the managers and members of all the Associations. One of the speakers expressed the hope that he might ' not find it a fall to cease to be a Professor at King's College and to become the Principal of the Working Men's College ' : on that evening the new venture was, as Ludlow phrases it, ' spiritually founded.'   Maurice was free to follow up the suggestion : a house was available owing to the closing of the Needlewomen's Association at 31 Red Lion Square : [1] knowledge of the requirements and capabilities of the probable students had already been obtained : further details could be learned from the authorities of the People's College at Sheffield upon which Lloyd Jones had reported to the Promoters some time ago : among their own body a nucleus staff could be collected and they were in touch with a number of others who would be willing to help. How Maurice regarded the proposal has been already seen in the letter to Ludlow quoted above. It was ' Divine direction ' ; everything pointed to the duty of accepting it as such. They decided to do so without delay.

One obvious preliminary was to obtain particulars of the College in Sheffield, a body originally started in August 1842 by the Rev. R. S. Bayley, a Congregationalist minister, and revived by working men in 1848.[2] Neale wrote to its secretary for details and at the meeting of the Council of Promoters on January 11th, 1854, his reply was read ; and on the motion of Hughes, seconded by Lloyd Jones, it was resolved that ' it be referred to the Committee

[1] The College was moved in 1857 to Great Ormond St. and in 1905 to Crowndale Road, Camden Town.

[2] An excellent account of the early history of this Sheffield College is given by T. Rowbotham in the *Working Men's College Magazine* (a periodical issued monthly during the three years 1859-61), i. pp. 71, 72, and 98-101.

of Teaching and Publication [1] to frame, and so far as they think fit to carry out, a plan for the establishment of a People's College in connection with the Metropolitan Associations.' Maurice was asked to draw up a scheme : he set to work at once, and on February 7th submitted to the Council an elaborate proposal which had already been considered by the Committee and printed as a twelve-page pamphlet. This was accepted with some modifications as the basis for the future College, and a circular was drawn up embodying its chief points and explaining the purpose of the proposal. Both the scheme and the circular are printed in Furnivall's articles on the ' History of the College' in the second volume of its *Magazine,* for the year 1860.

To arouse public sympathy with the project and if possible to interest those who might be willing to assist the scheme either by financial support or by offers of service, Maurice was invited to give a set of public lectures, and these were delivered in Willis' Rooms in June and July. They were subsequently published as part of the volume entitled *Learning and Working* and dedicated to Ludlow in a letter from which we have already quoted.[2] From the result of these lectures they felt encouraged to make a start ; for the proposal had been received favourably, and £87 had been collected by this means alone. A syllabus was carefully constructed : a teachers' meeting was held : circulars were issued : an inaugural address by the new Principal was given on October 30th in St. Martin's Hall, and fully reported next day by Brewer in the *Morning Herald* : and on November 2nd the first term was begun with an entry of 176 students,[3] William

---

[1] A list of the members of this Committee is given in Appendix B.

[2] See above p. 72.

[3] *Working Men's College Journal,* iii. p. 240—an article based on the original register. Furnivall (*W. M. C. Magazine,* ii. p. 168) gives the number as 120, though later (p. 190) he states it as 145.

Newton among them, these being about equally divided between operatives and clerks.

A very full account of these early days has been published in the magazines issued from time to time by the College, and in the jubilee volume already quoted. To recapitulate the story belongs rather to the future historian of the College than to a writer upon Christian Socialism. But a glance at the curriculum is enough to show how deeply the group whose work we have been considering was involved in the new branch of their activity.

Maurice lectured three times a week; on Sundays on St. John's Gospel, on Tuesdays on 'Political terms illustrated by English literature,' and on Fridays on 'The reign of King John illustrated by Shakespeare's play.' Ludlow lectured on 'the Law of Partnership,' a course intended specially for the members of the Associations. Hughes proposed to deal with 'Sanitary legislation,' but no candidates wished to take the subject. Furnivall had a group of strong shoemakers to instruct in English Grammar; Walsh dealt with 'Public Health'; Hose, by this time a London curate, taught Geometry; John Westlake [1] and Richard Buckley Litchfield, two recent recruits, neither of whom were Promoters, Arithmetic and Algebra; Brewer, anxious to throw himself into this branch of their work, undertook 'the Geography of England as connected with its history.' Of the other three who were strangers to the Christian Socialists, Ruskin, who had received a circular from Furnivall and had offered to take a drawing class, was the most famous, and as an advertisement to the College was of much value.

---

[1] Westlake met Maurice on coming down from Cambridge to Lincoln's Inn in the autumn of 1852 : he was from the first a supporter of their work, but did not take a prominent part in it until this time.

Hitherto he had written none of his sociological books [1]; and it appears that the experience of working men which he obtained during the years of his connection with Red Lion Square gave him his first impulse in this direction. He taught in the College until 1860, and during the next five years produced the three books which, whatever may be thought of their economics, always seemed to him the most important of his writings. Certainly their influence was immense; and here again the ultimate origin of that influence is the Christian Socialist movement.

In the next term the number of students increased and several fresh teachers were secured.[2] French, Latin, German, and Greek appear either then or shortly afterwards on the syllabus. All the lectures were of course given in the evenings, from 8 to 9 and from 9 to 10 p.m., so that students could go home after their day's work and come on to the College after their evening meal. Amusements were not neglected, Hughes' sparring classes and Furnivall's Sunday walks being prominent features at an early stage in the life of the place.

A word also must be said upon the broad principles underlying the foundation of the College. It was, as all their work had been, an attempt to embody what they had called Christian Socialism in a concrete form; that is, to teach men by practical experience that they were brothers, united as sons of God under the headship of

---

[1] Hitherto he had been known solely as artist and art-critic. The only forecast of his future work was the chapter in the *Stones of Venice* on ' the Nature of Gothic ' which treats of the function of the workman (vol. ii. pp. 149-228). This chapter separately printed was distributed to the audience at Maurice's inaugural address before the opening of the College.

[2] Huber, *Reisebriefe*, ii. p. 355, gives the total as only 175 : but this is not in keeping with other narratives cited above. He states the attendance at the various classes as follows : Bible 50 ; Algebra 49 ; English 42 ; Drawing 33 ; Geometry 19 ; Law of Partnership 4.

Jesus Christ, and fellow-workers with Him in the promotion of His Kingdom among men.   Like all the subsequent schemes of which it has been the forerunner, schemes ranging in their scope from the Settlement or Mission to the Workers' Educational Association, the College had a double object.   Not only did it exist to benefit the workers, by bringing within their reach opportunities for development hitherto regarded as the sole privilege of the upper classes, and so to train them to take a fuller share in the life of the nation and in the reform of social and industrial conditions ; but it desired to influence the wealthier and more fortunate, by giving them the means of coming into personal contact with the lives of those from whom they had been separated by birth and circumstances, and so to teach them the responsibility of their position, the joy of service, the value of friendship with the poor, and of sympathy with aspirations to which ignorance had hitherto kept them strangers.   Maurice had seen both these aspects of their work from the start, and had not hesitated to proclaim that the second of them was fundamental.   ' It would be a pretence,' he declared, ' to say that benevolence to the working men was the primary impulse of those who sought their alliance.' [1]

To-day this ideal of mutual education (in which it must be confessed the rich have the most to learn and receive the larger benefits) has become universally familiar.   The phrases in which it is expressed are truisms.   We all accept, at least in theory, the belief that it is part of the duty of every citizen to understand

[1] *Working Men's College Magazine*, i. p. 109.   He begins this article by stating that ' the College was established first for the benefit of us the teachers, secondly for the benefit of those whom we taught.   The statement sounds discreditable ; but I maintain that it is true and should not be concealed.'

from direct contact the conditions under which his fellows pass their lives. Every school and college is linked up with some social service : and in any place where there is vitality and vision the connection is something more than nominal or financial. But in Maurice's time all such ideas were unknown. 'Slumming,' that fashionable vice of the eighties, was as yet the secret of a few real lovers of the poor like Shaftesbury. Settlements were unknown ; and the Mechanics' Institutes, which to some extent took their place, did not touch any but prosperous artisans. Sporadic efforts of a highly pietistic sort, in night-schools or on Sunday afternoons, inculcated the reading of the Scriptures and the doctrines of Samuel Smiles—that strange compound which in mid-Victorian days passed itself off upon the middle classes as Christianity. But of all that we now mean by social service, of all that the Christian Socialists designed their College to promote, there was then no trace at all. Here too they were pioneers—and here too others, Toynbee and Barnett and a score more (to whom be all honour), have been credited with what is due to their predecessors.

And this twofold task the Working Men's College was admirably fitted to perform, and has performed with marked success.

So far as the benefit of the workers is concerned, the College was intended to fulfil an ideal put into words by Ludlow in the article in the first number of the *Christian Socialist* [1] in which, outlining the principles of their movement, he had written : ' We shall all agree, probably, that our Universities must be universal in fact as well as in name ; must cease to be monopolised for the benefit of one or two privileged classes ; we may differ as to

[1] Vol. i. p. 2.

the means by which that monopoly is to be broken up, that universality attained, whether by lowering the benefits of university education to the reach of the many, or by drawing up to them the pre-eminent few of every class,'—an ideal which is still far from being adequately realised. The Christian Socialists could not hope to break that monopoly so far as the old universities were concerned : the power which can compel reform in that quarter has yet to be discovered. But they could do something to bring a university education and the spirit of university life within the reach of the many : and this the College was intended to achieve. They aimed at no merely technical training ; they did not want to turn out skilled workmen, or to enable their students to become clerks instead of operatives ; their teaching was not to be estimated by its commercial or utilitarian value. Rather they wished to give the workers the opportunity of obtaining all that is meant by a liberal education ; to give them not knowledge only but wisdom, not attainments but character ; to make them not necessarily cleverer at their own trades nor more fully equipped for success in their careers, but better men, better citizens, better Christians ; above all to build up in them that spirit of corporate life, of brotherhood and membership one with another, of which in Maurice's eyes the very word ' College ' was symbolic, and which he and his followers believed to be the true meaning of Socialism. This was and has always been the purpose of the Working Men's College.

The novelty and audacity of the enterprise is admirably brought out by Litchfield, who had joined the group in February 1854 after coming down from Cambridge, and was intimately connected with the College for forty-seven years. In a paper on ' the Beginnings of

the Working Men's College,' written in 1902, he surveys
the facilities for education open to the workers at the time
of its foundation and the attitude of the public towards
it, and concludes, ' The idea that the sort of education
enjoyed by the " upper classes " could be of any interest
or use to men who have to earn their bread by common
daily work, seemed fantastic to ninety-nine people out of
a hundred. . . . It is no stretch of language to say that,
in 1854, the infant College offered working men what they
had not had offered them before : it was virtually a
unique institution.'

But if the scheme was almost startlingly bold, if the
attempt to supply an education of a university type to
men whose previous lives had left them no leisure for
obtaining more than the elements of knowledge and who
could not be expected to possess or even to desire
culture of a higher kind, might seem quixotic, if the mere
suggestion that it was possible to reproduce the rare
and subtle atmosphere of the older universities, among
casual groups of artisans meeting for evening classes in
a house in Red Lion Square, savoured of absurdity,
nevertheless it was rewarded with an astonishing measure
of success. ' What has this College of yours done ? '
a sceptic once asked Litchfield. ' Well, it has produced
George Tansley'[1] was the reply; and those who accept
the test of fruits will be satisfied. For in Tansley and
many another is to be found that peculiar *ethos*, that
nameless but quite tangible quality, which Oxford and
Cambridge in their arrogance have sometimes claimed
as the heritage of their sons alone. Generation after
generation of students at the College is infected with it :

---

[1] Tansley served the College all his life, and when he retired from
business gave himself wholly to it. In 1888 he was given the degree of
M.A. by Archbishop Benson. When he died in 1902 he was Dean of
Studies, and controlling all the educational work.

to some it appears from the first to be their native air ; others resist and hardly respond at all ; but none are wholly uninfluenced. The sympathy which learns to call nothing common or unclean ; the versatility which is not confined to a single subject or set of opinions ; the sense of perspective which sees its own pursuits against a background as wide as life itself ; the judgment which knows and can state its own convictions without refusing to recognise those of its neighbour ; the ability which combines the patience and accuracy of the ' digger ' with the freedom and imagination of the ' builder ' ; these characteristics of cultured manhood have been produced as richly there as in localities apparently far more favourable. And along with culture has developed, as Maurice had hoped, a corporate spirit among the students, revealing itself in a loyalty to the College and a fellowship with one another such as any *alma mater* would be proud to discover in her sons. Few, if any, educational institutions have so quickly developed a tradition or so steadily maintained their hold upon the affections of their members. Almost from the first, out of the small band who applied in the opening years, the College secured three men, Tansley being one, who went through the course with marked success, were duly elected Fellows, and proved themselves ' fit to stand beside Charles Mansfield and Walsh, the best and purest.' [1] There can be no more signal testimony to the personal influence of Maurice than the passionate devotion to his memory which has inspired and unified the whole history of his foundation. Conscious as he always was even here of his shortcomings, disappointed though he might be on many occasions by developments of which he disapproved, no founder has ever imparted to his

[1] Furnivall in *Working Men's College Magazine*, ii. p. 170.

offspring a fuller measure of his spirit, or more truly lived on in its career. Despite many influences hostile to all that he prized most and many changes which he would have deplored, his character has consecrated the work from its birth to the present day.

And if the College has fulfilled the more direct purpose of its existence, its success in educating its teachers has been equally notable and perhaps even more important. During all the earlier period of its history nothing is more significant than the number and distinction of the men who have undertaken voluntary work on its staff, and so been brought into contact with working men and given interest in social problems. In this way it has had an influence upon the conscience of the nation and a share in the promotion of progress, which can hardly be over-estimated. Young men fresh from the universities, like Litchfield and the two Lushingtons, or older men with reputations already made, like Ruskin and Rossetti, have from the first been drawn into the teaching staff, converted by experience to active sympathy with reform, and sent out as missionaries in the cause. Some few have kept up their duties there through a lifetime of service : for most this has been impossible ; pressure of other work has obliged them to retire after a year or two : but their places have been taken by newcomers ; and thus a stream of fresh supporters has been passed through its gates and has carried its lessons out into the life of the country.

Typical of its effect upon such visitors is the case of one of its original teachers, C. Lowes Dickinson. He had been in Italy painting from 1850 to 1854, and while there had made firm friends with Archibald Campbell. On returning to England he met several of the Christian Socialists, and running into Charles Mansfield one day in London was carried off to Maurice's, presented to the group who were discussing the plans for the College, and without further ado constrained to join them. ' My first introduction to the Working Men's College changed my ideal of life,' [1] he wrote fifty years later. ' He was an influence for good in the midst of a somewhat disturbed atmosphere,' writes a pupil,[2] comparing him with his two famous colleagues in the art classes. He, like so many of us, found his soul in the fellowship of those less fortunate than himself; and the devotion to Maurice, which comes out so nobly in his letters and in the portrait, was one acknowledgment of the debt.

The work of the Christian Socialists had been begun in the night-school in Little Ormond Yard; it ended, for the group though not for its members, in the Working Men's College. There, at least until Maurice's death, they had still a bond of common service, though after 1854 their corporate contribution to social history may be said to be over. With education they had started; to education they returned.

Yet it is to miss the whole purport and value of their ' Socialism ' if we regard their adventures in the field of co-operative production as an episode, or set them down, as Maurice in his modesty was ready to do, as the work of a body of academic and unpractical theorists. The strength and permanence of their message comes just from this, that they were in the best sense of the word educators in all that they did. They possessed, and are almost unique among social reformers in possessing, that twofold capacity which is the quality of the true educator: they had an expert knowledge of their subject, and at the same time they were in closest

[1] *Working Men's College, 1854-1904,* p. 26.

[2] J. P. Emslie in *Working Men's College, 1854-1904,* p. 46.

contact and sympathy with the human lives to whose service their knowledge was to be applied : they escaped the cold and inhuman logicality of Marx and the Fabians and the emotionalism and mental chaos of William Morris and the Anarchists. Combining these two gifts, the understanding of social theory and the understanding of human nature, they were able to construct a philosophy of industrial reform and a creed of progress, to which after two generations we are now slowly returning.

There are in the history of any new movement of human aspiration three definite stages to be traced. After the discovery of the fresh fact or principle, there is first the period of experiment, when data have to be collected and the scope of the problem surveyed and mapped out : this empirical phase usually ends with some great thinker, or group of thinkers, who draw together the results hitherto obtained and construct from them a complete and often a singularly perfect system. There follows a period of discussion, when the system thus developed is subjected to criticism and elaboration ; and in this second phase two contradictory schools of thought appear, representing the two standpoints, individual and collective, human and universal, from which every problem can be considered. After acute controversy the third period begins, in which an attempt is made to synthesise the alternatives and to fashion out of them a scheme which shall, so far as is possible, combine and reconcile the truth of each— a scheme which when complete often bears striking resemblance to that with which the first period closed.

A clear instance of this normal process of growth can be found in the history of Christian theology in the first five centuries. After the close of the Apostolic age there was a time of experiment. The Gospel had to be studied in all its bearings and interpreted empirically in terms of differing temperaments and different modes of thought. It was an epoch of guess-work, more or less intelligent, often wild and fantastic, often revealing a real anticipation of future discoveries. It ended with Origen, the greatest thinker and the greatest teacher of antiquity, who combining in himself the two necessary qualities of intellectual ability and moral depth, neglecting neither the universal or divine nor the individual and human point of approach, succeeded not only in bringing order out of confusion, but in fusing together into a harmonious and balanced system all the elements requisite for a solution of the problem.

On his death there followed a period of detailed study and controversy in which two schools became prominent. The Alexandrians, laying stress upon the divine aspect and magnifying the intellectual at the expense of the moral, produced a theology brilliantly logical but practically sterile and inadequate : they composed an admirable ' paper ' system, but their efforts were vitiated by bad psychology : as a scheme it was excellent, but it did not work. Their rivals, the Antiochenes, were strong just where they were weak ; approaching the problem from its human side and with a strong sense of its moral bearings, they were able to criticise their opponents' theories with crushing effect, but when they tried to set up a system of their own they fell into inconsistencies and uncertainty.

Finally, after some two centuries of discussion, the attempt was made to achieve a synthesis, and in the Creed of Chalcedon the two elements which had been separated since the days of Origen reappear side by side. As a solution it may lack, as in the last resort Origen's theology lacks, complete logical consistency. To reconcile the outlook of the two standpoints appears to be a

task transcending the powers of human logic ; they over-
lap, but they do not wholly coincide. But even if at
the heart of every problem there lies a paradox, at least
the synthesis provides what is lacking in the alternatives,
a satisfactory working hypothesis : men can use it for
the practical business of their lives. It may not supply
a cut-and-dried answer to all the secrets of the universe ;
it surpasses, and thereby stimulates, human reasoning ;
for man's feet are set in a large room, and the horizon to
which he must travel widens ever before him. But at
least it summarises for him those indispensable elements
in the problem of life, which he can only neglect at the
peril of self-imprisonment within the cell of a one-sided
rationalism. And he can test its validity in his own
experience and in that of the race by its results.
Apply it to the needs and difficulties of life, and it
works.

Even so it has been in the history of Socialism during
the past century. It began with the empiricists, St.
Simon and Fourier in France and Robert Owen in England,
men who realised the problem to be faced, and in their
various ways made or suggested experiments for its
solution. The influence of their environment and the
force of their reaction against it biassed and distorted
their efforts. Owen, for all his devotion and constructive
ability, was hampered by his intellectual weakness. He
seized upon an old and bad philosophy, the elements of
truth in which certainly needed restatement, exaggerated
it, and proclaimed it with the shallow dogmatism of a
mind untrained to think. But despite this he had much
real genius, and many of the fruits of his empiricism were
permanently valuable. He was a pioneer, and as such
the flaws in his work can be understood.

This first period closed with the group of great thinkers

and teachers with whom we have been concerned. They possessed very fully as individuals, and still more so in their corporate capacity, both the requisite qualities. They were students and men of notable intellectual power, familiar with the lessons of history and possessing a large and consistent philosophy of life : in them was contained all that was best in the teaching of Buchez, the Saint-Simonian, of Leroux, the Fourierist, of Proudhon and of Louis Blanc, as well as of the English thinkers and experimenters, Thompson and Gray and Owen, who had outlined constructive schemes for the reformation of society. And they were equally gifted with the understanding of their fellow-men, with sympathy for human weakness and with vision of human aspirations ; they knew the material with which as social reformers they had to work, and they knew the end to which that material should be devoted. They grasped both the intellectual and the moral aspects of the problem ; and so were saved alike from the danger of theorising in the void and of experimenting without any clear or sufficient purpose in view. Starting with a definite ideal of what a true social order should be, they were able to adapt the means to the end and to outline a programme which should achieve the desired result. They realised that the process of achievement must be long, that the pattern could not be copied universally at once, and so having exhibited it in a ' working model ' they were content to devote themselves to the task of preparing for its future acceptance.

And after them began the second phase. The different elements in their solution had to be analysed out, precipitated, and crystallised. Marx, whose brilliant analytical gifts and ruthless if vitiated logic conceal the defects of his thinking, his unsound economics and his lack of construc-

tive power, is reckoned the father of ' scientific ' Socialism.[1]
So far as he shows any constructive thought, he represents
the collective or universal standpoint, the deification of a
mechanical system. His Jewish birth, German training
and life of loneliness and exile robbed him of breadth and
balance, of sympathy with human ideals and knowledge
alike of his material and of the end to which it should be
shaped. He is essentially a spirit in revolt, passionately
stirred by the evidences of social evil, ruthless in analysis
and denunciation of its causes ; and lacking the qualities
most necessary to the genuine reformer. His own thought
is almost wholly critical and destructive : he has no
policy for the morrow of the revolution. And his successors
have been content, either in common with the Syndi-
calists, to perfect the machine for the overthrow of the
existing order, or, like the early Fabians, while rejecting
mere catastrophics, to elaborate in his spirit a social
mechanism which would stultify the faculties and enslave
the souls of mankind. For the latter the warnings of
Maurice and Ludlow against treating human lives as if they
were the cogs and wheels of an engine, and of William
Morris against degrading the craftsman into an instrument
of production, seem almost immoral. They dream only of
the absorption of the individual into the life of the whole,
of the sacrifice of his freedom in the interests of bureau-
cratic efficiency. It may be logical and academically
perfect : it is inhuman, and no motive save blind fear
could make it practicable. Characteristic of the quality
of Marx and of the Fabians is the degradation of the word
Socialism : to Ludlow it stands for a great spiritual and
moral ideal, brotherhood ; to them it signifies little more

[1] For a strong criticism of Marx's right to this title, and for proof
of his indebtedness to the British Socialists, and his lack of candour
in acknowledging his borrowings, see Menger, *The Right to the whole
Produce of Labour*, p. 101, etc.

than an economic and political programme, the national-
isation of the means of production.

And opposed to them stand the Anarchists with their
great but one-sided principle of the right of every individual to a free life. Outlined somewhat incoherently by
the fitful genius of Proudhon and defined more clearly
by Bakunin and Kropotkin, it represents individualism
applied to social conditions. The impulse from which it
starts is human and by no means ignoble ; Marx's treatment of its first teacher brings out its contrast with
his own outlook ; and William Morris in *News from
Nowhere* has done full justice to its elements of value.
But as an answer to the problem it is pathetically inadequate. Like the older Evangelical theology, it is driven
by the hopelessness of its task in this world to concentrate
upon the vision of a Utopia where the practical difficulties
shall be removed ; its thinkers become mere visionaries
like Tolstoy, or mere destroyers like the Nihilists. It is
significant that in Russia alone, where the complexity
of life and the interdependence of one individual upon
another is less obvious, has Anarchism ever attracted
serious students. There, in an ill-developed and un-
industrialised country, the notion that each citizen can
be at liberty to do exactly what he likes, or under the
loosest form of communistic control, may seem less absurd.
But the Christian Socialists were right when they protested that such individualism was a return to the level
of the brutes.[1] In its Western form the nearest approach to it is Syndicalism, which aims at the destruction
of the State and the control of industry by the *Syndicats*
or Trades Unions of operatives, and which shares with
the Anarchists a belief in the necessity for revolutionary

[1] Cf. *e.g.* Walsh's lecture on ' Co-operation in Sanitary Matters,'
Christian Socialist, i. p. 238.

methods, if the individual liberty of the proletariat is to be secured. In a sense they are followers of Marx; for from him they have derived the fallacy that the hand-workers are the only true producers. But they are in revolt against that belief in the rigid subordination of the human unit to the efficiency of the community, which is the legitimate descendant of his mechanical logic. State Socialism has a philosophy, which may be complete in an economic sense but fails to meet the needs or satisfy the ideals of mankind; Syndicalism has hardly got a philosophy at all, but it recognises that we are men and not the Selenites of Mr. Wells: the one has a definite objective, clear cut, logical, inevitable, the hell of pure intellectualism; the other is the product of the heart without the head, chaotic, instinctive, ineffectual, the blind groping of prisoners after freedom, dependent for its realisation upon those who know what freedom means, and who from their studies of the prison-house have discovered how it may be achieved.

The need for a synthesis of these two standpoints has thus become plain. Somehow the two methods have got to be combined, the elements of truth which each contains brought into harmony. For man is both an individual with his own peculiar gifts and requirements, possessing a personality which however much it may be devoted to the service of his fellows yet is never merged in theirs; and he is a member of society, unable to reach his fullest development except in comradeship, and bound indissolubly to those who share his family and national and human life, under obligation to consecrate in the common service whatever he has of special capacity, and finding in that service his perfect freedom. And no system which disregards either of these facts will meet the case. It may be surprisingly ingenious and perfect, with the rigid beauty of death upon it : test it and it will fail to work. As the Christian Socialists saw, the social reformer must do not one thing but two, and the two together. He must train the individual citizen, so as to develop.not only his peculiar abilities but also those qualities which are essential to a life of membership ; and he must have before him a large and definite vision of the goal at which society must aim, and a clear knowledge of the steps by which that goal may be attained. Each separate unit, and the system under which they co-operate, must be changed ; to change the one without precise purpose is folly, to change the other in the hope that men will automatically adapt themselves to it is equally folly. Furthermore there is need not only of an objective but of an incentive ; for to know what changes we ought to make is fruitless if we are left impotent for their making. Something is needed which shall supply both the programme and the power, which shall itself both satisfy the aspirations and inspire the purpose of mankind. Christian Socialism was an attempt to supply alike a social policy constructed with a due regard for individual and corporate need, and a motive force adequate to accomplish its fulfilment. The appearance of Guild Socialism, which seems to combine in some measure the two elements of the required synthesis and is in so remarkable a degree the revival of that which the Christian Socialists first formulated, seems to indicate that we have begun the third and final stage in the history of the movement ; does it possess, can it find apart from Christianity, the power not only to will but to do ?

At least we would suggest to all serious students of social and industrial questions that the thought and work of the Christian Socialists is worthy of far closer study than it has at present received. Nothing is more discreditable than the narrow spirit of jealousy and scorn with which they have been regarded by many who profess themselves to be labourers in the same field—a spirit which dares to express itself in the sneer that they owe it solely to their station in life and literary ability that they have received any attention at all. Quite apart from the merits or demerits of their actual schemes of reform, few will venture to dispute that they are infinitely the most highly qualified, alike in intellect and character, of all those who have studied such problems in this country, and that they need not fear comparison in these respects with the world's greatest sociologists.

We have no desire to depreciate the value of the services to social reform, rendered by the many heroic and often self-taught workers, who have laboured for the betterment of their fellows ; nor indeed would we neglect the claims upon our gratitude of those who, on the strength of an expert acquaintance with statistical and economic problems, have intimated that they alone are the guides of the people. But the construction of a sound philosophy of progress demands something more than honest effort or expert knowledge. That is the task of the greatest and most gifted, of those rare and pre-eminent leaders who combine wisdom and depth of thought with learning and grasp of detail, whose general principles are clear and consistent and yet are the product of experience and minute study. Ludlow, with his ' well-stored mind,' his massive knowledge of economic, social, and political theory, his wealth of ideas, his insight into human. nature, his energy and practicality ; Maurice, ' that spiritual splendour ' with his profound understanding of the eternal principles of life, his untiring quest for truth, his breadth of sympathy, his familiarity with the lessons of the history and philosophy of the past, his consistent courage in applying his whole self to meet the needs of the present ; Kingsley, ' a genuine poet if not of the very highest kind,' with his ardent imagination and keen sensibilities, hatred of all that was mean or degrading, and intensity of speech and life ; Hughes, the incarnation of breezy manliness, with his wholesome sanity of outlook, his unostentatious ability, and simple love of righteousness ; Neale with his mastery of resource, life-long faith in the cause, patient and persistent will, subtle and original intellect ; any one of these would strike an impartial observer as worthy of a place among the most talented of reformers. And as a group it is no exaggeration to maintain that they are unique, standing out high above the ranks of social thinkers and workers, and claiming from their successors a full measure of attention and of reverence. In such men and their message our generation, with its burden of opportunity and responsibility, can find an example and a hope.

APPENDIX A

In the periodicals issued by the Christian Socialists almost all the articles were unsigned, except those published over the familiar *noms-de-plume* of the two or three regular contributors. Thanks to the kindness of friends, I have been able to obtain annotated copies of their first two volumes, in which the names have been inserted. These are to the best of my knowledge unique, and as the list of authors is interesting to students of the subject it has seemed advisable to include it here.

Politics for the People.

For the marked copy I am indebted to Mr. G. J. Gray, the compiler of the bibliography of Maurice's writings. It originally belonged to John W. Parker, the publisher, and contained the suppressed pages 65-80 (for which see below, p. 110, *note*). Mr. Gray discovered it in 1893, at the shop of Messrs. Myers and Co., Booksellers Row, and presented it to Mr. Bowes, after transcribing the names into his own volume of *Politics*. From Mr. Bowes the late Bishop of Truro, C. W. Stubbs, obtained the list of contributors which he has printed in his *Charles Kingsley*, p. 108, though he inserts the name of Bishop Thirlwall, for which I can find no evidence. Parker's original volume seems to have been lost ; and the index here printed has been compiled from Mr. Gray's copy. In order to show the character of the periodical I have included the titles of all contributions ; those that are signed are marked with an asterisk ; those in verse with a dagger ; *noms-de-plume* are inserted between brackets.

Author.	Title of Contribution.	Page.
Bellenden Ker, H. (' Dodman ')	' One law for the rich, and one for the poor ' * - - - -	100
Brickdale, M. I.('B.')	Common Objects* - - - -	98
	The Saving of the Oak* † - -	141
	Rajah Brooke* - - - -	149

In addition there are three numbers of a report of the Rev. A. J. Scott's lecture on ' The Development of the Principle of Socialism in France ' (pp. 24, 41, 89) ; reports of a lecture by the Dean of Durham (p. 12), and of a Meeting of the Society for the Improvement of the Labouring Classes (p.107) ; letters from ' One of the Wicked Chartists ' (p. 45), ' A Working Man but no Chartist ' (p. 62), ' A. B. C.' enclosing verses (p. 159), and from ' T. H. C.' a working man (p. 282) ; extracts from the Press on ' The Social Condition of the Americans ' (p. 91), on ' A Decree of the National Assembly of France for an Enquiry into the State of Labour ' (p. 117), and on ' Emigration ' (p. 281) ; and an article ' Words from a Vicarage,' signed F. J. (p. 207).

Christian Socialist: Volume 1.

The bound copy originally belonging to J. M. Ludlow was presented by him to the Oxford University branch of the Christian Social Union, and has been lent to me by the Rev. J. Carter. It contains an index of ' Contributors and Correspondents,' written in Ludlow's own hand, and practically complete. As this publication is much more fully devoted to technical matters than *Politics*, and as it would take much space to print the titles in full, only the references have been inserted : most of the chief contributions will be found named in the body of this book. The marks are as before.

APPENDIX B

THE only complete list of the Council of the Society for Promoting Working Men's Associations, so far as I am aware, is that contained in the *First Report of the Society*, dated July 26th, 1852, and submitted to the Conference of co-operators. The *Report* is a rare document ; and it seems advisable to reproduce the list here. It is as follows :

COUNCIL OF PROMOTERS.

PRESIDENT.
Rev. F. D. MAURICE.

TREASURERS.
E. VANSITTART NEALE, Esq. THOMAS HUGHES, Esq.
F. J. FURNIVALL, Esq.

MEMBERS.

*G. BRADLEY, Esq., Rugby.
*Rev. T. P. BARLOW, Market Harboro'.
*A. M. CAMPBELL, Esq.
H. P. P. CREASE, Esq. (Barrister).
*Rev. J. ELLERTON.
C. E. ELLISON, Esq. (Barrister).
F. J. FURNIVALL, Esq. (Barrister).
Viscount GODERICH, M.P.
G. GROVE, Esq.
Rev. S. C. H. HANSARD.
HENRY J. HOSE, Esq.
G. HUGHES, Esq., D.C.L.
T. HUGHES, Esq. (Barrister).

*WILLIAM JOHNSON, Esq., Eton.
Mr. LLOYD JONES.
*Rev. C. KINGSLEY, jun., Eversley.
A. L. J. LECHEVALIER (*St. André*), Esq.
*Rev. T. G. LEE, Pendleton.
*W. LEES, Esq.
A. H. LOUIS, Esq.
Lieutenant Colonel LUDLOW, H.E.I.C.S.
J. M. LUDLOW, Esq. (Barrister).
ALEXANDER MACMILLAN, Esq., Cambridge.
C. B. MANSFIELD, Esq.
D. MASSON, Esq.

MEMBERS—(*Continued*).

Mr. J. MILLBANK.   *Rev. A. B. STRETTELL.
E. V. NEALE, Esq. (Barrister). A. A. VANSITTART, Esq.
ALFRED NICHOLSON, Esq.   C. R. WALSH, Esq.
J. C. PENROSE, Esq.   Mr. J. WOODIN.
*Captain LAWRENCE SHADWELL.

* Those marked with an asterisk are corresponding members of Council.

A list of the Committee of Teaching and Publication, to which was referred the preliminary business in connection with the foundation of the Working Men's College in January, 1854, is given by Furnivall (*Working Men's College Magazine*, ii. p. 46). It is :

Rev. F. D. MAURICE (President).
Viscount GODERICH, M.P.
Rev. H. J. HOSE.
WM. JOHNSON, Esq., Eton College.
Rev. C. KINGSLEY.
A. H. LOUIS, Esq., Law-Student.
J. M. LUDLOW, Esq., Barrister.

EDWARD LUMLEY, Esq., Publisher.
A. MACMILLAN, Esq., Publisher.
C. B. MANSFIELD, Esq.
E. VANSITTART NEALE, Esq., Barrister.
Rev. C. KEGAN PAUL.
C. R. WALSH, Esq.
JOHN WESTLAKE, Esq., Law-Student.

THOMAS SHORTER (Secretary).

APPENDIX C.

In view of the existence of such bibliographies as the very complete record of early socialist literature given by Professor Foxwell in the appendix to Menger's *Right to the whole Produce of Labour*,[1] the more specialised list of authorities for Christian Socialism added to Seligman's article *Owen and the Christian Socialists*,[2] and the elaborate catalogue of all the Christian Socialist publications in Brentano's *Die christlich-soziale Bewegung*,[3] it seems needless to print here a formal description of the books and papers bearing upon our subject. The account of the Christian Socialist publications in the text, and the very full references in the footnotes, will give a more precise idea of the authorities for the various phases of the history than could be supplied by a list ; and I believe them to include most of the available information. But a few words as to the character of the various materials may not be out of place.

The chief sources of our knowledge are the following:

(1) The contemporary writings of the Christian Socialists themselves. These are of two kinds. There are first the periodicals, tracts, lectures, and reports published by them ; and containing a pretty complete record of the events of the years 1850-52, and much information as to the ideals, plans, difficulties, and environment of the movement. They supply the great bulk of our material : but the task of piecing together the isolated scraps of news into a history is by no means an easy one. Secondly, there are the letters preserved in the biographies of various members of the group. Those of Maurice and to a less degree of Kingsley are storehouses of information, when one has learnt to understand the allusions and see the whole movement in perspective. Fortunately Ludlow collected the correspondence of his two friends with care and contributed it to the respective *Lives*, thus preserving for us a picture of the actual feelings of the leaders of the

[1] Pp. 195-263.   [2] Pol. Sci. Quarterly, i. pp. 246-249.
[3] Pp. 75-78.

movement, and helping us to study it ' from behind the scenes.' It is a sad thing that his own side of the correspondence has been lost. Several other biographies, notably those of Daniel Macmillan, William Cory, formerly Johnson, and Octavia Hill, contain contemporary references to phases of the work.

None of these documents with the partial exception of the *First Report*, gives anything like a connected history of the movement. The only narrative of this kind written by a member of the group is the curious apologia of Le Chevalier, or, as he now calls himself, St. André, written in 1852-3 after he had left the Society and founded his rival establishment, and published in 1854, with the title *Five Years in the Land of Refuge*. It is confessedly an attempt to vindicate his own character and sagacity, to attract customers to his new venture, while defending himself against the charge of ingratitude to his former employers ; and takes the form of a letter to the Christian Socialists, and of an Appendix of selected papers and reports. The human interest of such an impostor's defence gives it a value quite apart from its evidence as to facts ; it has much of the quality of a Browning monologue— of ' Mr. Sludge ' or of ' Bishop Blougram.' The turgid English, the complexity of motive, the combination of effrontery and pathos, the outbursts of bitterness amid pages of laboured plausibility, the naked commercialism and self-seeking that peep out from behind the veil of pious and altruistic language, —these make the book a fascinating contribution to the literature of the subject. Obviously its historical value is not great ; large allowance must be made for the personality and circumstances of its author ; but the collection of papers in its Appendix contains some material nowhere else preserved, and although it deals only with the distributive side of the movement, is for this of unique importance. The self-portrayed hero of the book stands as the incarnation of that ' commercial part of the business ' [1] against which Maurice and Ludlow from the first, and in their later lives Neale and Hughes also, waged truceless war.

(2) Closely akin to this last are the pictures of the movement provided by the writings of contemporaries. There is here a mass of material, drawn from widely different sources, from official documents like the blue book of Slaney's Committee, from the files of the press, from the attacks of critics like Greg, from the correspondence of friends like Hort,

[1] Letter of Maurice to Ludlow (*Life*, ii. p. 550).

and from the narratives of detached students like Huber. The first of these has been described and quoted at length in the text : the second and third are singularly barren : the fourth gives us some delightful sketches of the group at work, but little of any historical importance or novelty : the last is much the most interesting ; and the books of the two or three students of co-operation repay careful study.

Holyoake, whose writings are those of a contemporary, though his references are full of interest, was at this time heavily biassed against all things Christian, and in addition knew little at first hand of the earlier phases of the movement. Moreover his work is often inaccurate in details, discursive and ill-arranged, and permeated by its author's vigorous and assertive personality. Nadaud, who had been for a short time a working member of the North London Builders' Association, though he subsequently published in 1872 a book, *Histoire des Classes ouvrières en Angleterre*, and in 1873 a pamphlet, *Les Sociétés ouvrières*, has little of importance to contribute. In both cases his treatment of the subject is general and impersonal, and though he mentions the Society of Promoters and their work, he does so without adding anything to our knowledge. Huber is vastly more valuable, both because he gives us evidence of the doings of the Christian Socialists at a time when their own publications had ceased, and from the quality and standpoint of his work. As literature his letters are possessed of a rare charm—they are among the most interesting human documents in our period. His work seems to have been neglected by almost all writers on the subject,[1] and a brief account of it may well be given here.

Victor Aimé Huber, born at Stuttgart and sometime professor at Berlin, had visited England first in the winter of 1824 and stayed some two years. He returned in 1844 and in 1847 ; and employed his knowledge of the country for the composition of several books, a treatise on the Universities and a volume of Irish sketches being the best known. He has been called the father of co-operation in Germany, and was keenly interested in its progress. In 1852 he had published in Berlin a pamphlet of 35 pages *Ueber die cooperativen Arbeiter-associationen in England,* in which he noticed the

---

[1] There are two references to his *Reisebriefe* in Seligman's article (*l.c.* p. 239) and one in *Life of Maurice* (ii. p. 2) : Valleroux cites his account of the "London Associated Enginery" (*Associations co-opératives,* pp. 150, 151) : Holyoake mentions him in *History of Co-operation,* ii. pp. 521, 526.

Society of Promoters, the Central Agency, and the Redemption Society at Bury, and mentioned Maurice and Kingsley, Neale and Le Chevalier, but without showing any personal knowledge of them or their work. Two years later he visited England for the express purpose of studying co-operation, was introduced to the group at Lincoln's Inn, and received from them not only much information but introductions to the centres of co-operative effort throughout the kingdom. He toured through these, visiting Rochdale, Leeds, Coventry and several other towns, inspecting stores and workshops, and attending the Annual Conference at Leeds. Of the work of the Promoters in London he obtained a more detailed acquaintance.

The record of his impressions he embodied in a series of letters filling the second volume of his *Reisebriefe aus Belgien, Frankreich, und England im Sommer 1854*, published in 1855 at Hamburg. His observations are very shrewd and his knowledge of English conditions quite remarkable. He writes with a wide outlook upon continental problems, and with a lively interest in all that he sees. Though he was evidently greatly struck by the character of Maurice and by the work of his ' friends at Lincoln's Inn,' his account of them shows a detachment and discrimination that adds greatly to its value. Moreover he has a keen eye for a situation, and in spite of a love for strings of cumbrous adjectives a gift of racy description : the scene of the great cricket match between Price's Factory at Belmont and an eleven of Christian Socialists,[1] and that of the ' live German professor among the Mustos '[2] are masterpieces—the effort to reproduce John Musto's idiom in a mixture of German and weirdly-spelt English being particularly piquant.

(3) The evidence of later writers, biographers and historians, is considerable. Maurice's part in the movement is admirably told in his *Life* and in Masterman's book. Kaufmann and Stubbs have narrated Kingsley's connection with it. But for the *personnel* of the group, far the most useful authorities are the papers by Hughes and Ludlow in the *Economic Review* and the *Atlantic Monthly*.

Of the histories, Holyoake's *History of Co-operation*[3] does not give any connected account of their work, and only

---

[1] ii. pp. 40-47.   [2] i. pp. 484-492.

[3] ii. pp. 339, 389, 538-543. He sums up their work in the words of *Fors clavigera* (above p. 79) : and yet admits that ' their influence was the most fortunate that has befallen the movement.'

mentions it at all in a few scattered paragraphs. His book is not strictly a history at all, but a collection of notes and anecdotes. He makes no attempt to survey the subject as a whole or to see it in perspective ; and his references to the Christian Socialists are neither adequate nor accurate. Benjamin Jones' *Co-operative Production* is a painstaking example of the use of scissors and paste, but his attitude to the Christian Socialists is one of ill-concealed hostility. Catherine Webb's *Industrial Co-operation* contains a short but by no means unsympathetic chapter descriptive of their efforts and influence. Woodworth and Kaufmann have written pleasantly, but without intimate knowledge ; most of the material seems not to have been familiar to them. The two most satisfactory and complete accounts of the movement are those already mentioned, by Seligman in the *Political Science Quarterly*, and by Brentano in Schmoller's *Jahrbuch für Gesetzgebung, Verwaltung, und Volkswirthschaft*, both of which have been reprinted and published separately. Both books contain a few unimportant mistakes, but are careful, thorough, and unprejudiced. Seligman's is a model of condensation.

Of more general treatises several, notably Fay's *Co-operation at Home and Abroad* and M'Cabe's *Life of Holyoake*, contain judicious and suggestive remarks on the subject. The histories of Socialism almost invariably dismiss the Christian Socialists with a few lines of calumny and contempt.

INDEX

Agriculture, associative methods in, 179-81.

Aikin, J., 24.

Albee, E., on Bentham, 34.

Allan, W., secretary of A.S.E., 132 ; supports association, 235 ; and Windsor Ironworks, 238 ; joins committee with Christian Socialists, 238 ; A.S.E. letter, 255.

Alton Locke, origin of, 166-7 ; publication, 168 ; reviews of, 168-70 ; influence and quality of, 171-4.

Amalgamated Society of Engineers, 232 ; favours association, 234 ; approaches Christian Socialists, 235 ; and Windsor Ironworks, 236 ; lock-out of, 242-4 ; resolves on co-operative production, 250, 255-7 ; reverses its policy, 310.

Anarchism, 366.

Annual Co-operative Conference, in London, 277-9 ; second in Manchester, 314-5 ; third in Leeds, 316-7.

Arnold, M., on Maurice, 78.

Ashburton, Lord, 244 ; joins Christian Socialists, 280 ; deputation, 297.

Association for Promoting Industrial and Provident Societies, its religious position, 306-7 ; its end, 316 ; *see* Society for Promoting, etc.

Associations ouvrières, at Paris, 143, 182, 260.

Associations for co-operative production, Ludlow's scheme for,

143, 146 ; Tailors' founded, 150-3 ; difficulties, 183 ; constitution, 186-94 ; communism and, 190 ; finance of, 193-4 ; Tailors', history of, 194-200 ; Shoemakers', 200-3 ; Builders', 203-8 ; Printers', 208 ; Bakers', 208 ; Needlewomen's, 210 ; Piano-makers', 211 ; City Tailors', 212 ; Smiths', 212, Southampton Tailors', 216-9 ; Manchester Hatters', 220-2 ; in the provinces, 222-3 ; Engineers', Windsor Ironworks, 236-8 ; East London Ironworks, 252-3 ; Atlas Ironworks, 254 ; changes in constitution, 261-3 ; legal position of, 286-9 ; failure of, 308-14 ; its causes, 317-38.

Ateliers nationaux, 142.

Atkinson, C. M., on Bentham, 33.

Atlantic Monthly, Ludlow's articles in, 72, 383 ; cited 103, 138, 142, 148, 317, 326.

Atlas Ironworks, founded, 254 ; fails, 309-10.

Babe Christabel, by Massey, 152, 161.

Bagehot, W., 36, 40.

Bakers' Association, history of, 208-10.

Bakunin, M., 366.

Ballard, H. J., manager Southampton Tailors, 218.

Bannister, J., of Southampton Tailors, 219.

Barton, J., and Ricardo, 41.

Bayley, R. S., founder People's College, Sheffield, 350.